Filmmaking for fieldwork

A practical handbook

ANDY LAWRENCE

MANCHESTER UNIVERSITY PRESS

Published by Manchester University Press
Altrincham Street, Manchester M1 7JA
www.manchesteruniversitypress.co.uk

British Library Cataloguing-in-Publication Data
A catalogue record for this book is available from the British Library

ISBN 978 1 5261 3155 3   paperback

First published 2020

Typeset
by doubledagger.co.uk

Printed in Poland
by Opolgraf SA

Jón Bjarki Magnússon
filming near the
Sauðanes Lighthouse
on the northern coast
of Iceland

Rachel Webster recording the geography of a Bakarwal valley for her PhD research in northern India

I think of myself as an amateur filmmaker, not a professional,
in the sense that 'amateur' means love of something, for the form.

Jim Jarmusch

Contents

Kevin But filming in Manchester, UK

About this book

This handbook is intended for anybody who wants to use ethnographic documentary for broadcast, research or personal filmmaking projects. Its focus is practical and theoretical with a degree of technical advice appropriate for those making their first films. It will also suit media professionals aiming to convert established practice into research. The aim is to encourage exploration through practice, and the book adopts a pedagogy that I have developed over the past twenty years while teaching filmmaking to research students and professionals and by making my own films independently for TV, festival and internet broadcast. It is intended to inspire the development of core skills in camera use, sound recording and editing that can be applied to sensory, fictive, observational, participatory, reflexive, performative and immersive modes of storytelling.

In his landmark text *Ethnographic Film*, first published in 1976 and now available as a revised edition, Karl Heider finds a 'degree of ethnographicness' – meaning the balance between description and analysis as it is contextualised from within the lived circumstances of others – that may or may not be evident through the content of a film. This has proved useful in social anthropology, but one of the intentions of this book is to extend the reach of ethnographic filmmaking into other areas, and for this reason I have looked for different ways to describe the purpose, ideas, equipment and techniques associated with ethnographic documentary. The handbook also aims to simplify and update existing practical introductions to ethnographic film, such as the comprehensive *Cross-Cultural Filmmaking* by Ilisa Barbash and Lucien Castaing-Taylor (1997), which concentrates mainly on the production of celluloid film.

Section 1, *Why make a documentary film?* describes a way of doing research through filmmaking, and as such it is concerned with data gathering as well as analysis and theory making. The main aim of the book is to provide practical help as we connect theoretical ideas and technical considerations to the task of ethnographic filmmaking. This first section describes two techniques that help define filmmaking as a research practice, and demonstrates how these can be applied to the most common filming situations found in processes, testimonies and events. This will help readers to practise the foundational elements of cinema craft as they are outlined in this book in situations similar to those they might find in the field. It then looks at how other filmmakers have used collaborative, observational, reflexive and expressive methods to produce a core of approaches that can be refashioned to suit your own research subjects. Finally, a discussion of ethics and good practice is central to any endeavour that frames the lives of other people and exposes their vulnerabilities.

Section 2, *Preparation* looks at what is required to ensure the success of a film project before you arrive on location. A written proposal deepens our engagement with a subject area and helps to tackle the obstacles that commonly threaten to derail a filmmaking and research journey. Due to lengthy production schedules and the limited funds available to research projects, hiring equipment can be impractical, so ethnographic filmmakers tend to favour lightweight gear that can be carried easily and is affordable to own. This section considers how to find the most suitable equipment for your project and how to practise using it with the manual functions that help to create high-quality images and sound.

Section 3, *Recording* looks at how to apply techniques for gathering image and sound on location to serve the core ideas discussed in Section 1. Before looking at technical matters it addresses the fundamental skill of establishing good fieldwork relationships and maintaining a rapport with research participants to ensure your documentary project remains viable. Filmmaking for research purposes relies on a variety of recorded material that covers the demands of both cinematic grammar – the shots that create coherence in a film through description – and theoretical analysis. Alongside technical advice about operating a camera and sound devices, it includes a discussion of situations that commonly present a filmmaker with opportunities to gather important material, such as daily activities, discussions, journeys, performances, reflexive moments and major events. I encourage filmmakers to begin working in small crews, in order to gather hands-on experience in the specific technical requirements of quality image and sound recording. Working in a dedicated sound and camera team will ensure the highest standards of cinematographic craft, but it will also help you to develop confidence for working solo, which for most researchers becomes their modus operandi.

Section 4, *Editing* describes storytelling as an integral part of the ongoing research process, as well as a means to reach cinematic expression. The focus is on the practical stages involved in an entire post-production workflow, but this also involves a degree of understanding about human perception and expression, and in particular the way that humans comprehend time and space. The section discusses how recorded material is put to work through the narrating of a film, in order to extend an understanding of fieldwork, especially in terms of affect, bodily sense and experience. Although the opportunities that exist in broadcast television for documentary are well defined before a film is made, a research film is in a constant state of evolution right up until the final cut. To choose a mode of storytelling and cutting techniques that suit a project, you need to use carefully positioned feedback screenings of work in progress and develop the ability to receive editorial advice.

Section 5, *Distribution* discusses when it is appropriate to write about your filmmaking. Typically a written statement will help a researcher to elaborate on methodology, ethics or personal and descriptive aspects of their ethnography that have escaped the confines of a film. A short written statement such as this will help peer reviewers of online video journals to assess the unique contribution that your film has made to an area of study. Also in this section, the role of film festivals and distributors in getting your film out to a wider audience is assessed, as well as some of the pitfalls that may be encountered along the way.

I have added a number of **Appendices** that will be useful to a practising filmmaker. These include a summary kit list and templates of important forms and documents to organise the bureaucracy of a film project. I have also compiled a list of films in chronological order and texts in alphabetical order, including works that I have cited in this handbook, in the hope that these might inspire readers with a wide range of interests.

The handbook is designed to accompany filmmakers into the field in the pocket of a camera bag. I hope that it will inspire your own documentary practice, so please put it down once you have arrived at a stage in the filmmaking journey that interests you and pick it up again when you get stuck.

Good luck!

Photomontage of daily life on the river Ganges
in Varanasi, India, with spiral galaxy

SECTION 1
Why make a documentary film?

Images and written texts not only tell us things differently, they tell us different things.

David MacDougall
author of **Transcultural Cinema** *(1998: 257)*

We write to test our thinking, and the same is true when we film. A modern approach to social research requires us to think about human action through its affect, bodily sense and experience, and for this we need techniques that work in real time as well as those that operate retrospectively. We cannot know the experience of another person completely, even if we share the same time and space, because of the way that things feel differently for each of us. A filmmaker, however, seeks proximity to others as a way to interpret their thoughts, emotions and actions through images, sounds and stories that are eventually shared in a different but related cinematic experience. Opportunities for these documentaries are found in daily processes, spoken words and critical events, or they might be discovered outside of our existing conceptual frameworks as we encounter new things along the journey.

Filmmaking for fieldwork is more than using a camera and sound devices to gather data on location. It is about a collection of procedures and skills involved in cinema praxis that can inspire our thinking and transform our ability to understand the world. It is a simple method that relies on the belief that good construction

material for a film can also provide rich terrain for growing new ideas, and as such it is informed by just two principles:

1   Knowledge is explored and expressed using techniques that operate at the level of sensory perception.

2   Ethical considerations about the lives and experience of others inform the style and approach of the work.

The emphasis of this handbook is on the practical and technical aspects of documentary filmmaking. However, in this section we will look at some theoretical ideas and their associated techniques that demonstrate the relevance of cinema practice for academic research. The text uses ideas that have supported the making of my own films in order to inspire readers to think about their reasons for using a particular filmmaking method. Equally, you may wish to reflect on an already established cinema practice where you are required to think about filmmaking in new ways.

In *Argonauts of the Western Pacific*, Bronisław Malinowski (1922) described how a wealth system based on the exchange of seashells informs the daily lives of island people, beyond their simple economic needs. The so-called 'kula ring' required that in order for shells to retain their monetary value they must be in perpetual circulation, which required various means of direct interpersonal communication. When this work was first published it presented an interesting alternative to a Western audience who were more familiar with depersonalised systems of hoarding capital in banks. Malinowski's research ethics and findings were brought into question when his personal diaries revealed a colonial sensibility that is anathema to contemporary

The author (right) consulting research participants about framing for his film, *The Lover and the Beloved: a Journey into Tantra*

research, but his methods have survived to this day. During an extended stay on the islands of New Guinea, Małinowski developed an approach to understanding other cultures that he called 'ethnographic'. This involved participating in the lives of other people, alongside a more detached, observational and academic analysis of their customs and practices. Filmmaking for fieldwork draws on this ethnographic tradition by using a camera and microphones to describe the ways that people become involved in and affected by processes, such as the kula ring, from a position of close involvement. It uses the procedure of narrative editing as an analytic tool, in order to explore ideas about the relations between people and objects, with the ultimate aim of developing documentary stories about the complicated feelings and emotions that extend from such intersubjective activity.

Filmmaking for fieldwork is an empirical art where each stage of the method contributes towards the creation and adaptation of knowledge. Today people share films across the internet that have the potential to convey physical, emotional, performative and experiential aspects of social life in ways that other media cannot. However, film*making* should not be seen as a way to merely illustrate people and practices, but rather as a means of ethnographic discovery. There is a general need for fieldwork techniques that can produce audiovisual material with the potential to extend our understanding, through the editing, towards whatever mode of storytelling is best suited to the topic. Fortunately, material that makes good research can also make a great film. The requirements of anthropology, for instance – a detailed understanding of the relations between people and things – also contribute the vital elements of filmic grammar. By using the camera and microphones to look closely at what is happening around us, we can begin to see how experience is woven through individual processes that combine strategic action with emotional feeling and their collective impact on our wider environment.

The words 'film' and 'making' were first used to describe how images are rendered in celluloid, but in an era of digital technology they have come together to denote a praxis that involves ideas, human experience and technique, as they are enacted and narrated through sound and image. In a filmmaking approach, the physical and interactive elements of cinema craft help a practitioner to look more closely at everyday situations. Some have suggested that a process of mimesis or enskillment happens when a research subject is engaged through a documentary filmmaking method. According to Christina Grasseni (2009), seeing is shaped, directed and attuned, instinctively and cognitively, by our physical and social engagement with our environments. In this sense, seeing and hearing are epistemic practices that shape and are shaped by our practices. It is not possible to represent a moment of fieldwork for all those involved because of the difficulty in sharing experience, but we can aim to evoke a sense of it through an illusion of proximity that might introduce others to our way of seeing. What we see refers directly to how we see, and thus perception and expression are in a relationship that is mutually influential. This is demonstrated to the audience of a film by our choice of camera and microphones, the way these are handled and how the associated images and sounds are used in the eventual narrative. Our own feelings are embedded in a film, coexisting with the sentiments of the people who are the main focus of the documentary work. The aim of ethnographic research is to explore these subjectivities and find balanced and nuanced ways to represent them. By looking closely at how emotion and intellect are expressed through strategic action we can even work with spoken languages that we do not fully comprehend, simply by following the emotion of a scene. By editing these recordings into an ethnographic story a filmmaker can explore how personal actions become social or political, and how experience reinforces or challenges a person's ways of being in the world.

Writing field notes requires a reformulation of experience as it is happening. Experience as it is lived soon turns into experience as it is narrated. Ethnographic writing tends to happen on the margins of fieldwork events and it relies on the researcher to continuously conceptualise what is happening around them. A camera and microphone, on the other hand, work at the speed of light and sound, not only framing what occurs in front of the lens and around the pickup, but also preserving the embodied reactions of the filmmaker. In written ethnography our own emotion and sensitivities as they were recorded in the field can be edited in an attempt to create narrative coherence. In filmmaking 'sentences' are cast as the film is being recorded, and the personal and experiential cannot be removed because they overlap in each element of the recording.

Filmmaking and writing should not be set against each other – they should be seen as complementary practices. For example, the ethnographer Richard Werbner (2011) has shown that when filmmaking is undertaken before writing, a continuous re-engagement with emotive moments of fieldwork that have been recorded can help us to develop a more evocative and situated written ethnography. What is important for an ethnographic story is not that it attempts to tell the whole truth about something or someone, but rather that it aims to convey a sense of the lifeworlds of others. The relationships that eventual audience members create with the protagonists of a film then become something altogether new, 'an experience' entwined in the broader context of public viewing. In this way an audience contributes to the recreation of meaning through their own immersion in the film's content. Filmmakers are encouraged to reflect on their work and develop written accompaniment to their films when necessary, but the primary mode of enquiry and the main output of the work can all be achieved through the filmmaking medium.

The intention in making my own films (Lawrence 2008, 2011, 2012, 2016) was to understand situations involving childbirth and death that arose through proximity and involvement. I was not assuming to know the experience of being born, giving birth or dying; rather, I wanted to receive wisdom from those who had made it their profession to be involved in these activities. Filming in the UK with midwives for *Born* (2008) encouraged me to engage with existential experiences that are aroused in childbirth, and this forced me to think about how to evoke this cinematographically. To achieve a successful birth, a woman must harness the fear that pregnancy can encourage and use this new-found ability to overcome obstacles in her path. Midwives help women deal with the uncertainty that childbirth brings about through coordinated action which requires long-term training and the use of specific techniques. I came to realise how similar the task is for ethnographic filmmakers working with the people they encounter in fieldwork situations. Throughout my travels with a camera I have found it necessary to evoke the way other people act and speak, summarise their actions and truncate their histories, and in doing so I have also considered my own part in their lives. I will attempt to convey some of the difficulties, as well as the pleasures, of this journey by using examples from my work.

Daniel He, appearing in the first public screening of *British Born Chinese*

Technique

A documentary film develops through a continuous process of analytic thinking and enactive recording, where new ideas are created with each interaction. Academic researchers who choose audiovisual methods to express their ideas encounter problems if there is a lack of recorded material available to describe their theory in a cinematic way. A filmmaker must record images and sounds that both support and generate ideas. If certain grammatical shots are neglected while in the field then it may not be possible to create effective new sequences later on when editing. This is an important difference between filmmaking and writing, where it is much easier to elaborate on actuality at the writing-up stage. In this section, I will describe some foundational techniques for recording and editing a film that can be applied equally well to research and documentary storytelling.

Describing human experience: the triangle of action

The moving picture makes itself sensuously and sensibly manifest as the expression of experience by experience.

Vivian Sobchack
author of ***A Phenomenology of the Film Experience***
(1992: 3)

A filmmaker mediates between those who have first-hand experience and those who develop a related experience by watching the film. We cannot know the experience or bodily sense of another person completely because we cannot *be*

that other person. However, it is possible to gain a proximity to others, and through this closeness or distance we can develop an understanding of how they feel. There are two quite distinct types of experience. 'An experience' that unfolds in real time requires different techniques for recording it than 'narrated experience', which is explicitly retrospective and presented according to a conceptual logic that is already pre-formed when we first encounter it in the field. At this gathering stage we collect evidence of experience as it unfolds through time and space in physical actions and processes – rather than evidence of how it is talked about after the event that developed the experience has taken place. This is how we *show* rather than *tell* an audience about what has happened. The late philosopher, Hannah Arendt, emphasised how meaning is created through subjective human actions and interactions, and in the same way, ethnographic films make use of processes to build an impression of what constitutes human action and the experiences that extend from it.

Films that are concerned with affect, bodily sense and experience often try to get close to their subject. The first and most pressing question when recording any film is where to direct the camera and microphones and how to move fluidly to gather the variety of shot sizes and compositions that are necessary to build the narrative of a film. One solution to this problem, which can also help to build a foundation in cinema craft, is to imagine a triangle of action to help us explore a subject. At the three points of this imaginary triangle lie aspects of human action that can be materially evidenced in single shots with synchronised audio. When these shots are combined in a single edited sequence they help us to describe how an activity feels to the person performing the action, as well as the consequences for others who might witness it. Let us consider the expression of emotion as the first point. Emotion is easy to frame on a human face or through verbal sounds. Emotions tend to provoke strategic thoughts, so for the second point we can show the hands as they operate tools or manipulate materials. Actions have consequences, so the third and last point in our imaginary triangle describes the impact that this activity has on our protagonist's immediate surroundings, perhaps in the reactions of others or through the products of their labour.

Through medium and close-up shots, this triangle technique provides indexical material to 'cover' the grammatical requirements of a film sequence, and in doing so it also uncovers significant potential to explore the social rules that govern human behaviour. At any given moment in a process, the face of a protagonist offers an emotional description of their experience. Here we see, face to face, if the activity provokes feelings such as fear, anger, happiness and so on. Secondly, the person's strategic use of their hands or feet describes how they think in relation to the action. When these two shots are connected in a film sequence we start to see how emotion provokes a strategic response, or vice versa. Thirdly, we observe how this mixture of action and affect can impact a wider environment. These 'triangles of action' are not confined to one actor; they intersect and multiply in the intersubjective spaces that help to generate them. We can use this same triangular technique to record anything that moves, from one person or group of people to another, or machines and animals. The camera and microphones demand accountability from these three points according to how they connect in real time, and this in turn helps us to demonstrate the temporal, as well as the spatial and sensory relationships between actions, feelings and consequences.

Filmmakers are themselves actively engaged in these performances. Emotional gestures and verbalisations, strategy in using the camera and microphones and a filmmaker's impact on protagonists and witnesses are all recorded, adding an important reflexive dimension to the technique. One can start at any point in the imaginary triangle, moving between nodes in whatever order they appear to connect. The technique can be used to record unfamiliar processes without knowledge of the spoken language or context, simply by following the movement and emotional sense of the scene. It is not always desirable to direct action in a research-led documentary film, so instead we exploit repetitions in parts of the activity, to create temporal and physical space that allows us to move between shots. Altering the way we choose to frame a scene can help to compress the process to suit the narrative constraints of an edited film. To arrange frames of emotion, strategy and impact in sequence an editor must experiment extensively with how they are positioned – editing then becomes a tool for analysis, leading to new and original theories about a field site. As individual shots are placed within a film sequence we begin to see their unique descriptive potential and how this might change as they are brought together. Importantly, ideas arise from a continuous engagement with actual recordings – not solely from imagination – leading to new discoveries that we may never have made without practising the empirical art of filmmaking for fieldwork.

Kevin But (left) and Daniel He (right) filming in Manchester for *British Born Chinese*

Establishing shots describe where and when
an action is happening

Medium or wide angle frames
describe geography and positionality

Emotion is expressed with a
close up on the face

The camera can pan
in any direction between
these frames

Impact of an activity can be
seen in medium or close up

Strategy can be seen in close up detail
by recording the movement of hands

A point of view can also be achieved
by filming over the shoulder

Figure 1 *Visualising the triangle of action
through a process sequence (see pp. 7-8)*

Jón Bjarki Magnússon filming with
his grandmother for *Half Elf*

Editing as an analytic tool

It is the task of the translator to release in his own language that pure language that is under the spell of another, to liberate the language imprisoned in a work in his re-creation of that work.

Walter Benjamin
author of **'The task of the translator'** *(1999: 80)*

A film is not a reproduction of reality. It is a representation of experience that looks, sounds and feels real. A successful ethnographer uses the language of cinema to translate their own experience, and that of their collaborators, into a related experience for the audience of a film. I think of an ethnographic filmmaker as a messenger, or translator, who interprets what has been entrusted to them privately in stories for public audiences. This type of authorship involves an interpretive process that we call editing, where moments of recorded actuality are arranged into sequences that explain our own and hopefully also our participants' ideas about a fieldsite.

Editing is a way of thinking through ideas as a route towards a narrative conclusion. In a documentary puzzle aimed at discovery rather than illustration one can never be certain that all the parts of the game are available. The process is similar to solving a scattered jigsaw that has no box to contain the pieces and no picture to suggest a solution. When there are no instructions to follow, the editor must act like a child, feeling shape and texture and trying them in position until they make us and those around us feel more or less happy. As we experiment with new ways for this to work, we learn how society is organised and imagined for the people and subjects we study. Editing helps us to understand what materials are needed to construct a convincing

film, and so the process can also inspire great improvements in the way you acquire images and sounds in the field. In short, we learn to record a film through our efforts when editing a film.

Filmmaking is an enactive art where the relationship between practising and thinking about creativity becomes a way to challenge our preconceptions about the world and generate new ideas about it. It can be off-putting to review raw material that at first glance does not live up to expectations. Sounds are merged inseparably and images might include details or camera movements that are not easy to eradicate. In order to progress at the editing stage we must control our initial frustration, as we attempt to force together what we perceive to be imperfect elements. At this stage, there may be many ideas for a potential narrative, but they do not necessarily connect with individual shots and sounds. But as we work through the many iterations, or 'cuts', which are necessary to complete a narrative expression in film, our understanding of this raw material gradually changes. Recordings that were initially thought defective because of a wobbly camera or a momentary disturbance in the sound can become key to solving cutting problems.

Editors use a post-production workflow (see Section 4) to help them experiment with incomplete ideas, with some reassurance that the process will eventually deliver something coherent. There are few, if any, variations to this workflow because each stage is built upon the previous one, so it is with some reassurance that a filmmaker, who hopes to make the transition from camera-director to editor of their own work, can follow each stage to a successful end. Preparing for the editing process is key to that success. Cataloguing field recordings, in written camera and sound logs and verbatim transcripts, helps us gain a new perspective on fieldwork experiences. This in turn develops the narrative potential for the raw material and its ability to communicate broadly and effectively. If you are working as part of a team, these logs also provide a structured way to engage with a significant body of data, which may be useful for an editor who is new to the project.

Creative editing aims to discover the film hidden within a body of raw material, and at some point you will inevitably have to leave your initial ideas behind to accept this new destination. The most difficult part of cutting a film is finding a place to begin – we will elaborate on this in Section 4. It is not advisable to rely too heavily on spoken word material as a structuring device early on in the editing process. Narrated experience is useful in all sorts of ways to support an edit but it can divert your attention from looking closely at how experience is formed intersubjectively through action. Also, for the same reason, it is not advisable to return immediately to the field to record more material if you encounter a blockage while editing. Part of the cutting process in research-led filmmaking is to work with what you have in order to look more deeply into the reasons that the material has arrived in its current shape, and then make a story from this actuality. If you shoot more, then you risk not finishing the film and only covering the surface of your subject. The task of the documentary maker is to engage with life as it is and then cultivate the patience to work with that, however imperfect it may appear at first glance.

Rajive McMullen's bookcase

Creative practice as research: four useful exercises

A 'cryptographer' is needed, someone who can at once account for nature and decipher the soul, who can peer into the crannies of matter and read the folds of the soul.

Gilles Deleuze
author of **The Fold** (2006: 3)

People join and separate things through myriad interconnected processes designed to extend the possibilities of life. Because we are constrained by time and limited in our ability to move in space, so are the activities that give meaning to our lives, which makes them easier to film. Using process as an empirical lens is therefore both possible and interesting for an ethnographer. These opportunities extend to a close and involved real-time examination of what people actually do and how they feel about it (see also pp. 7-11). Processes translate well into the scenes of a film, especially when they have a discernible beginning, middle and end – so they are a good place to start learning how to make films for research and documentary purposes. Once skills have been acquired in this way they can be applied to more complex and critical events, involving networks of intersubjective relationships and broader historical, political and geographical factors. Such events may also be well expressed through conversations and in the way individuals speak about their lives.

Recording a process does not mean that your film's narrative must follow a processual logic. Similarly, recording spoken word does not imply that your story is structured only around words. Filmmaking for fieldwork is an imaginative horizon that requires experimentation through each stage to explore the practitioner's vision. Learning how to record in key situations will provide you with audio-visual material that can be fashioned into any mode of documentary to suit the development of your research ideas. For example, a process recorded with a variety of shots and sounds can be edited chronologically, or intercut with a completely different process – whatever suits your ethnographic story and preferred mode of storytelling.

Filmmaking is a practice, so a student's first day of learning the method begins with a filming assignment. The **one-shot** exercise requires students to record a single camera take along with synchronised sound for the duration of one minute, without significantly altering the visual framing or moving the microphone. I ask trainees to search for images and sounds that express the spatial and temporal dimensions of human or non-human activity, such as a queue of people or a grass lawn being cut. The exercise demonstrates how a camera and microphones can be used as an extension of the eyes and ears, and as a catalyst to thinking through frames of dramatic action. The aim while recording is to train students to look and listen closely, so that they do not miss the potential of a situation.

A subsequent exercise extends the single shot to a narrative sequence and introduces the need to control the recording equipment in order to better express cinematic ideas. For this I suggest that students record a **process sequence** – perhaps making a cup of tea, repairing shoes, cooking a meal or chopping firewood. Any process can be considered as the folding of human activity into a particular arrangement. It follows therefore that all processes also offer the filmmaker a way to explore human experience through their unfolding. Trainee filmmakers are encouraged to develop an understanding of cinematic grammar through a variety of shot types and sounds recorded using the triangle of action technique, designed to bring them closer to human experience as it is enacted. Elements of emotion, strategy, impact and context convert to close, medium and wide shots that students then experiment with during the editing of a story about the process (see Figure 1, p. 10). Course participants are encouraged to express a sense of proximity and detail in their edited sequence, using simple techniques involving synchronised clips and hard cuts with linked sound and picture and without the use of special effects. This exercise helps to develop awareness about the fundamental building materials needed to construct a cinematic scene. It also helps trainee filmmakers to recognise mistakes in microphone positioning, image composition and shot selection as they struggle to use compromised recordings in edited storytelling.

The word 'interview' suggests a structured, interrogative mode of questioning that is controlled and channelled by the filmmaker. Interviews are useful when addressing a clear set of targets or if you are dealing with people who are unwilling to be filmed in natural settings. However, to break new ground we sometimes need to understand how words extend from individuals as expressions of a strategy to deal with broader, situated and historical issues. The third exercise involves all forms of the spoken word under the banner of **oral testimony**. Testimonies are also processes, so skills learnt in the previous exercise are extended as students begin to unlink sound from picture in the edit and make use of titles, inter-titles, archival material and credit sequences. This exercise is designed to help trainee filmmakers learn how to build fieldwork relationships and introduce them to more complex narratives. I often ask students to interview each other, with the aid of storytelling props which I ask them to bring along to the class, such as photographs, memorabilia, gadgets and toys. Whereas this has less to offer in terms of preparation for fieldwork, it does help to build an empathetic understanding of how it feels to be a person who is filmed and questioned.

The fourth exercise is constructed around an **event**. Events provide an empirical lens through which the filmmaker can attempt to understand a person's experience within a broader community. Events involve more than one person, they occur over a longer period of time than the simple process and they have a more complicated structure. They often involve some sort of ritualised behaviour or they might be considered crtical to supporting or destabilising the status quo. Students are encouraged to look beyond the individual performative and experiential aspects to uncover the social and cultural dimensions of human activity, while honing their technical skills in real-life situations. An event is a collection of process sequences, often punctuated by testimony. In terms of learning the nuts and bolts of narrative filmmaking, developing the cinematic skills associated with processes, testimonies and events will prepare a filmmaker for pretty much any situation that can occur on location.

I will return in more depth to each of the issues raised here in subsequent sections of this handbook. For now, these exercises provide a context in which to practise with your equipment locally, to prepare for similar situations that will certainly occur further afield. You could also watch some of the films listed in the back of this book and observe how processes, testimonies and events are incorporated into the overall narrative.

Andy Lawrence (far left) and Rajive McMullen (centre left) filming with Ma Durga Nath (centre right) and Shobha Nath (far right) at their house in Haridwar for *The One and the Many*

Approach

The ideas that inform the overall method and style of our work are often referred to as a methodology, or more simply as an 'approach'. They are important because they help an ethnographer answer practical and ethical questions such as what type of camera and microphones to use, what fieldwork techniques, which editing style and mode of storytelling to choose and how to safeguard the wellbeing of research participants. To connect the thoughts and emotions of protagonists with our own and render this meaningful for an eventual audience, each new project requires its own unique method that suits the subject matter. The elements of this task are drawn from approaches that emphasise collaboration and participation, observation, reflexive awareness about how a filmmaker shapes context or the expressive possibilities of a cinematic encounter. A filmmaking for fieldwork project often aims to realise self-expression through observation, but it does this through a deep connection with others and a certain awareness of self.

An ethnographer should have a variety of techniques at their disposal that can serve the approach they have chosen. The potential of a filmmaking method grows with each advance in technology. It is part of the creative process to explore what is on offer but it is also necessary to develop control when doing so. We must not unintentionally digress from our pursuit of reality into the realms of fantasy, or allow the careless use of effects and gimmickry to get in the way of an audience's sharing in knowing, sensing or feeling the lives of others. For example, it is not recommended to make strong and irreversible artistic choices before entering the field, such as shooting in black and white or recording only with a lavalier microphone (see p. 48). Whereas monochrome may eventually turn out to be the best choice, it is contrary to our purposes to commit to the associations of black and white recordings before we understand better how they connect to the subject matter. Similarly, recording audio at the specific distance required by a lavalier microphone might limit our ability at the editing stage to develop a nuanced sound environment that speaks of the unfolding relationships between people and objects. For this reason filmmaking for fieldwork often makes use of the constraints of the observational method (see p. 22) to interrogate the narrative choices that a filmmaker must make. Techniques learnt through such limitations can be relied upon when things get complicated in the field; they allow for quick and appropriate reaction in a fast-paced documentary scenario, and most importantly they work with a variety of editing styles and modes of documentary.

Aesthetics and ethics are closely related. In my own filmmaking I reveal my presence reflexively at moments that are 'risky', transgressive and ethically problematic in terms of my own cultural boundaries. By connecting an audience with the fieldwork through a networking of vulnerabilities, I hope to show how each person involved in the cinematic encounter is seeking to make some kind of sense of the situation. The intention is not to remove the audience from a moment, but to lead them into closer proximity with fieldwork situations. Our own aesthetic choices are interwoven with the aesthetics of our fieldwork participants and also with a potential audience, at least at the level of perception. The active nature of filmmaking as a method encourages the researcher to try some of the techniques and styles of those who collaborate with them, to better explore and express the different ways of experiencing a field site. For the second film that I made on the subject of Indian tantricism I attempted to narrate the material according to a central tenet of that belief system. *The One and the Many* (2012) begins and ends with the funeral of a revered teacher and the story develops through ideas and associated actions of other tantric practitioners that have influenced the main protagonist in his search for enlightenment. The title of the film refers to *many* expressions that unfold from and then fold back into *one* single source. By physically immersing myself in this way of thinking I started to understand the nature and intimacy of relationships that are governed by a set of beliefs other than my own and articulated in a spoken language that I could barely comprehend.

In the following sections, I identify a 'core' of traditions in ethnographic and documentary filmmaking that privilege one particular style or approach: **c**ollaboration, **o**bservation, **r**eflexivity and **e**xpression. This is intended to help readers understand how their own work is in dialogue with a history of ethnographic filmmaking and how to select techniques from any tradition that might suit their own project.

A tantric adept who had taken a vow of silence communicating ideas for *The One and the Many* in the cremation grounds at Tarapith in north-eastern India

Collaboration

> *Tomorrow will be the time … of a camera that can so totally participate that it will automatically pass into the hands of those who, until now, have always been in front of the lens. At that point, anthropologists will no longer control the monopoly on observation.*
>
> Jean Rouch
> *filmmaker and author of* **'The camera and man'**
> *([1974] 2003: 46)*

Notions of participatory, shared, collaborative and co-directed cinema vary in approach, but they all engage the creativity of others as a way of sharing knowledge and foregrounding ethics. Fieldwork always involves relationships that are collaborative to some extent, but the power to effect change in productivity is not necessarily equal for all parties. Although the late French ethnographic filmmaker Jean Rouch did support his indigenous co-fieldworkers in making their own films, their primary role in films credited to him was one of participation rather than collaboration or co-direction. In *Chronicle of a Summer* (1961) Rouch worked with the sociologist Edgar Morin, a fellow Parisian academic. There is a moment when one of the protagonists of the film, Marceline, takes the camera to talk about her experience as a holocaust survivor. Even though this is her story, spoken in her own voice in words she has chosen, she does not in any way control the direction of the film but remains complicit in the filmmakers' story, which is credited to Rouch and Morin as authors. Nonetheless, we learn from Marceline how her experience of the Second World War shaped her life in subsequent years.

Research participants can be unaware of the future consequences that will result from their collaboration, so it is important to seek fully informed consent (see p. 28) for projects of this type. Adopting a collaborative approach should not become an excuse for filmmakers to gather material of an exploitative nature that they no longer feel solely accountable for. Equally, a collaborative approach does not necessarily imply that the power relationships governing the direction of a film are balanced – only that protagonists become involved in the process to a lesser or greater extent. This can take the form of pre-shoot meetings or script development for semi-fictionalised work, or could mean placing the camera directly into the hands of participants and using their ideas to inform the editing. This is how Elena Barabantseva, an international relations scholar based at the University of Manchester, directed her film *British Born Chinese* (2015). For this collaborative research Barabantseva worked with Daniel He and Kevin But, two young Chinese boys living in Manchester, to see how they unified a sense of their Chineseness with their Mancunian identity. Elena engaged a team of filmmakers, that I co-ordinated, to provide the boys with training in filmmaking techniques so they could film some of the scenes themselves. During the editing of the film Barabantseva decided to include visual references to herself, both during fieldwork and in feedback screenings, as a way of sharing the vulnerability of being on film with the participants of her research. We then elaborated this approach in a journal article discussing the ethics, and mechanics, of collaborative research (Barabantseva and Lawrence 2015).

Participatory approaches are common to most ethnographic fieldwork but they do not always extend to the type of collaboration described above. Sometimes the researcher comes to understand a fieldwork site through their own audiovisual involvement in actions with and through the recording equipment. For *Born* (2008), I spent four years working alongside an independent midwife in a type of apprenticeship, which I hoped would give me an insider's perspective that I could use to direct the narrative of a film authored by myself. Similarly, when spending time with tantric practitioners in northern India the sound recordist and I were drawn into events to a much greater degree than I had at first imagined we might be. It was impossible for me to access the subject to the degree I wanted by rational means alone, so I had to abandon my ambition to make a film about Tantra and instead attempted to imbue the film with a sense of tantricism garnered through my own experience.

Elena Barabantseva consulting Kevin But for *British Born Chinese*

Observation

Observational filmmaking was founded on the assumption that things happen in the world which are worth watching, and that their own distinctive spatial and temporal configurations are part of what is worth watching about them. Observational films are frequently analytical, but they also make a point of being open to categories of meaning that might transcend the filmmaker's analysis. This stance of humility before the world can of course be self-deceiving and self-serving, but it also implicitly acknowledges the subject's story is often more important than the filmmaker's.

David MacDougall
filmmaker, writer and educator (1994: 31)

Observational techniques offer us a way to describe the actuality of others from a position close to their own experience, with attention to the things that matter for them. Observational films take particular notice of the subtleties of gesture and reaction and how these are embedded in everyday processes, and they mostly attempt to progress a narrative without recourse to voice-over narration or other devices outside the context of the narrative and the awareness of the film's protagonists. This approach to filmmaking is closely linked to the method of participant observation, which has dominated written ethnography, and the films themselves can resemble fictional drama. Material that has been gathered in this way, with long takes and detailed scenes, allows one to extend the research process throughout the editing, revealing things that would be missed if the account had been limited to a script or pre-established idea. However, David MacDougall himself noted the difficulties for a filmmaker of staying purely in an observational mode as the vagaries of human activity draw them towards participatory encounters. Jean Lydall and Kaira Strecker's film *Duka's Dilemma* (2001), about the experiences of a Hamar woman living in southern Ethiopia, describes this process well. The film uses the participation of Strecker, as cameraperson, in events involving her life-long friend Duka as she struggles to understand why her husband has chosen to take another wife – an opportunity permitted by the Hamar people but rarely invoked. A triangle of action technique is used by the filmmakers to build a narrative that describes the experiences of fieldwork participants through emotional and strategic responses to their social surroundings. This culminates in a cinematic sharing of experience, where alterity (being 'other' or different) is mediated by the filmmaking process. The filmmakers translate this intimacy by focusing on daily rituals that a Western audience might be familiar with, such as conversations, food preparation, building projects and even the birth of a new member of the community. This is both informed and supported by the strength of field relationships developed over a lifetime.

One of my teachers in this method, Paul Henley, developed a three-stage pedagogy based on a broad interpretation of Observational Cinema. He began by telling students 'ten commandments', or rules, of observationalism, which I have summarised overleaf. Here, Henley pointed to a number of considerations that can improve the technical qualities of a film and the integrity of research. Rules are simplifications, and are useful when attempting to establish a foundation in ethnographic and cinema craft, but in the 'second stage' they must be challenged, to allow space for the use of collaborative, reflexive and expressive methods. In the 'third' or final stage, Here, Henley instructed students to search for their own style in the production of a graduation film. This was thoroughly researched and made over a prolonged period of fieldwork with a lengthy editing schedule, during which the 'ten commandments of

Martha-Cecilia Dietrich filming observationally in Ayacucho, Peru for *Entre Memorias*

observational cinema' provided the guiding principles for further experimentation that is necessary to both explore and express a field site. An observational-type film might result from this process, but equally any other mode of documentary can develop because recording observationally allows for a wide variety of narrative interpretations. My other teacher at the Granada Centre for Visual Anthropology, Anna Grimshaw (2001, 2009), notes how observational filmmaking, especially in the way it is described by MacDougall, becomes a method for academic researchers to balance their epistemologies with those of research participants and see deeply into the shared nature of living and experiencing.

The ten commandments of observational cinema

1　No scripts
Scripts constrain research to what is already known and they may even divert our attention away from a serendipitous opportunity to extend our understanding. It is, however, good to have a practical plan and a strong research proposal.

2　No direction
Telling people what to do removes their agency and thus the authenticity of their actions. Instead, work collaboratively with co-fieldworkers to explore filmmaking possibilities. If you miss something, then look carefully at how this is repeated in different ways rather than getting hooked on singular expressions.

3　No tripods
Tripods limit how we express our reactions to what is happening in a filmic encounter and they slow us down as we attempt to keep pace with what is happening. However, they are useful for recording establishing material, skylines and general views, where a wobbly handheld shot would itself create a distortion.

4　No interviews
Even semi-structured interviews equate to direction as the subject is led by the preconceptions of the filmmaker. Instead, testimony should be allowed to flow in a natural way through conversations and other spontaneous verbal activity.

5　No virtuoso image or sound recording
Recording should be simple, naturalistic and discreet, aiming for long takes that capture the 'distinctive temporal and spatial configurations' of the location. A filmmaker can move nearer to a subject physically rather than use technology such as a zoom lens that is not akin to the human experience.

6　No narration
Voice-over commentaries that appear from outside the location recordings again reduce the agency of fieldwork collaborators by rendering them as objects for study. Inter-title cards or first person commentary that emerges from location recordings are therefore preferable.

7　No music
Replacing synchronised sound with extra-diegetic music is perhaps the greatest of all sins as this says more about the makers of the film than it does about those who inform the work. However, music played on location or which emerges from the action in some way is fine, even if it extends from the synchronised recording across a sequence of other related images.

8　No special effects
Slow and fast motion effects, vivid colour changes, achronological and spatially unrealistic sequences all position co-fieldworkers as hostages to your own aesthetic agenda.

9　No virtuoso editing
The style and technique of cutting a film should be appropriate to the subject matter and suit the direct engagement of an audience with the content of the film rather than the skills of the filmmaker.

10　No deviation from any of the above, except when necessary or appropriate
And of these, the last commandment is the most important. 'Despite the fierceness of these commandments, actually OC is a very forgiving religion. It's like Catholicism, you can always come to an accommodation and still get into heaven.'

*from unpublished teaching notes by Paul Henley, Director of
The Granada Centre for Visual Anthropology 1987–2014*

Reflexivity

The deeper we go into ourselves, the wider we go into society. For me, this is where the challenge lies in terms of materializing a reality, because the personal is not naturally political.

Trinh T. Minh-ha
filmmaker, literary theorist and composer
(Chen and Minh-ha 1994: 435)

Reflexivity in filmmaking involves cinematic techniques that are used overtly to both explore and express positionality and affect. Positionality is how your own race, class, gender, sexuality, abilities and so on affect the way you see and comment on the world around you, and affect is your ability to move emotions and instigate feelings. Documentaries that emphasise reflexivity tend not to seek an external subject but instead they make a feature of the mechanics of the film and the experiences of the filmmaker in the ways described above. When a filmmaker becomes the principal character or narrator in their story they might consider their own experience as the most reliable authority from which to examine the construction of knowledge, both cinematic and ethnographic. Techniques include turning the camera or microphone onto the filmmakers, to make explicit the mechanics and intersubjectivity of the filmmaking process or extending a scene to include material that would commonly be cut from the final film, as Kirsten Johnson did in her film *Cameraperson* (2016). Johnson used this technique to demonstrate the personal impact on her family life when she attended upsetting news events as a media professional. Because of its enactive qualities there is always a degree of reflexivity in filmmaking. In the era of silent films Dziga Vertov,

the revolutionary Soviet filmmaker, used the camera as a physical eye in his film *Man with a Movie Camera* (1929) to demonstrate a world in motion that was literally changing before his vision. Had he made this film thirty years later he may have used the advances in lightweight cinema equipment to provide himself with a cine-ear as well. Today this idea can be extended into the immersive realms of virtual reality, with ambiasonic and 360-degree technology (see p. 42), and it is the modus operandi for the internet phenomenon of vlogging, where video bloggers use small handheld cameras and mobile phones to recount highly personalised stories.

Reflexivity is used to question structures of power, including those adopted by the filmmakers themselves. The avant-gardist Maya Deren was interested in how experience could be conveyed by cinema and she used her own performance in films such as *Meshes of the Afternoon* (1943) to blur the boundaries between author and actor. Her ideas were inspired by ethnography through her involvement with anthropologist Gregory Bateson; in turn, she had a considerable influence on the genre of ethnographic filmmaking and in particular Bateson's film collaboration with Margaret Mead, *Trance and Dance in Bali* (1952). This film adopts handheld camera positions and rapid montage techniques previously unseen in documentary work, to convey a sense of the field site through a tension between the filmmaker's involvement in and observation of events.

Trinh T. Minh-ha combines a sophisticated philosophy of cinema, influenced by Maya Deren, with a tendency for introspection. In films such as *Reassemblage* (1982) and *Surname Viet, Given Name Nam* (1989), through her style of editing, she cross-examines the language of power and influence using a detailed and personal approach to field exploration and an innovative analysis. This amounts to an explosion of the grammatical tropes of ethnographic cinema, resulting in disjointed montages of extreme close-ups, sometimes rendering the work difficult to watch but nevertheless leaving a lasting impact. Techniques for the reflexive exploration of cause and effect helped to shape feminist thinking, by bringing into question arbitrary structures of power through the legitimisation of individual perspectives. This in turn has ensured its place as a core approach in mainstream documentary and ethnographic filmmaking.

Expression

I thought this shore had a special meaning. I sensed a quite forbidding mystery about it. It was a shore as much in the metaphorical sense as any other, something that all of us must finally reach.

Robert Gardner
Director of the Film Study Centre at Harvard University
1956–97 (2001:16)

Filmmakers form impressions about the world and seek to express them in cinematic ways to a wide audience. In the quote above, the US documentary filmmaker and pedagogist, Robert Gardner, was describing his personal experience at the edge of the River Ganges during the making of his film *Forest of Bliss* (1986). The film is a beautifully crafted and inspiring meditation on death that focuses on cremation practices in the Hindu holy

city of Varanasi. Its ethnographic value, however, was brought into question because of the absence of agency afforded to the people with whom Gardner filmed, underlined by a general lack of subtitled dialogue. The missing local perspective in *Forest of Bliss* derives from Gardner's own reticence about the ability of one person to understand another human being in a meaningful sense, a point he outlines in his reflections on the making of the film (Gardner and Ostör 2001: 99). For Gardner, attempting to get an audience to relate to the experience of his protagonists was an impossible task, so instead he chose to explore his own existential concerns through a direct observation of others and then express this in a singly authored film. In doing so he emphasises his experience of Varanasi as unfamiliar, exotic and intriguing. Gardner constructs a sensory landscape of the holy city that is beautifully evoked, and it is left to the audience to imprint their own accounting for the events onto the film.

Robert Gardner was the director of the Film Study Centre at Harvard for a period of forty years, before it became the Sensory Ethnography Lab (SEL) as it is currently known. A sensory turn in ethnography inspired films such as *Sweetgrass* (2009) and *Leviathan* (2012), both of which are film collaborations by the present director of SEL, Lucien Castaing-Taylor. Such poetry in film aims to reach beyond the limits of seeing and hearing to create an organic sense of fieldwork. In *Leviathan*, which narrates the experience of being on a commercial fishing boat, we may actually feel damp and fishy through our engagement with the film. In this way the film can itself become a haptic (sensed as if through touch) and transformative experience lived by the filmmaker, subjects *and* the audience, albeit in different ways. Overtly authored films make use of the artistic vision of the filmmaker to connect the audience with a sense of the field

ite, rather than achieving this through direct observation, or participation in the lives of others. The difference between a reflexive approach and this type of expression lies in the emphasis placed on a clear critical awareness of the procedures that led to authorship, which in *Sweetgrass*, for instance, can only be found in the extra items included in the DVD release.

The expression of perceived actuality, required in filmic praxis, blurs the distinction between film and reality. Dai Vaughan, an experienced editor of ethnographic films who worked on the Granada Television series *Disappearing World*, noted the importance of recognising that film is about something, whereas reality is not (Vaughan 1999: 21). However, when our emphasis is on provoking the involvement of an audience in the subject matter of a film, then maybe the film ceases to be about something other and instead itself becomes a real and transformative experience lived by the filmmaker, subjects *and* the audience.

Remnants of human life gather in the Manchester Ship Canal, UK

Ethics

Understanding, as distinguished from having correct information and scientific knowledge, is a complicated process which never produces unequivocal results. It is an unending activity by which, in constant change and variation, we come to terms with and reconcile ourselves to reality, that is, try to be at home in the world.

Hannah Arendt
*author of '**Understanding and politics**' (1994: 307)*

Ethnography relies on fieldwork relationships, and it is how we negotiate these relationships for the benefit of all parties that develops the most substantial parts of our research. Ethical considerations and good practice are therefore closely linked. The relationships that govern our work are most commonly human but occasionally they might concern other forces that allow or forbid one from filming. This was the case when I was working with tantric practitioners in northern India, where complicated and often contradictory rules, sometimes ordained by supernatural powers, legislated over my behaviour in cremation grounds and temples. Some of the issues that arose from this were negotiated 'on camera' to good effect, but to avoid upsetting people on location I also needed to understand what was acceptable before I turned the camera on. It is important to suspend judgements that have been developed at home and instead allow ourselves to be informed by the context we are now operating in. We need to think carefully how our techniques will be perceived in these new settings and consider whether our overall approach suits the context. Good practice requires us to inform collaborators about the impact a project could have for them and then gain consent for their participation from this informed perspective. There are examples of documents that can be used for this purpose in

Appendix 2, along with a brief explanation of each and a guide to more detailed reading on the subject of ethics in documentary making. Because of their practical importance to the job of filmmaking, I have included in this section information about how to seek permission and when to post notices or apply for visas and criminality checks.

Establishing good practice

What are ethics and why consider them?
The word ethics is derived from an ancient Greek word meaning habit or custom. Our contemporary use of this word extends further but its origins underline the importance for an ethnographer of considering ethics within the cultural context of a field site. Considering ethics in filmmaking involves distinguishing between what is right from what is wrong in terms of human interaction. This is an underlying question that remains present throughout a project. We consider our ethical approach in ethnographic documentary in order to avoid unpleasant, illegal and damaging consequences that can arise from our work. Most universities promote a code of good practice that is informed by ethical considerations and agreed by a committee of research professionals. This does not cover methods and other approach-related issues – it is a set of principles about how to act towards others, which can be applied to different methodologies and in different situations. Ethics committees are at liberty to set their own standards and requirements, but they usually centre around the notion of informed consent as a way of protecting fieldwork participants and the researchers operating within their remit.

Can we protect fieldwork participants?

You are obliged to consider the wellbeing of your filmmaking team and also those who inform your work. Ultimately you cannot ensure their safety and happiness any more than you can safeguard your own, but you can make significant steps in the right direction by implementing the following measures:

- Make sure that participants give consent to use their contribution to your work from an informed position. Be clear about your objectives and who has the final say over the work.

- It is not easy to anticipate the impact your work will have, so explain your ambitions to publish, distribute or broadcast your ethnographic story. Participants can then understand the contexts in which your work might appear.

- Consider carefully how you act in the field, as the consequences of any decision can impact negatively on yourself and your co-fieldworkers.

- Avoid moral judgements about behaviours that are different from your own.

- Anticipate how a witness might respond to your actions in the field, or how an audience could react to the finished work, and include this estimation in your participant information sheet.

- Store recorded material on encrypted hard drives for data protection and confidentiality. Do not use Cloud storage or share data either willingly or unwittingly with third parties.

- Remember to also consider funders, producers and academic backers. You should attempt to guarantee their stake in your work by obtaining appearance release, location and intellectual property rights clearance documents – in some instances these may be recorded on video – so the work is not prevented from being released publicly for legal reasons.

What is the relationship between ethics and reflexivity?

A reflexive approach to filmmaking acknowledges the subjectivities, mechanisms and associated power structures that have influenced the narrative of your film. A degree of reflexivity, made explicit on screen or in a supporting statement, is expected when working with creative practice as research. Even if you are the central and only character in your film and you make the unusual claim that you acted entirely alone while making your film, you must still consider ethics and good practice because the work will eventually have viewers, who will be affected by it.

Accountability

Filmmaking requires the development of a triangular relationship between filmmakers, the people whose lives are the subject of the film, and those who view the work as an audience. Once you have initiated a film project you have a responsibility to complete the work in a safe and timely manner for the sake of everyone involved in the production. You must accept authorship for the work but also acknowledge other people who have collaborated with you along the way. Most filmmakers see a hierarchy in this tripartite relationship in which they position either themselves, the subjects or the viewers at the top. For instance, a filmmaker working for broadcast television must satisfy their audience, a political activist will attempt to address the needs of their informants and an artist will try to remain true to their own subjective vision. Ethnographic filmmakers often think of their work as collaborative and so privilege the relationship between filmmaker and fieldwork participants. In doing so, they often relegate the audience to a distant third place. We are aiming here at a balanced consideration of all three parties.

If you feel that the material you have recorded may cause damage then you can choose to destroy or withhold it. But this is very much a last resort, as there is usually a way through the difficulties and giving up on a project may make it harder for funders and commissioners to have faith in your abilities in the future.

Payment

It is a questionable practice to offer people cash incentives before they act or speak in your film, but it is acceptable to compensate them for expenses or any loss in earnings that they incur while working with you – so long as this is not used to covertly influence the nature of their involvement. People who feature in your film, or who become co-authors, may have a right to a share in the profits generated by the work, so it is important to establish some sort of agreement about this from the outset. *One Long Journey* (2016) is an ethnographic story, set on the English waterways, about the role of adventure in the life of a man in his seventieth year. During the making of the film, I and the crew agreed to pay some of the expenses encountered by Vik Pengilly-Johnson as an acknowledgement of our involvement in Vik's adventure. We were careful that these did not divert the

story and only agreed to pay for things that were pre-arranged, such as craning Vik's boat into the canal. Material that has been cut from a film remains precious for those whose lives it has been carved from, so as a proxy for payment I have sometimes gifted a complete set of the recorded material to principal protagonists, as I did with Vik once the cutting was complete.

Most people become involved in a documentary project without expecting any payment, but this can change as the project develops. If your film becomes widely successful, having already made a formal agreement can prevent a legal battle of the sort that developed between Georges Lopez, the principal protagonist in *Etre et Avoir* (2002) and Nicholas Philibert, the director of this film about a French rural village school, who both claimed authorship over the work. It is good practice as well as a politeness to credit your collaborators in the title sequences of your film and in accompanying statements.

Informed consent and other production documents

The emphasis here is on the word 'informed' to describe the type of understanding a potential participant has about how you will become involved in their life and they in your work. Aim to give as full an understanding as possible by preparing a 'participant information sheet', such as the one in Appendix 2. Take time to help participants consider each question on the sheet. You do not need to do this for everybody that you meet, only those who are central to your work or who might be directly affected by it. When you both agree that a full explanation has been given, then filmmaker and participant both sign and date the 'informed consent' document. This process will help to ensure the continued wellbeing of your fieldwork participants throughout the various stages of your production and it may be all that you need to consider if you are working in a research environment. However, this process can sometimes fail, as people may change their minds or may not have fully understood your intentions despite your best efforts. This is particularly the case when filming with children and vulnerable adults, who may not be able to comprehend the implications of your work. In this case additional procedures are necessary, such as finding a caring adult to act on behalf of the vulnerable person.

If your work is intended for broadcast then you will need appearance and location release documents (see Appendix 2). These can be invoked if participants later object to your work and attempt to prevent broadcasters from screening it to a fee-paying audience. You must also acknowledge the authorship of other people's work, such as music and archival material, and there are special documents that will give you the right to use these. The copyright of older images and music may have expired or be covered by a copyleft or fair use policy. But as you will almost certainly be re-versioning this material to serve your own narrative you must make sure that you have researched its status well and considered the implications that this change of use may have, or you may not be able to show your work legally in public. A quick internet search will usually lead you to copyright holders.

In a research project with a rigorous ethical approach, *informed* consent is gained as early as possible in the production process, with any caveats over the release of material established from the outset. Broadcast release, if this is required, can be obtained at the editing stage before the picture is locked and in consultation with your co-fieldworkers, or as many of them as you can consult. I have found that an approach such as this gives me more confidence to explore controversial material. If your intention is to broadcast your work from the outset then the producing company will set the terms for how you go about gaining release. They usually request that you secure unanimous rights before any filming begins.

Permissions and notices

If you are working with children and vulnerable adults then you will probably need to apply for a criminality check, where a government official searches to see if you have been convicted of a crime or registered as a dangerous person. These checks take a varying amount of time and money depending on the country in which you are working, so make sure you apply early on in the development phase to ensure the necessary documents are available for when you want to start filming.

You may also need to request permission to film in a country that requires consular approval to do so. Media production visas are an extra cost to consider and again they take time to arrange. If you are unlucky, they can be declined close to the start of your filming schedule. Most bureaucracy that surrounds filming has been developed to deal with the production of news, or the influx of large crews for high-budget films. These present different problems to a host country than you will pose as a researcher using filmmaking as a research method, so you may be better advised to request a study visa. Recent incidents of students being accused of operating as spies have also complicated this process in some countries. The recording equipment that we use is not dissimilar to that used by wealthy families to record their holiday adventures, so a simple tourist visa is another option. Whatever you decide, make sure you are aware of your legal status in the country you are visiting and be clear about what risks you are taking on. Take care how you present the aims of your project, as some communities will not welcome people seeking to criticise their authorities or government. The outcome of a decision on whether or not to allow you to film on location will certainly be influenced by your choice of words to describe your intentions, as well as by fluctuations in global and local politics. This is one of the few aspects of a research project where it pays to be vague about your objectives. For instance, someone who wants to make a film about civil disobedience will provoke different bureaucratic concerns to an academic researcher who intends to use a video camera to record research data.

Entry visas are designed to allow control over foreigners and to protect the state and its governance, but they do not ensure the wellbeing of your collaborators or yourself. Some administrations claim that they operate a checking system to safeguard their citizens and the visa will ensure that the relevant authorities know about you and your activities – but this does not necessarily imply a duty of care on their part. Permits can be requested from any authority but you may not wish to draw attention to yourself at this early stage in your research. The nature of your relationship with fieldwork collaborators will alter if you arrive on location wearing an official name badge of any sort. Think about permission in relation to whose story you are attempting to understand. Similarly, at this early and unresolved stage in your work the decision to post notices on walls that detail your objectives or advise people to avoid you if they do not want to be filmed may also shine unwanted light on your already cumbersome presence.

Kiera photographed by her father in hospital moments after she was delivered by caesarean section. Video still from *Born*

SECTION 2
Preparation

I had no crew. I filmed, operated sound and camera as well as interviewing drug users on camera. This was a type of solo work that took me to new levels of creativity and pressure. Taking equipment in and out of drug markets and areas where prying cameras are definitely not welcome meant I had to go with lightweight and discreet cameras that could work in very low light. Everything had to fit in a bag that did not look like camera gear. I had a mini studio on my back that could go unnoticed with a Sony A7r2 mirrorless camera, Zhiyun Crane gimbal, Røde shotgun mic, one Zeiss Batis 25mm full frame lens, a mini tripod & batteries tucked away.
Lloyd Belcher (PhD University of Manchester, 2019)
filmmaker and fieldworker

Documentary is driven by ideas but it is navigated with technology that is in a perpetual state of innovation. The task of selecting cinematic equipment is best approached with a strategy for locating the technical features that suit your project rather than having a specific brand in mind. There are many self-updating references on equipment, such as internet forums, user reviews and blog sites. This handbook complements these sources of information by concentrating on the practical and theoretical aspects of cinema craft – which change more slowly – and some of the relevant technical innovations that have appeared in recent years. I will describe in detail two popular camera and sound-recording systems that suit the job of ethnographic filmmaking and point to others that can extend your work in interesting directions. We will then spend some

time looking at how to place this technology under manual control, so that you are ready to begin practising. Do not worry if you cannot follow all of the text; you may need to begin your first film project before you understand its relevance. You can skip on and then refer back at any point to clarify areas of uncertainty.

Selecting equipment and placing it under our control helps filmmakers to become aware of how we choose to see and hear our environments and why we make those decisions. Think about the core elements of your approach when considering what equipment you will take to the field, and about how you might use it. Collaborative approaches seek to involve participants in the making of a film, so consider equipment that is easy to use if you expect people with no filmmaking experience to operate it. Observational filmmakers often record long uninterrupted handheld camera takes with high-quality synchronous sound, and need to follow focus in moving subjects. For this task a portable system that balances the requirements of image and sound as well as comfort and weight is important. A reflexive approach sometimes needs more than one perspective, so extra cameras with supports and stands as well as various types of microphone may be useful. For those hoping to recreate the rich aesthetics of a field site, then extra lighting, tripods and a camera with a large sensor that can accept interchangeable lenses will help.

Filmmaking requires the physical and active engagement of the author in the subject matter. If you wish to move unhindered, alongside your fieldwork participants, then you will need to know your equipment well and understand how to operate it in a variety of circumstances, both handheld and on a tripod. Developing cinema skills is like learning to dance with a partner.

Ethnographers and documentary filmmakers are often guided by fieldwork participants who are significantly more skilled at navigating the terrain than they are, yet they must move sympathetically and elegantly if they expect others to engage with this cine dance. A proficient dancer will spend hours moving in front of a mirror or guiding a pillow around a room before they take to the stage. Likewise, the time you spend practising with the equipment prior to arriving in the field will increase the enjoyment of everyone who encounters your work throughout the stages to come. Use the practical exercises outlined in Section 1 (pp. 14–15) to develop cinematic craft skills and competence when recording everyday processes, oral testimonies and critical events.

A strong central question is useful when beginning a research film project. Jean Rouch believed that a documentary is in a constant state of evolution, and he followed the Soviet filmmaker Dziga Vertov in his edict that you should edit before leaving, while in the field and on your return. Putting down ideas about technique, approach and research ethics in writing before you go on location is a good way to test how they may function in practice. As the work gathers momentum, your thoughts will become sharper and your methods will grow stronger.

Lloyd Belcher working on his PhD research film, *Nepalese Drug Users in Hong Kong* (2017), with Sony Alpha 7R II mirrorless camera mounted on a gimbal

Writing a film proposal

Typically, a documentary film proposal intended for fieldwork research is about 4,000 words in length. The word counts given in brackets in this section are a guide to how you might organise ideas under useful headings. Work that you undertake now will also be useful when you come to write a final statement about how you arrived at your finished narrative and what ideas carried you there (see p. 179).

Title and log line

A name and short description for work in progress help readers of your proposal to place the work within a simple context. In more academic-related work this is called the research question. A common strategy is to use a poetic phrase or play on words to grab the attention of your readership and then elaborate on the subject using as few words as possible. For example:

One Long Journey: One man's dream to build a boat and sail home

The title will often change as the project progresses, but for now it will help to frame your initial ideas.

Introduction and background (500 words)

Set the scene for your fieldwork and include a map and other images if these are relevant. Tell readers what you are interested in and why. Develop a hook by elaborating your research question and explaining in brief why this is of interest to an audience. Why does your chosen field site provide a good context in which to explore your interests? Why have you chosen

filmmaking as your method? You will elaborate on this later, but for now keep it short and exciting.

Literature and audiovisual work review (500 words)

Describe texts, films, artworks, photographs and sounds that relate to your field of study and why you consider them important. Balance these between theory and method – 'texts' that develop ideas about your subject area and those that discuss techniques for exploring or expressing these ideas. You will return to these works under the headings below and describe how your own work is in dialogue with them. Don't hide your ideas behind the citations of others; instead, cite to make your own ideas more understandable.

Research question (750 words)

This section is about your ideas and how you will test them. It is a place for you to further explain your research question beyond its title and log line. Demonstrate how you conceptualise your field of study and how this will develop through your ethnographic fieldwork. Explain how your ideas extend or respond to the works mentioned in the literature review. How do you imagine your final piece of work will look, sound or be installed? Think of filmmaking for fieldwork as a means of exploration and a way to express ideas, and write about both these aspects of the craft.

Methodology (1,000 words)

Here you can explain the ideas that inform the need for specific techniques in your work and the overall style of your approach.

In this section, the reader becomes convinced that your research question is testable and that the exploratory techniques you have selected will extend an understanding of your subject. Each point made under this heading underlines why you have chosen filmmaking as a method to achieve what cannot be done in writing. Discuss how your methods will help you explore the conceptual ideas that you have already outlined in the research question section. Talk about how you will use the equipment you have selected and why. Discuss how you will approach your field sites and collaborators, elaborating on any personalities that are of central importance to your work and how they might contribute to the development of an eventual narrative. If your work is not driven by a character, then talk about what other devices you will use to organise a narrative, such as daytime chronologies, a journey or an event (see pp. 139–42). This will assist in developing a schedule, which will help to ensure that you gather the material required for editing a film. Will you adopt a collaborative, observational, reflexive or expressive approach, or take elements from each? Will you use interviews, and if so will these be structured, semi-structured, or recorded conversations? How will you ensure that lighting and sound environments are suitable, or can be controlled to make your work of a high enough standard?

Ethical considerations (500 words)

In this part of your proposal set out any potential issues of vulnerability, for instance where participants may be too young, old or incapable of giving you their informed consent. Demonstrate that you have considered the wellbeing of your fieldwork participants and specifically how your work might affect them. Include participant information sheets that you intend to use to explain your work to potential collaborators and suggest how these will allow you to obtain informed consent (see Appendix 2). Try to explain your approach from the perspective of your subject(s) or cite the work of others as an example of how you will conduct your own fieldwork. Also think about possible collaborations with your participants or other experts and how this will affect the authorship of your work. Consider using feedback screenings to prepare your participants for the eventual broadcast of your film and as a way to develop your narrative ideas.

Practicalities (750 words combined)

It is most commonly a lack of attention to practical issues that derails a project. In this section you are encouraged to think about all the stages involved in making a film and plan for any potential pitfalls. Use the headings below to organise your thoughts and actions.

1 **Schedule**
   Developing a schedule will help you to make important decisions about where to focus your attention and how to refine your ideas, and ensure that your energy is well spent. Do you have enough time to achieve your goals? Be realistic and specific in your intentions. Your schedule can point to any clearances that will take time to obtain, such as intellectual property rights, visas and criminality checks. Plan enough time in the field to obtain all the materials you need and allow for the possibility of delays. In a post-production section consider: archiving (backing up), logging (recording data about each shot in writing), transcribing, paper editing, rough cutting, fine-cutting, colour correction, sound mixing,

writing your statement and planning the exhibition or screening of your work.

2   **Equipment (for recording, editing and exhibition)**
Make a detailed list of all the equipment you intend to take with you into the field and also the equipment you need to edit and present your work. This will underline your understanding of the methods you are using and ensure you have selected equipment that suits your approach. This section will provoke practical considerations such as budget, portability, travel arrangements, baggage allowances, insurance, how to back up original material and charge batteries on location.

3   **Areas of technical weakness**
Help may not be accessible on location, so think about how you will use the equipment that you have listed and if there are any areas of fieldwork craft, technique or technology that you need to practise or require assistance with.

4   **Budget considerations**
Create a detailed and accurate financial breakdown to cover each stage of production and exhibition. This will help you, your supervisor or your funders to develop confidence in your project, no matter what the scale of your budget is.

References

Only reference texts, films or other media cited in your proposal. Think about developing this resource throughout your project so that when you arrive at the final statement or essay, you will have considered all the works relevant to your subject.

Selecting equipment

Most ethnographic filmmakers look for lightweight, unobtrusive and budget-friendly equipment to balance the requirements of high-quality sound and picture when operating alone. For my own filmmaking, especially when working solo, I find the simplicity of a camcorder, with its integrated lens and audio recording functionality, suits a fast-paced observational approach where I need to respond quickly to the movements of protagonists. Optically superior and technically more demanding mirrorless and DSLR equipment, with additional sound interfaces and multiple microphones, work well in a more controlled environment, when I have the opportunity to work as part of a small crew, especially on sensory and semi-fictional work. And a smartphone has the advantage of being light in weight and usually at hand when something important happens. It is important to be aware when advances in technology help to shape our ideas, and each camera system will have a different impact on the cinematic experience of viewers, so select one that will help you to relate your own experience of a field site to that of participants. The theoretical and methodological parts of this book can be applied equally to any system, including formats just coming into use in the research environment such as 360-degree, action, drone and smartphone cameras.

The kit list in Appendix 1 can be used to further simplify the following information and as a checklist to prepare your equipment.

Martin Ccorahua directing *The Curse of the Inca*, on location in Ayacucho, Peru for *Horror in the Andes*

Budget and complexity

The amount of money you have to spend on equipment tends to have the greatest influence on what you decide to purchase. As a general rule, higher quality sound and picture requires more detailed settings and controls, and this will increase the cost of both the system and its peripheral attachments. For sound equipment, it is the quality of pre-amplifiers and limiters that lie hidden inside field mixers and recorders that are important. For microphones it is the pick-up, or transducer, that determines the price. With cameras, the size of the electronic sensor that processes image data, manual functionality and the ability to connect professional-level sound equipment are all important. Accessories are valued by their build quality and how this translates to an overall balance of strength, weight and usability. Research projects can take a long time to complete and you may spend only a small fraction of this time using the recording equipment. Technology dates quite quickly, so a good option is to buy and then re-sell a year or two later, as most kit will hold its value unless you have damaged it in some way. When buying second-hand, look for obvious signs of wear that indicate the conditions in which equipment has been used. If you hope to fund your research activities with commercial filmmaking projects then build a versatile set of kit, adding new items as you need them. A good option if you need to borrow extra kit cheaply, or if you want to earn some cash by loaning out your own equipment, is to join a peer-to-peer lending group.

The following list represents the minimum amount of kit you will need to begin making high-quality films. Try to borrow or hire this basic equipment to familiarise yourself with the possibilities before you buy.

1	Camera body
2	Lens – cheaper camcorders use an integrated lens
3	Battery
4	Data storage
5	Headphones
6	Microphone
7	Tripod

Care and maintenance

None of the following camera systems need any technical maintenance by the user because they have very few moving parts and the sensors are cleaned automatically. Sound equipment is similarly user-friendly. Ethnographic and documentary filmmakers often find themselves shooting in challenging environments; camera bodies are fairly sturdy but lenses in particular will not respond well to drops or knocks. Most cameras can withstand a small amount of water and some are even housed in a 'weather sealed' body, but do protect them from heavy downpours of rain or sea spray and do not submerge them in water unless they are in a suitable waterproof case. Even a simple solution made from plastic bags and rubber bands can give that extra protection in rain if you are working in challenging conditions. Do not leave kit outside or in a vehicle during excessively warm or freezing weather and take special care to keep dust away from glass or sensors by ensuring that plastic caps are replaced on lenses and the camera body when not in use. If you are carrying lenses and cameras in a bag then consider purchasing one with soft dividers to prevent them from being knocked, and whenever possible remove the lens from your camera before transporting it. If you are working in a humid environment, seal your equipment up when you are not using it, with silica gel bags to soak up the moisture. These can be heated to remove the moisture and then re-used. Most care and maintenance issues are common sense but do look at the technical manual for your camera to check for any specific issues.

Batteries will leak or deplete if they are left inside accessories or attached to the camera, so remove them after you have finished filming and place them on charge ready for the next day. Label batteries and data cards numerically or according to their status, as they can be hard to tell apart when they are thrown into a bag. Ditto for the sound recording equipment. Check every bit of kit before *and* after you use it against a list like the one in Appendix 1, because each item is vital to the production of your film. Don't trust hire companies to deliver the equipment that you requested, nor friends to lend you functional equipment in good order. Instead, build in contingency to resolve problems that are likely to occur.

Anja Vogel using a Sony NX7 camcorder at the University of Bern

Camera types and terminology

Camcorders

After celluloid film gave way to tape at the end of the 1980s and up to about 2010, ethnographic films were mostly made on videotape cameras with a fixed zoom lens that balanced the requirements of audio and picture. These became known as camcorders. Current ultra high definition (UHD) digital models are direct successors to the analogue tape cameras of the 1980s and the digital video (DV) tape versions that appeared in the mid-1990s. Solid-state recording, which requires no moving parts to transfer images and sound directly onto small secure digital (SD) cards (as opposed to tape-based recording that makes use of a mechanical recording head), was introduced to the market in the 2000s.

Older camcorders record two separate image fields as one interlaced frame, creating a smooth 'video look' that became a staple of TV documentaries at the time. Today, most camcorders record images by progressively scanning each frame to produce the 'film look' that independent filmmakers want. Camcorders are simple, affordable, light in weight and combine quality sound recording with adequate but not fantastic image technology. For teaching we use a semi-professional model that incorporates full manual functionality. The controls are on the outside of the body and it has professional XLR audio interfacing, allowing an audio mixer or microphones to be attached directly to the camera. A camcorder is a good choice for mobile shooters who want the flexibility to work either on a tripod or handheld. The system is simple and reliable, and less technically demanding than the DSLR and mirrorless systems. Lenses are fixed on cheaper models, so it is less important that you understand about sensor size and lens mounts, and for this reason I have taken more time to explain these in the following section. However, the way that each system develops an image is based on the same principles of exposure to light, so it is worth reading this entire section, regardless of the camera that you select.

Digital single lens reflex (DSLR) and mirrorless interchangeable lens (mirrorless)

Photographic cameras with a single lens and reflex mirror (SLR) that save digital images to data cards instead of rolls of film are known as Digital SLRs, or DSLR for short. The addition of high-quality video recording capabilities, in the form of interchangeable lenses and a large digital sensor, separated these video-oriented DSLRs from camcorders. Such advances in image quality meant that documentary filmmakers on a

Andy Lawrence operating a Canon 5D Mk3

tight budget who wanted to share their films on the cinema screen could dispense with the hassle of shooting on celluloid. However, the makers of early DSLR cameras paid little attention to sound quality, and this became a limiting factor in their use until professional audio interfaces and camera controls were added to address the problem. These cameras are a good choice if you are shooting in consistent low light or if you need a modular, flexible and portable device that can also act as a high-quality photographic camera.

Other than the way that a particular camera feels in your hands, another key feature to consider when purchasing a DSLR is the sensor. Sensor size has an influence on the cost of a camera, the quality of the images that it produces, the type of lenses that can be used with it and the way that the camera is operated. The sensor is an integral part of a DSLR camera. It is positioned behind the lens to receive light, in order to process a digital image that can be recorded onto a data card. In film cameras the task of the sensor was undertaken by a mechanical gate and a removable roll of negative celluloid film. The sensitivity of the sensor is controlled by a setting known as 'ISO', which is the same standard used for the sensitivity of film stock. This helps to compensate for the amount or lack of light that enters the camera – this was previously controlled by a mechanical gate, but now falls directly onto the sensor according to the speed of a digital shutter and the width of the exposure aperture. Even the smallest sensor in DSLR cameras is larger than the one inch-sized sensors used in professional camcorders, allowing more light and therefore also more detail to be captured, creating cinematic depth previously only available with film equipment.

If they are operated with skill, these cameras can increase our ability to describe the relationship between seeing and experiencing. For example, by placing a subject in sharp focus while blurring distracting backgrounds viewers are drawn closer to your point of enquiry. The full-frame sensor used on cameras like the Canon 5D takes the old still photography standard of 35 mm film and brings it into the realm of video shooting. DSLRs that use a crop sensor, such as APS-C and micro four-thirds (MFT/M43), are easier to focus but not so capable in low light. Continuously chasing focus in shallow depths of field can be a problem for observational filmmakers, where the focal distance is often shifting. Crop sensors are favoured in this scenario for offering more manageable focus control, although this is at the expense of image quality.

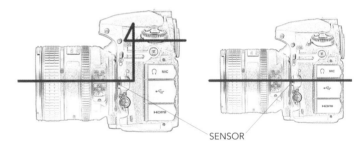

SENSOR

Figure 2 *A DSLR mirror structure compared to a mirrorless structure*

The reflex mirror mechanism inside a DSLR camera is a photographic feature that has no function when recording video, where images are monitored directly from the sensor. For this reason the mirror has been removed by some manufacturers to reduce the overall cost, size and weight of the camera and improve stability. Cameras such as the Panasonic GH series became a popular choice for independent filmmakers even though they lacked the depth of field and ultra low light capabilities afforded by a full-frame sensor. Soon mirrorless full-frame cameras, such as the A7S from Sony, sought the best of all worlds. These cameras have a small body with large lenses; they produce superior quality pictures but can be awkward to handle without a rig or a gimbal (see p. 56). Affordable cameras like these blur the once clear distinction between DSLR and camcorder, as do the more expensive and bulky professional hybrids like the Canon C300 and Sony FS7.

See Appendix 1 for a typical DSLR or mirrorless camera kit.

Smartphones and other small devices

Our online and physical worlds have become entangled in a form of digital wayfaring (Pink et al. 2016) – this has changed how we think about research encounters and uncovered new ways to make films. Camera phones allow researchers to record images and sounds with a device that is part of their everyday life, but the benefits of being at hand should be weighed against the compromise in sound and image quality and overall usability.

Some smartphones include high-quality optics, sophisticated menu-based controls and the ability to record in low light using ultra high definition that can approximate the results of the systems mentioned above. The year 2017 marked a paradigm shift in phone-based videography with the release of Apple's iPhone X. Other brands soon followed, offering comparative value for money at only a slight reduction in standards. An expensive phone can become a cheap and lightweight filmmaking for fieldwork solution when one considers how this single device now incorporates professional-level video and photographic cameras, a sound recorder, navigation and communication tools, facilities for note-taking and internet research, word-processing and video-editing software. However, manual functionality, recording versatility, storage capacity and audio recording functionality remain compromised even in so-called 'Pro' devices, which is significant if you are considering making a film that will appear on a big screen. Framing, composition, handling and movement are all more difficult when using a small device that is susceptible to camera shake and inadvertent gestures, even when recording in ultra high resolutions that allow for stabilisation in post-production. In short, it is harder to craft a cinematic film with a small device of this type. There are pieces of equipment and software available online that you can add to your phone to increase its usability for filmmaking purposes, such as omni- and uni-directional microphones, clip-on lenses, wraparound battery packs or cages with additional storage that also improve handling. Software apps that allow more manual control over aperture and white balance are included as standard on 'Pro' phones, or available at cost for download on other devices. If you wish to lighten the weight of your kit and carry a single device that performs all the basic functions you need to make a film, including editing, writing and communication, then it is worth considering a top of the range phone. Look specifically at its video capability and how sound can be recorded, either with plug-in microphones or on a separate device. Opt for the model with maximum storage capacity and develop a solution to back up your recordings each day. Trial any equipment you are considering purchasing through a complete production workflow – pay particular attention to the quality of images as they appear on a big screen and how the audio sounds through amplified monitors. The techniques described in this book, both in terms of cinematographic practice and ethnographic approach, can be applied equally to a small device such as a smartphone.

Eleanor Featherby filming with a smartphone at the Cross Bones graveyard in London

360-degree cameras

Intended for the production of virtual reality (VR) and other individualised cinema experiences, these devices record an equirectangular image. As with most documentary technology, innovation in 360-degree is driven by the desire to immerse an audience in an approximate 'experience' of actuality, which is why it is of interest to us here. One important difference from the systems described above is that 360-degree media is experienced alone, with the viewer wearing a headset, such as that seen opposite, in which they place a handheld device or hardwire it to a computer. It is important to record material from a first-person perspective that a viewer can easily slip into. 360-degree cameras use an omnispherical lens to record all around them but there are also 250-degree cameras that suit a vérité or observational approach. It becomes easier to move a camera and edit shots together if the viewing perspective is limited to what lies in front of the lens, but anything less than 360-degree is unconvincing as a surround viewing experience. Sound is recorded with an ambiasonic microphone from a perspective of 360-degrees, which can be separated into four tracks and mixed in post-production in a similar way to 'flat films'. Mono audio recording is not an option if you intend the viewing experience to be immersive, and special attention must be given to sound design, particularly in relation to spatial orientation. A cheaper alternative to ambiasonic – suitable for those experimenting with a first-person vérité approach – is to use a binaural system, where each stereo microphone also acts as an in-ear audio monitor to create three-dimensional audio. VR films are edited and audio-mixed using plug-in software included as standard in most editing systems. These use specialist motion graphics, titles and transitions that allow you to switch between flat and equirectangular views of the virtual experience.

360-degree technology offers an extension to the usual 120-degree maximum visual experience of 2D films but its use does not present the praxis of possibilities described in the previous section of this book. It is not possible to explore a field site using the same grammar of wide, medium and close shots that is used to develop a flat film. Consequently, navigation of the triangle of action shifts from the filmmaker to the viewer, through the orientation of their gaze from within the VR experience. Similarly, the montaging of grammatical shots to explore the puzzle of fieldwork and express new ideas through editing is altered by the need for an uninterrupted description intended for an individual viewer rather than a collective audience. The *i-docs* collection of essays (Aston et al. 2017) presents some interesting ideas about how this format can engage people in academic ideas, but at the time of writing the format appears to offer only limited possibilities as an ethnographic research method. Ambiasonic microphones, however, can be used for observational-type documentaries to record sound from multiple perspectives. The large variety of configurations that ambiasonic microphones offer means that in the future this could become the single microphone of choice for budget filmmakers.

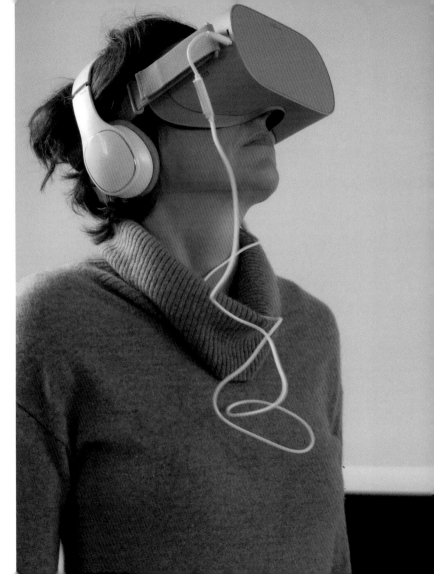

Michaela Schäuble immersed in a VR experieince

Action and drone cameras

Strapping cameras to moving objects and finding ways to obtain aerial views is not a new idea; in fact it was the underlying principle of Vertov's *Man with a Movie Camera* produced in 1929. The availability, size and capacity of technology that can perform this function has greatly improved since the early days of filmmaking. Lucien Castaing-Taylor and Véréna Paravel used waterproof action cameras to good effect in their film *Leviathan* (2012) to produce a literal sense of immersion into the experience of commercial sea fishing. Action cameras are versatile, relatively cheap and usually arrive with a waterproof housing that can be connected to human or machine, allowing for all sorts of new ways to describe perception without the need to risk the safety of your principal camera. Airborne drone cameras are particularly useful for establishing a scene, for moving between wide and close shots, or if you need to demonstrate the proximity or location of a protagonist within their environment. Drone cameras can be used to mimic the effects achieved by expensive cinematic equipment, such as a rolling dolly, helicopter fly-by, crane or jib arm. Laura Coppens includes a number of shots recorded with the help of a drone in her film *Taste of Hope* (2019), simultaneously broadening the scope of the film's context and increasing the cinematic appeal of the work. These cameras do not, however, record sound at a high enough quality for professional use and if they are not placed well, or if the recorded sound does not connect with the images, then they can distort rather than augment a viewer's experience of your film. Experimentation prior to fieldwork is recommended if you are thinking of adding textures such as these.

Peter Ndagi filming with a camcorder at the F4F™ Summer School in Manchester

Sound recording technology

The aspect of filmmaking that has changed the least and continues to be undervalued most is sound recording. The quality and sensitivity of audio recordings define the way an audience experiences a film, so sound must not be a secondary consideration. In documentary work audio data is commonly picked up by a variety of omni- and uni-directional microphones and recorded via a mixer to a camera or solid-state recorder, and then saved onto secure digital data cards. Fiction filmmakers think as much about what occurs off screen as they do about what is happening in front of the lens, but most sounds that occur in a documentary happen in the near distance and occupy a central, or mono, position in our audio field. In my own films, I have recorded in stereo and sometimes surround sound but the skills associated with these more advanced applications were built on foundational mono techniques of microphone positioning, audio monitoring and establishing recording levels.

If you intend to work alone by positioning a microphone on top of your camera, perhaps via an audio interface, then you will need to control the levels and monitor the recordings yourself. If you choose to work with a dedicated sound person, using a retractable boom pole to push the microphone closer to the source of sounds, then this person will control audio levels and listen to the recording with headphones through a field mixer or recording device (see Figure 13, p. 107).

Jon Tipler recording atmospheric sound for *One Long Journey*

Stereo and mono

A stereo microphone incorporates two audio pick-ups that mimic the human capacity for binaural hearing, so like a human being the microphone must also remain upright. If the left and right stereo patterns are inverted then the audio space will become confused. Consequently the microphone positions that one can adopt when using a stereo system are limited. Anyone wishing to use 360-degree media will need to extend their sound craft beyond stereo into quadrophonic recording, using something akin to an ambiasonic microphone that records sound from a number of different positions surrounding an object or person. Voices and other synchronous sounds that occur at close quarters to the filmmaker generally occupy a position of centrality in our imagination and can therefore occupy a similar place in the audio mix of our films. Mono recording is a simple way to learn basic skills in location sound environments which will be applicable to all microphone types.

A dedicated sound recordist, working with a single mobile stereo microphone and using either an X-Y pair or Mid-Side (MS) configuration, has to think about where sounds are located and ensure that the microphone is correctly positioned and upright at all times. When recording in mono you need only worry about levels and not spatial configuration. That makes it a good place to begin answering the main challenge of documentary filmmaking, which is how to record good, clear synchronised audio by positioning the microphone as close as possible to the source of a sound and selecting the correct recording level. Some filmmakers record synchronised sound with a mono microphone and atmospheric sounds in stereo, so that there is a stereo feel throughout the film even if most of it has been recorded in mono. If you run into problems when working in

stereo, you can simply sum the two tracks into one mono track in post-production, so that all sounds extend from the same perspective.

A common misunderstanding is to assume that a mono signal can be made into stereo by doubling it onto two tracks of an editing timeline and then positioning these to the right and left channel of an eventual audio mix. This will ultimately result in two identical signals extending one from each speaker, which is not stereo but what we refer to as dual-mono. A film can only be received in stereo if it has been recorded in stereo, or if a stereo atmosphere has been created in post-production by positioning separate audio recordings to the left, right and centre of the mix.

Microphones

Microphones are transducers that transform sound into electrical signals. Those that are built into cameras range from very poor to passable for recording sounds that occur close to the camera. In-built microphones are weakest when they are recording the human voice, so consider adding one or two quality microphones to your kit.

Directional microphones shield global sounds from the edges of the pick-up, using a hypercardioid recording pattern that concentrates on sound that occurs in front of the microphone. Omni-directional, as the name suggests, refers to mics that record sound equally from all of the near global environment of the mic. Video incorporates two audio tracks that can be separated to record two independent mono microphone signals or one stereo or MS signal that uses both the left and right audio inputs on the camera for a single microphone. Choose microphones that best suit your field site; many people opt for a directional as their primary microphone and an omni-directional in the form of a radio-controlled lavalier microphone for occasional use, or more consistently when working solo.

Directional microphones have either a narrow or wide pattern, and some are switchable between the two. A narrow pattern is referred to as super-hypercardioid and it allows you to record more distant sounds. More skill and sensitivity are required when positioning and moving this microphone in order to create a naturalistic sound environment, and because of this they do

not work well when mounted to the top of a handheld camera. A directional microphone with a wider hypercardioid pattern allows more extraneous sounds to enter the recording but it is much more forgiving when it is unintentionally panned or tilted away from the axis of sound. For beginners I recommend a microphone of this sort, such as the Sennheiser MKE600 or the Røde NTG-1. Microphones need a 48 volt power supply and most audio interfaces and mixers that are designed for video deliver a 'phantom' power supply of this type (usually shown as 'PH' or '+48v' on the equipment), so you can choose a microphone that does not have its own independent power supply if you wish.

Figure 3 *Patterns for common microphone types*

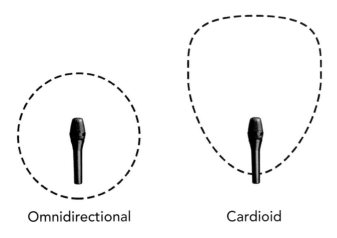

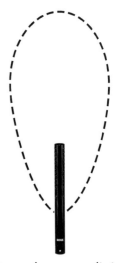

Omnidirectional

Cardioid

Hypercardioid

Super-hypercardioid
or shotgun

DSLRs, mirrorless cameras, cheaper camcorders, smartphones and some audio recorders do not have this feature, so you will need to choose a microphone that uses a rechargeable or disposable battery when phantom power is not available. Videomics that have been designed specifically for use with DSLR and mirrorless cameras are smaller and lighter in weight and they carry a small cell battery. They connect to the camera via a 3.5 mm jack plug and offer a sophisticated range of features aimed at highlighting sounds within a vocal range or eliminating sounds that are very low pitched, such as road noise. The audio quality is not sufficient for professional use because the pre-amplification is weak and their type of connectivity means they are less versatile when used off-camera with other devices, but if you are looking for something lightweight and inconspicuous to work with a specific camera then they are a good solution.

Remote lavalier microphones use radio frequencies (RF), or channels, to transmit audio between a subject and a receiver across a variety of ranges, according to their sophistication and cost. When working alone you can clip the microphone discreetly to a principal protagonist to achieve closeness without the use of a dedicated sound recordist. Remote microphones help preserve mobility with the camera, so they are popular with observational-type filmmakers. However, contrary to the tenets of observationalism (see p. 22), the nuances of a sound recording that varies in perspective as images draw closer and further away are lost when pinning a microphone to a single position. When used in combination with a camera-mounted microphone some semblance of atmospheric sound can be retrieved. Radio-controlled microphones vary greatly in cost. You do not need the top of the range, but equally avoid the very cheapest, as the main compromise is in loss of audio quality. You

should check what frequencies are available for use, as these vary between countries and in some places it is illegal to interfere with certain channels.

Ambiasonic microphones are not solely for recording audio that accompanies 360-degree images. These microphones unite the capabilities of stereo and mono sound recording from a 360-degree perspective that encompasses the entire sphere surrounding the sound recordist. This is a significant improvement on other microphone types because humans experience sound continuously from all perspectives in varying intensities. Images, on the other hand, are seen in single blinked frames from a maximum of 180 degrees. Ambiasonic microphones need to be interfaced through a four-track recorder to take full advantage of the possible configurations they offer, and they are usually mounted in an upright position, which can be moved by a single-person operator or by a dedicated sound recordist. Because of this, ambiasonic equipment can be difficult to operate; but advances in this technology will develop fast, reducing the cost and size of the peripherals needed and of the microphone itself.

Suspension and mounting

Microphones are designed to be sensitive, so you will need to protect them from unwanted disturbance. A variety of cradles, 'pistol grips' and suspension mounts exist for this purpose. Again, consider your approach. If you are working alone then you will need a low-profile suspension to hold your microphone on the top of your camera. If you are dedicating yourself to sound recording and working alongside a camera operator then you can opt for a more robust pistol-type grip, which can be handheld or attached to a retractable pole. Another solution is to find something in between that can be attached to both your camera and a boom pole, like the Rycote Lyre mount.

Wind protection

Most microphones arrive in their box with a foam cover included. This will prevent draughts from affecting the quality of a recording but it is grossly inadequate for anything that will occur in an exterior environment, so you will need to purchase some sort of additional wind protection. A popular choice is a furry sock with a silk liner that fits over the microphone and foam shield, sometimes referred to as a 'dead cat'. This has the benefits

Hlín Olafsdóttir operating a shielded, boomed microphone with Zoom recorder attached

of being cheap to buy and suitable for moderate exterior conditions. They are, however, apt to slide out of place, exposing the pick-ups to serious audio distortion, even in the lightest wind conditions. For stronger wind you will need a 'softie'-type cover, such as those made by Rycote. These have a cellular foam inner housing and a fur outer windshield, with a strong rubber collar to hold them in place on the microphone. However, unless you contain the whole microphone within a protective housing wind will still find a way to destroy your sound. If you are operating in extreme conditions then a full cage wind cover is the only reliable solution. These are expensive but most professional sound recordists will not work outside without one. They are also highly conspicuous and will place your filmmaking in a professional context, at least in the eyes of people observing you. Slightly smaller, cheaper and less easy to operate versions of wind cages, like the one shown here, are available but they are just as conspicuous as their professional siblings. Positioning yourself is as important as selecting the correct protection – wind is pervasive, but there are ways that you can shield your microphone from the worst effects of this, such as recording in the lee of a building.

Boom pole

Retractable poles are used to position a microphone when a production includes a dedicated sound recordist. Boom poles are useful to push the microphone ahead of the image, ensuring precise and clear recordings and making possible a wider range of options for framing images. To use a boom effectively one must build strength and learn how to 'fish' for sounds from below or above a frame without getting caught in the image. For documentary purposes a lightweight retractable carbon-fibre

OPEN

LITRES

Jon Tipler listening to rust and metal with his microphone
fully protected from the unwanted interference of wind

pole about 2 m in length at full extension is ideal. When considering portability look for the best collapsed to extendable ratio but also make sure you can operate it easily and intuitively in a fieldwork situation. Internal cabling features can help reduce handling noise but they are not necessary and are more suited to controlled productions where more time is available for set-up and breakdown. In documentary work it is best to learn how to wrap a cable quickly around the outside of the pole to reduce noise.

Cables

Whenever possible, cables should be connected with high-quality shielded and balanced connections that lock into place, such as the industry standard XLR system. Many variations on this exist, sometimes using a smaller, scaled down version of the XLR that is also lockable. DSLR-type cameras often join sound via a weak and friable unbalanced mini-jack connection that is subject to electrical interference. I recommend purchasing high-quality cables and developing a way of securing these in place, for example with a cable tie attached to the camera strap loop. Make sure that you coil cables carefully using a loose half-turn method rather than wrap them tightly around devices as this will damage the cable and lead to constant tangles.

Headphones

To listen carefully to what is being recorded look for 'field monitors' that can recreate sounds accurately using a flat, unenhanced response. These headphones suit a documentary project because they use a closed-back system that covers the

Lana Askari recording an event at the F4F™ Summer School

entire ear, preventing extraneous sounds from entering your interior recording space. Some people opt for earbuds as they are inconspicuous, easily carried and allow you to also hear what is happening around you. Unfortunately this is all that earbuds achieve. Significantly, they will not help you to hear what you are recording, alert you to fluctuations in sound or help you to recognise unwanted noise and be sensitive with microphone placement and recording levels. While we live in hope for affordable noise-cancelling earbuds with a flat response, in the meantime it is best to acquire a cheaper and more robust pair of closed-back field monitors to listen to your audio recordings.

Audio adapters, pre-amplifiers, external recorders and mixers

A microphone signal needs to be amplified before it is channelled through noiseless connections in order to produce high-quality audio. Camcorder manufacturers incorporated professional audio interfacing and microphone pre-amplification from the outset, and recently these have also become available

Emma Harris demonstrating how to organise cables on her Canon C100

for DSLR and mirrorless cameras. Passive adaptors – those without pre-amplification – simply add XLR connectivity and they are of limited use because they do not increase the microphone signal. Adapters in the form of a small box that connects to the top of the camera body via a powered housing, sometimes called a 'hot shoe', draw phantom power from the camera to supply passive microphones. These devices give you the benefits of professional XLR connection for a variety of microphones, manual level controls and slightly better pre-amplification than is offered in the camera. They will enable you to connect two mono microphones, such as a uni-directional and an omni-lavalier, that can be independently controlled and targeted to two separate tracks. Alternatively, you can link the channels and record with a

professional Mid-Side (MS) or stereo microphone. If you want to use an ambiasonic microphone you will need an audio interface and recorder capable of receiving four separate inputs, unless you dispense with some of its functionality. Higher quality pre-amplifier and mixer units designed for camera mounting tend to include a peak-level display that is useful for monitoring audio levels. These tend to be higher in price but more robust in their build quality and contain superior pre-amplification, leading to less noisy recordings.

If you need a device that can be used away from the camera, for example to record the entirety of a speech or musical performance, then handheld audio recorders are a good choice. Devices such as those in the popular 'Zoom' series provide manual mixing controls, four XLR inputs, good-quality pre-amplifiers, interchangeable microphones and the ability to record audio onto a secure data card. When recording synchronised sound alongside camera images these recorders have the option to take a 'line out' to the 3.5 mm mic input on your DSLR or mirrorless camera, so that you can lower the audio levels on your camera and make use of the far superior pre-amps in the recorder. Because you can record to the data card as well as to the camera, you can record another track at a lower or higher level (+ or – 12 dB) to avoid clipping or noisy recordings.

There are a number of more costly and advanced pre-amplified mixers on the market, aimed at DSLR and mirrorless users. These are built with the highest quality pre-amplifiers and limiters, which prevent your recordings from distorting when confronted by excessively loud sounds. They can be heavy and complicated to use, so not much help if you are a solo shooter operating handheld. But if you work regularly with a sound recordist, or if you can mount them on a tripod, they can dramatically improve the quality of your audio recordings. The Sound Devices MixPre-D remains the most versatile option. It is sturdy, relatively compact and more battery-efficient than newer models. It gives broadcast audio with the highest quality pre-amplifiers and usable analogue limiters. This device offers great possibilities to learn the craft of sound recording, because you can hear precisely the sound that you are recording. It involves a commitment to learn how to use a device of this type and there are a number of features it carries that you may not need, but it is well worth the investment if you can afford the time and money.

Zoom H4N recorder attached to a Blackmagic Pocket Cinema Camera rig

Peripheral kit

Lenses

Cheaper camcorders use a zoom lens that is fixed to the body of the camera, but if you are using a DSLR or mirrorless camera you will need to think about what lens or lenses suit your project. Lenses come in two types, at various cost. Prime lenses are those where you cannot alter the focal length or width of a frame from a fixed camera position. Zoom lenses, on the other hand, allow you to adjust the focal length to suit the shot size required from a single camera position. Prime lenses incorporate fewer glass elements, so they are lighter in weight and produce higher quality images in low ambient light. Zoom lenses appear easy to use but working with prime lenses forces you to 'zoom with your legs'. Actively engaging in the framing of a shot by moving yourself physically nearer to the action will position you closer to the experience of your protagonists. It also creates steadier images and improves the sound quality when working solo.

The size of the digital sensor in your camera determines the width of a shot with any given lens (see Figure 7, p. 70). For example, a 50 mm lens is considered standard on a full-frame sensor measuring 35.9 mm across, but on a smaller micro four-thirds digital chip, measuring 17.3 mm across, the same lens would translate to a long lens of roughly 100 mm. Along with the size of sensor, the mount system used to attach the lens is crucial in determining which lenses will suit a particular make and design of camera. Common examples of lens mounts are Canon EF, Nikon F, Sony FE, Canon EF-S, Sony E, Panasonic, Olympus and Blackmagic.

For documentary purposes, where content is unpredictable, a versatile zoom lens with a constant aperture is useful – for example, the Panasonic Lumix 12–35 mm f2.8, or Olympus M.Zuiko 12–40 mm f2.8 on a small sensor system. For a full-frame sensor camera 28–105 mm zoom lenses are available, but these can be heavy and low-cost versions do not use constant aperture, so you may also want to purchase a 50 mm f1.8 prime lens, which will be cheaper and lighter.

Stabilisation is important and it is worth considering whether a lens has this facility to help keep your shots smooth. Most camera bodies now have in-built stabilisation but some full-frame cameras do not, so it is a good idea to look for a lens with image stabilisation (IS).

Speedboosters allow you to adapt a camera mount to fit lenses from other systems onto your camera and also increase the focal length and aperture opening.

Macro lenses, which focus on very small objects, are not often used in ethnographic filmmaking because they exaggerate an image beyond what the human eye can see. The relationship between experiencing and seeing is a key element of anthropological understanding so when we distort an image we must consider carefully our reasons for doing so. However, such lenses might prove useful when exploring the imagined consciousness of other species, bees for example.

Filters
A neutral density (ND) filter will allow you greater control over your image in bright daylight. Darkening the image with ND allows you to open the iris for creative use of depth of field (see p. 67) where it would not otherwise be possible. Two- or

three-stage NDs come as standard on camcorders but they need to be added to a DSLR, mirrorless camera or smartphone. The most portable option is the screw-on type with a range of six stops. A popular choice for videographers is a variable ND, which allows a range of filtration for adjustment between slightly to very bright environments with a turn of the filter, in a similar way to adjusting a focus or zoom ring.

Polarising filters do a similar job to the ND but they are particularly useful when working in environments that produce excessive glare, such as snow or seascapes, where you may need more incremental adjustment. A simple UV filter or skylight can be used to protect an expensive lens when operating in windy and dusty environments, for example when you need to frequently wipe the lens clean. These filters slightly reduce the amount of bluish light entering the camera but they do not have a significant effect on the image. When purchasing filters check the thread size at the front of your lens – for example, ø58 translates as 58 mm. A good economy is to buy a single filter to suit the widest thread and then use a 'stepping ring' to convert for smaller lenses. Cheap filters produce visual banding, vignetting or a very noticeable grey tint or colour shift to your images, so if possible stick to quality brands.

Batteries and charging
You will need spare batteries for the camera, and also for audio interfaces, lights and microphones. It is better for you and the environment if you invest in good-quality rechargeables as these retain power for longer than disposable batteries and they produce less waste. Calculate how many of each type of batteries you need for the longest filming days, taking into

account the power demands of all of your devices. Lithium-ion batteries are preferable but nickel–metal hydride (NiMh) are an acceptable cheaper alternative. Treat rechargeable batteries with care, as excessive sunshine or dropping them can cause swelling and this will ultimately damage your equipment. For this reason, it is not recommended to use rechargeable batteries in devices where the battery is inserted into the unit lengthways.

Camera batteries are always rechargeable. Some use the camera itself as a charging device and some require a separate charger unit. Camcorder batteries can be quite heavy; they have a large capacity and are commonly charged on the camera. DSLR and mirrorless batteries are smaller because they fit inside the camera. They have a lower capacity and use an external charger, so the weight to power ratio generally evens out between the two systems. Consider purchasing enough power for at least eight hours' shooting for DSLR and mirrorless cameras (usually about four batteries) and more recording time if you are using an efficient camcorder. Cameras with large sensors need more power. If long, observational-style recordings or locked-off shots of entire performances are required, a camcorder or mirrorless camera that uses a micro four-thirds (MFT)-sized sensor might be a good choice. If you are intending to operate in very low light, then the benefits of a DSLR camera that has a full-frame sensor would outweigh the compromise over battery life and stability.

Smartphones tend to have a very short battery life when shooting video, so if you are using one as your principal recording device consider purchasing a back-up power supply. Portable USB powerbanks also charge microphones and lights that accept this type of charge. If you will be away from mains power for a considerable amount of time – at sea or in a jungle or desert, for example – where the sunlight is strong, a portable solar charging unit might serve you well.

Storing data

Most camcorders, DSLR and mirrorless cameras now use secure digital (SD) cards for saving recorded images and sounds, but some still use Compact Flash (CF), which despite their name are larger than SD cards. Fewer still make use of tape. In this handbook I will refer to data cards in general, as specific brands and formats come and go quite quickly, while the principle of saving material in a way that can be easily exported for archiving and editing remains constant. Smartphones commonly record to their internal storage, which can be a limiting factor when working with these devices. One way around this is to choose a smartphone that accepts micro-SD cards or the like, or to purchase a plug-in data expander.

The quality of recording media is important. SD cards can fail and cheaper brands may not live up to the elaborate descriptions on their packaging. There are three considerations when purchasing data cards: the capacity of the card, measured in gigabytes or terabytes; the speed at which data is transferred and 'written' to the card every second, which is measured in megabytes per second (MB/s); the type and capacity of card your camera will accept, for example SDXC 128GB or CF64GB. For answers look in the technical section of your camera manual and take note of the speed at which the hungriest format needs to write to a card and the amount of space needed for one hour of material.

Tripods and monopods

Carrying less is often a priority for fieldworkers and the first thing to be dispensed with is usually the tripod. Some images, however, are more useful in the edit when they have been 'locked off' on a tripod – for instance landscapes, horizons, architectural shots, some close-ups and anything that depicts writing. A compromise is to purchase a good-quality lightweight tripod that can be weighted down by adding extra ballast to it. A good tripod is easy to level, with a ball-mounted head that incorporates a spirit level and a twist grip on the underside that can be loosened, adjusted and tightened. Panning and tilting are best avoided, because unless you spend a great deal of money on a heavy tripod with a fluid head then these movements will often produce disappointing results. Think of your tripod as a stand for the camera rather than as a way to gain contrived and sometimes nauseating camera movements. Most tripods include retractable rubber feet at the base of the legs that can be lowered to protect flooring when working inside or retracted to reveal spikes for soft ground outside.

Some filmmakers use monopods, with tiny spreader feet and fluid head systems that help to hold a camera steady. Monopods do not have the rigidity necessary for interviews and establishing shots but they are useful for long takes in cramped spaces and when moving through crowds of people. Gorilla pods™ are useful for wrapping around trees, supporting lights or microphones and even carrying a lightweight DSLR camera, but they cannot replace a three-stage tripod for professional purposes. If you are using a smartphone or other small device then these tiny flexible tripods, with a mini 'ball head' on top to make levelling easier, provide the most appropriate means of supporting your camera.

Rigs, cages, brackets and gimbals

You may want to add accessories to your camera by using a lightweight scaffold, or rig (see opposite), which can also improve the handling capability of some systems. But beware of turning what ought to be a convenient lightweight set-up into something unwieldy. If you need to attach an extra light, microphone or field monitor, or simply extend the holding positions for your camera, then a better solution might be a modular aluminium cage. These are sold as an expensive accessory for most DSLR and mirrorless cameras. A significantly cheaper solution is the L-arm, or flash bracket (see also pp. 92–3). This will share the weight of a heavy set-up across two arms and help keep horizons level and avoid camera 'droop'. It also incorporates two 'cold shoes', unpowered slots on which you can attach accessories such as radio microphone receivers. There are other grip solutions to consider, such as a versatile 'magic

Jón Bjarki Magnússon setting up his tripod for a landscape shot in Iceland

Battling an Icelandic storm with a monopod

Using a rig to support a Blackmagic Pocket Cinema Camera

arm' (see p. 118) or the lighter and cheaper 'Dinkum clamp', which can be used for attaching cameras to moving objects or as supports for lighting. A gimbal has a floating hydraulic head on a short handheld pole, which can help to create smooth, balanced walking shots. It is particularly helpful for a small handheld camera with a full-frame sensor that requires large lenses, such as the Sony A7s (see p. 33).

Display and monitoring

There are two ways to monitor the image on a camcorder: a liquid crystal display (LCD) screen or pressing your eye to the electronic viewfinder (EVF). DSLR and mirrorless cameras use an LCD screen only, which can be converted into an EVF with a display loupe like the LCDVF from Kinotehnik (see overleaf), or the models from Vary-i. An EVF gives a sharper image, primarily because it is shielded from external light. Using the LCD screen can be tricky when filming outside in bright sunlight, but there are solutions available such as a clip-on sun shield. If you are tall, you may find it difficult to shoot effectively using the EVF; in this

Kevin But, Daniel He and their Tai Chi teacher seen through a Kinotehnik viewfinder loupe.

case try holding the camera lower and tilting the LCD screen so that you can gain a less intimidating perspective. The reverse might be true if you are short in height. An EVF is not the same as through-the-lens viewing on old-fashioned SLR cameras. An EVF screen works because it is close to the eye, so it can be uncomfortable to use for people who need glasses to see far away. To compensate for this, there is an optical adjustment under the viewfinder, but on a rapid-moving shoot it is not practical to keep removing and replacing your spectacles, so in this instance you are better advised to monitor your shots from an LCD screen.

Some filmmakers prefer to use an external field monitor that slides into the hot shoe of your camera, or is powered externally. These offer a larger and brighter screen for framing and monitoring your images and to help in finding accurate focus and exposure. In practice this is usually one step too far for a lightweight documentary crew. Some action cameras use a wifi signal so they can be controlled and monitored remotely from a smartphone or tablet using a third-party app.

Bags and portability

When you need to carry your kit over long distances in a variety of modes of transport you will need a comfortable and robust bag or case. It will also need to conform to hand baggage restrictions if you are travelling by air. Ensure that your equipment is well packed and easily accessible when you are working but unobtainable to others while en route. Hard shell suitcases are a good option for carrying peripheral equipment such as tripods, boom poles, reflectors and lighting stands that cannot be taken on board an aeroplane as hand luggage. Suitcases protect your equipment

adequately, they are usually cheaper and more spacious than bespoke hard cases and they do not draw attention to the fact that you are making a film. Expandable lightweight rucksacks, 40 litres in size, with webbing straps on each side, are particularly useful to carry your personal belongings, sound equipment, tripod and tent if you need one. Along with this you must also carry your camera equipment, ready to use in a bespoke bag, perhaps improvised so that it can attach to the strap system of your rucksack. I have travelled like this on a number occasions – I found that to achieve a portable weight I needed to reduce my personal belongings to a bare minimum and buy replacement clothes along the way. The non-filmmaking items that I was pleased to have retained, other than the rucksack, were a good pair of shoes, a compact but warm sleeping bag and a lightweight waterproof coat.

Lights and reflectors

Under this heading I want to consider items that can increase ambient light without straying into the territory occupied by professional lighting solutions. Due to budget and accessibility issues it is unlikely that even a two-person lightweight documentary film team will take a three-point lighting set-up into the field, especially now that sensors inside cameras allow low-light recording. Increasing light will greatly improve an image, so for this purpose I always carry a small LED cluster and a foldable reflector into the field. I have often found that the best solution actually lies somewhere in the field site itself, such as a local market where electrical cable, plugs, bulbs, reflective tinfoil and candles are readily available (see images on p. 145).

LED lights are an affordable solution if you are working in dark conditions and want to avoid flat, out of focus, grainy images.

They are available in units ranging from 100 to 1,000 or more individual LEDs, and can be mounted to the top of a camera, cage or L-arm flash bracket, held by hand or placed on a tripod or stand. Some are powered using camcorder batteries while others allow the option to use a mains power supply, USB or AA-sized rechargeable batteries. LED technology is efficient so batteries last well and they are lightweight and compact enough to fit into a camera bag. Find a unit that allows you to adjust the light intensity and colour temperature to suit the situation. I would recommend shooting with available light wherever possible or search for local light sources when working at night, but when this is not possible LEDs are a good option.

If you are operating in bright sunshine and using the shade of trees to avoid overexposing an image then a reflector, such as those sold by Elastolite™, can be used to reflect light onto a subject. This will reduce the possibility of your protagonist appearing darker than the background. Reflectors are sold in a range of sizes and materials; I use a 1 metre diameter, reversible white and silver version. They collapse with a twist, like a pop-up tent, into a flat circular bag about 30 cm in diameter, so they are quite easy to carry. Reflectors require precise and careful positioning to work effectively, so they are most useful when you have someone else to help operate them. In some instances the job can be done equally well with a roll of aluminium foil mounted onto sheets of cardboard.

Participants of the F4F™ Summer School scrutinising an Adobe Premiere Pro timeline

Editing gear

As with most equipment, do not purchase editing gear until you need it and then look for the simplest and cheapest solution that suits your needs. The summary information below will help you to understand what is important when selecting editing equipment – its use will be explained later in Section 4. Do not worry if there are terms that you do not understand on first reading. They will become clear as you search on the internet for what you require and as you make progress through this book.

Editing software

There are at least four major brands offering affordable editing software that all perform similar post-production functions. The cheapest and easiest to use tends to dominate both the professional and domestic markets and this is probably the best one to opt for. Some software, such as Adobe Premiere Creative Cloud, is purchased with a monthly or annual fee. For this you are allowed access – for as long as you continue to pay the subscription – to a variety of post-production applications via a desktop console that manages updates. Others are available by paying a one-off fee, such as the Apple product Final Cut Pro and Avid's Media Composer. Some software, such as the basic edition of DaVinci Resolve, is currently available for free download. Each brand of software has its relative merits, and the most important thing to remember is that they all allow you to cut your film very well. Avid use a traditional interface, which helps to manage media across multiple projects, especially useful when cutting a long documentary, but it is too technically demanding for occasional users. Adobe offer an intuitive suite of software that is useful for an independent filmmaker, with tools for processing photographs, mixing sound, grading colour, website design and hosting and graphics support. Final Cut Pro is fast, creative and intuitive, but like most Apple products it does not interface well with other systems. DaVinci Resolve is well known for its colour-grading capabilities. I tend to use them all at some point over the course of a year but most people opt to stick with one because it can be confusing to swap between the different interfaces and complicated to translate projects between different programs. You can download a time-limited trial version of each system for free; this will allow you to learn the software and possibly get your first film edited for free, if you work fast.

Computer

Many people choose to take a small laptop computer with solid state hard drives into the field to back up their daily shooting. The same device can be used to edit your material into a film if it is powerful enough to run the software. However, it can be fiddly to work on such a small machine so a good option is to extend your basic laptop with a large external screen, keyboard, mouse and audio monitors. A desktop computer will work equally well but you will not be able to carry this on location. Check the system requirements of your editing software before you select the specification of a computer and if possible include extra resources, such as memory or graphics capability, to cope with future advances in software features and image resolution. It is also worth considering how you will import your data – through a card slot or by attaching the camera – and whether the computer has enough ports of the correct type. It is key to test any system through the entire workflow.

Hard drives

Having completed the final cut of *Nanook of the North* (1922), a film many consider to be the first ever documentary, Robert Flaherty lit a celebratory cigarette and accidently set fire to the whole project. For Flaherty, this unfortunate incident became a motivation to return to the field and re-shoot a better film with a stronger central character. For an optimist, hardship and loss will always create new opportunity, but it is prudent to take good care of your work to avoid this eventuality wherever possible. Save your recorded material in three separate places and keep the hard drive that you have chosen to work from away from your other back-ups. Perhaps you have used solid state drives, with no moving parts, in the field. In that case these can become archives or equally you can transfer the material to less costly hard drives and re-use the more expensive lightweight drives for your next shoot.

Keyboard and mouse

If you are editing with a laptop computer then it is easier to use a full keyboard, to which you can map keystroke shortcuts. Silicone covers are available for most keyboards that indicate what each key does in a specific editing program. These are of limited use because they only present one option for each key and can make the keyboard more difficult to operate – so mine usually occupies a place next to the keyboard rather than covering it. An independent mouse or track pad will allow you to raise the laptop up to the level of your additional screen.

Additional video monitor

Extra screen space is essential if you are using a small laptop to run editing software but it is also useful when using a desktop

Using external luma scopes to assess brightness and contrast

correction, it is important to make use of the technical scopes for luma and colour that are included with software, or external ones such as those shown left. It is also a good idea to test the exports of your film using a variety of screens, monitors and projectors.

Audio monitors

Loudspeakers perform the opposite role to a microphone by transforming electrical signals back into sound waves. Search for a good-quality pair of powered desktop audio monitors with a flat response that can express high pitched and low frequency sounds across the entire audible dynamic range of a recording without compression or enhancement. I use a small desktop range of powered monitors made by Genelec in their 8010 series, which operate between 67 Hz and 25 kHz and are ideal for rough cutting. Sounds below 60 Hz or above 30 kHz are inaudible to most people and speakers that can accommodate these frequencies are significantly more expensive. However, in the final stages of an edit it is a good idea to listen to your film on monitors with a wider range if possible, in case there are sounds at a frequency above or below the limits of your own set that you have not noticed. Output power is less important than dynamic range if the editor is working near to the audio monitors; they are best positioned on either side of a video monitor. You will need more speakers if you are working beyond stereo, in surround sound or 360-degrees for example. Headphones can be useful for rough cutting but they do not represent how sounds respond in space and they often lack dynamic range, so they should not be used in the final stages of an editing project where the sound is mixed and exported at output level.

computer. An additional monitor will help when you need to refer to logs and transcripts, or view multiple clips in your project window when you are rough cutting, or to increase the size of your editing timeline for audio track-laying and subtitling. A calibrated screen is useful to assess the visual impact of colour and luma (brightness) correction (see pp. 160–2). Make sure the screen can handle the highest resolution that you are working with and that it can also be downscaled for lower resolutions. It is difficult to find a cheap screen that can be calibrated for colour and luma sufficiently for advanced colour grading but most are ok for basic colour correction, where shot-to-shot consistency is most important. If you are using a cheaper screen for colour

Establishing control

Control, control! You must learn control!

Yoda

Star Wars legend. **The Return of the Jedi** *(1983)*

Before fieldwork begins, it is a good idea to experiment with your equipment in a setting akin to your field site. If you are intending to work, like Yoda, in a galaxy far, far away then find a local context that mimics the conditions where you will be operating and practise there. Consider what lenses will suit your approach. Do you need more light? How many data storage cards will you need? How will you back up your material? Will you use a tripod? Always approach a situation with as much control over the camera as possible or practical. Use manual controls and menu settings to avoid unwanted effects, such as focus pulsing or exposure shifts. If you encounter problems, then put the camera in automatic mode in order to stay with the action, but take a break as soon as possible to think about what is happening around you and re-establish manual control.

Image format and menu settings

One of the most daunting aspects of starting to use a new camera can be understanding the menu system and how this is used to arrange all the settings that affect the image quality and storage size. Menus are navigated in a unique way for each camera, and numbers associated with these settings increase with each advance in technology, but certain principles hold true for most systems. Specific information about format

settings will be explained thoroughly in the manual that came with your camera, and if you do not have a physical copy of the manual, one is usually available on the internet. Before you select a setting, use the in-camera menu to prepare the data card for recording. When you select 'format card', the camera is prompted to write its own file system onto the removable data card so it can accept a selection of settings, as I have outlined below.

An example of a format setting is (4K/ALL-I/400M/50p) for a high-quality image or (FHD/20M/25p) for a lower quality image in the same menu. The letters and numbers in brackets vary according to differences in **image size / compression type / data rate / frame rate**. If you have enough space on your data cards or hard drives and a computer that can cope with high resolutions and fast data transfer, it is common to record a long-term project in the highest quality available and then downsize this for whatever output is eventually necessary. For training and internet sharing purposes 'lighter' weight, lower quality files can be used.

The first number in the example above refers to **image size**, or the quantity of pixels used to determine the resolution of an image. A 4K image has 3840 pixels horizontally and 2160 pixels vertically. Full high definition (FHD), which as its name suggests was once the best quality available, is 1920 x 1080 pixels. Both of these give a landscape aspect ratio of 16:9. Some cameras offer cinemascope features which produce a wider image of 4096 x 2160 pixels, sometimes referred to as C4K. Black bars will appear at the top and bottom, or the sides, of an image when played back on a monitor that doesn't match the aspect ratio it was recorded in. Ultra high definition (UHD) 4K, 8K and 16K pixel resolutions are available, but the majority of ethnographic filmmakers who film at higher resolutions tend to down-convert their images to FHD or lower, as not all research participants or audience members will own screens that can accommodate such a high resolution. Some filmmakers record using a high resolution so that they can crop various shot sizes from a wide frame. This is not common in ethnographic work, where choices about composition and the proximity of the filmmaker help to convey a sense of experience and knowledge.

Image compression refers to the type of video file, or 'codec', that a camera writes to its data cards. This affects the quality, size and usability of images and the way that a computer processes data at the transferring, editing and exporting stages. Examples of format include **ALL Intra**, where each frame is encoded separately (resulting in a very large file that is useful for editing but not very portable) and **Long GOP**, including codecs such as MOV, MP4 and AVCHD, where the file size is much smaller (resulting in a more portable image but at the expense of image quality and ease of editing). There are many codecs that have slightly different characteristics but share the same intent: to compress high-quality video into manageable file sizes.

The **data rate**, or speed at which information is transferred between a recording device and its storage media, determines the overall quality of your image. It is important because it affects the amount of detail available in an image in terms of colour and contrast. This is measured in megabits per second (Mbps) and so it is also referred to as the 'bit rate'. Higher numbers such as 400 Mbps indicate a higher quality and a significantly larger file size than the old digital video standard of 25 Mbps, which is still available for training purposes and internet sharing.

Frame rate is the number of still images, or frames, recorded each second. This affects the look and the motion of your images. Frame rate is largely determined by the electrical or 'system' frequency used in your geographic location. For example, the Americas use a system referred to as NTSC 59.94 Hz, which is sometimes rounded up to 60 Hz, while Europe and China use a PAL 50.00 Hz system. This setting can be changed in most cameras. If you select the wrong frame rate then you will notice flickering similar to that seen on images of computer screens and scenes lit by fluorescent lights. In this handbook we will stick to examples using the PAL settings. Filming in PAL requires a standard 25 frames per second (fps) , or multiples thereof if you want to slow down images. The way this image data is processed, either by progressively scanning each image or interlacing two image fields together, also has a bearing on how your pictures will appear. An interlaced image is indicated with an 'i' that appears after the frame rate, and a progressively scanned image uses 'p'. Most filmmakers opt for the higher quality and film-like progressive scan option.

Sometimes a setting relating to YUV/bit is available. This concerns the way colour is recorded, in terms of depth and separation, and has an impact on the possibilities available for secondary and tertiary colour grading, or if you want to give your film a specific 'look' (see p. 160). This is generally less important for ethnographic purposes, so it tends to fall into line with the settings mentioned above.

Whatever you opt for, format settings must be tested through an entire production workflow. That means: format the data card, select your settings, record a small variety of material, then import or reference the clips from your editing software and make some cutting decisions, and finally export the portion that you have edited and screen the resulting 'film' (see Section 4). Cross-reference the results with the information in this book and on internet forums and try to clear up any areas of uncertainty. Do not worry if you struggle to understand all of this to begin with – opt for a setting that you think balances usability with quality and stick to that for now.

Data storage

Try to anticipate the number of hours of audiovisual material that you hope to record between back-ups and then purchase enough data cards to give you the necessary capacity. For example, if your camera uses 50 gigabytes (GB) of space to store a single hour of material, then a 128GB card has the capacity to hold roughly 2.5 hours of material. You can opt to record more material at a lower quality but most filmmakers prefer to record at the highest quality and then downscale if necessary at the post-production stage. The speed at which data is transferred to the card is as important as its capacity – and this is where it gets even more confusing. There are eight megabits in one megabyte, so recording video at 400 megabits per second (Mbps) will require a data card of at least 60 megabytes (MBs), which will allow for some 'headroom' if the bit rate temporarily slips above this 8:1 ratio. Professional SD cards include a video class number – shown as V30, V60, V90 and so on – indicating their suitability for recording high-quality video files. If in doubt, ask other filmmakers what storage card they have used successfully with similar recording expectations.

With a single data card there is the danger it might fail, or get lost or damaged, so you may prefer to carry a number of smaller cards, especially if you cannot back up your material easily while in the field. If you need to store a number of cards then engage the write-protect tab and label each card before you stash them safely. Whatever you decide, back up this material on two separate hard drives before you reformat your card(s) using the camera menu. If you are using a camcorder at a lower bit rate, you can buy high-capacity SD cards and use these to back up your material. You will need a device that accepts two SD cards or similar in order to make the transfer. Store data cards in the slots of your camera and keep spares in a safe place, as they are small and easy to lose.

Operating a camera using manual functions

I recommend operating with full manual control over the camera, during the recording of your film and certainly when practising the exercises on pp. 14–15. This is important to ensure that you create an image that reflects your own understanding of a subject rather than the camera manufacturer's interpretation. You will also develop more aesthetically proficient pictures if you are able to control the ways that light enters your camera. Some cameras have dedicated switches on the exterior of the camera body that give control over the main manual functions, whereas others have selectable functions for a more limited array of buttons. The following six photographic functions have the greatest impact on the quality of images and they are relevant to all camera systems. Find these on whatever system you are using and learn how to set them accurately under a variety of recording conditions.

1. Exposure and depth of field

Contrast between brightness and darkness in video images is altered as the digital sensor is exposed to more or less light. This is controlled by changing the aperture of a mechanical iris housed within the lens, according to increments of focal-ratio called 'f-stops'. Exposure, iris, aperture and f-stop are all interchangeable terms used to describe the workings of a mechanical gateway that allows light to enter the camera. The width of this opening also determines the amount of an image that is in focus, sometimes referred to as depth of field. So a low f-stop, say f/2, creates a wide opening that allows a lot of light to pass into the camera and leads to a shallow depth of field. This means that the foreground and background are out of focus and only things at a particular distance are in focus. The reverse is true for a high f-stop of f/5.6 and above. A precise balance must be struck between the diameter of the iris opening and the speed at which the shutter mechanism opens and closes, in order to correctly expose an image. Shutter speed cannot be adjusted in videography in the same way that it can in photography – doing so will add an unrealistic blur or oversharpness to the image – which is why we add artificial light when not enough ambient light is available, or ND when there is too much.

Correct exposure avoids excessive brightness, which will limit contrast. Equally, try not to lose detail in the dark areas of an image by 'crushing' the shadows into total blackness. It can be difficult to strike the correct balance between light and dark in

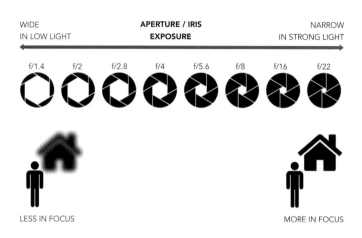

Figure 4 *Aperture size influences the amount of light that can enter a camera, which in turn impacts our ability to focus on a subject*

situations of high contrast. For example, if you were to record a person with dark skin in the shade of a tree, with bright sunlight behind them, then the situation will be 'backlit'. This results in either underexposure of the face or overexposure of the background, as the contrast is too great between the light and dark areas to achieve an overall balance. The same is true for a light-skinned person against a dark background, where the face can become overexposed or the background underexposed. As a rule, the subject of your recording should be given priority when assessing exposure, even if this means 'clipping' brightness or 'crushing' darkness in other areas of the image. It is best to avoid such situations wherever possible and try to operate where the strongest light falls directly onto your subject rather than behind them.

Most cameras have a 'zebra' function that highlights overexposed areas by adding visible stripes, or a histogram that shows the proportions of an image that are light and dark. This is similar to the Y-waveform graph available in all video-editing software and on some cameras and external field monitors (see p. 161). Remember to check the brightness of your monitor screen, preferably with the help of a Y-waveform graph, so that you can accurately assess exposure, and if in doubt use the zebra setting to show up any areas of overexposure.

A camera can perform the function of a light meter, helping to select the correct exposure by reading the intensity of light falling in the centre of a frame. The focus of such 'spot metering' can be adjusted in most systems, but it is best to keep the assessment area in the centre of the frame and move the camera to obtain a number of different readings from both light and dark areas. Once you have explored a scene in this way, you can select whichever reading you think best exposes the image. Camcorders incorporate a 'push-auto' button that allows you to temporarily engage auto mode to get a light reading before returning to full manual control for recording. For DSLR and mirrorless cameras this function is performed when the record button is half-pressed. Do not allow a camera to automatically control exposure as this can result in exposure shifts on-shot. If a dark cloud covers the sun or a moving vehicle obscures the light areas of a scene, resulting in a darker image, then our aim is to evoke how this dramatic change affects our subject, rather than attempting to cover up the shift by compensating for the change.

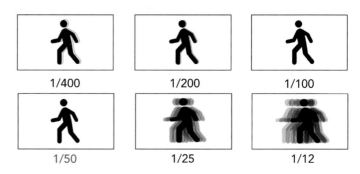

Figure 5 *Moving images become over-sharp and edgy if the shutter speed is too fast and blurred if it is too slow*

2. Shutter speed and frame rate

Video recording uses 'shutter priority', which means the speed at which a shutter mechanism opens and closes the iris should be kept constant. Variations in light are accommodated by adjusting the exposure ring, allowing more or less light through a larger or smaller aperture in the lens. Shutter speed helps to determine the amount of light that enters a frame, but in doing so it can affect the naturalism of a moving picture. In the PAL system the default setting for shutter speed is '50', meaning that the shutter is open for 1/50th of a second, allowing the 'film' to 'travel' at a desired speed of 25 fps. This is considered the frame refresh rate that most closely mimics human sight. If we increase the shutter speed then movement appears jagged and edgy, and lacks the softness that occurs when the human eye scans a scene. If we decrease the shutter speed by half, to 1/25th or less, then blurring will occur that gives the impression of drunkenness and disorientation. This technique can be used for effect if the content demands it but otherwise operate your camera in a way that mimics the way you see. A shutter speed of 1/50th works well when shooting at 24 or 25 fps but you will need to manually adjust this when shooting at other frame rates, such as 30 or 50 fps. For NTSC recording the setting is '60', which translates to a film progression speed of roughly 30 fps. Some DSLR, mirrorless and high-end hybrid cameras allow you to prioritise the shutter angle instead of the speed measured in fractions of a second. When the shutter angle is set to 180 degrees the shutter speed will automatically double to suit faster or slower frame rates. This gives a consistent film look, which is useful if you are swapping between frame rates.

Flickering can occur for images lit by screens or light sources that have a refresh rate higher or lower than the frame rate of your film, such as fluorescent strip lights and computer monitors. To overcome this, adjust the shutter speed up or down until it corresponds with the 'frame rate' of the light source and the problem will disappear. Some cameras include a 'synchro scan' function in the menu that allows finer adjustment to the shutter speed, specifically aimed at overcoming this problem.

Be careful not to confuse shutter speed with slow or fast motion effects that are created by increasing or decreasing the frame rate along with an associated change in shutter speed. Think carefully about your reasons for using fast or slow motion effects beyond the fact that they look cool.

3. Focus
Sharpness helps to highlight detail in your composition. Most cameras have advanced autofocus features but I recommend that you learn to use manual focus. Focus can be used creatively

within a single shot to add timed emphasis, something an automatically focused camera is incapable of doing. Make sure that assign buttons for 'Manual Focus' (MF) or 'Autofocus' (AF) on the camera body or lenses are set to MF, and disable any continuous focus functions. Camcorders that suit the pedagogy of this handbook tend to have a focus ring that can be rotated infinitely in both directions, which makes the job of focusing quite difficult. Try to work out which direction brings a distant object into focus and which does the opposite. Lenses that are intended for use with DSLR and mirrorless cameras usually have a more precise, and therefore easier to use, focus ring.

When using a zoom lens, the most reliable method for finding critical focus is to zoom in fully on a discernible part of an object, like a strand of hair or the glint of an eye, find your focus and then pull out to the desired shot size. DSLR and mirrorless cameras have a 'punch-in' button dedicated to critical focus, and on some cameras this is triggered automatically when you adjust the focus ring. This is useful when recording with prime lenses

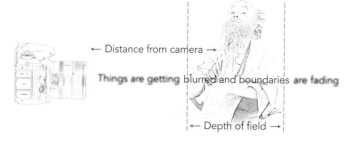

← Distance from camera →

Things are getting blurred and boundaries are fading

← Depth of field →

Figure 6 *Judge distance correctly, or temporarily engage auto-focus, to ensure that your subject remains sharply in focus*

that can't be zoomed, although this function is not available during a recording.

All cameras struggle to focus in low light, as this forces a wide aperture with a shallow depth of field. If you are recording at dusk or dawn, operate from static positions, as this will reduce the need to follow focus. Focal length is measured between the subject and the digital sensor of the camera, so as long as these two points are static then your image will remain in focus, no matter what shot size you select. If either the subject or your camera move, then you will need to 'follow focus' by manually manipulating the focus ring. Do not use automatic focus, especially in low light, because when a subject or person moves position your camera will search to focus on whatever is occurring at the centre of the frame, often resulting in an unnaturalistic shifting back and forth of focus. If you want to create more depth of field by reducing the aperture to a number greater than f/5.6, you will also need to introduce more light – by altering your position, reflecting natural light onto the scene, or if this is not possible by adding artificial light. It is acceptable for an image to be out of focus temporarily when the content is compelling but it should return to its focus before you cut away.

It is difficult to focus a smartphone using manual controls, even with the additional software apps mentioned in the previous section. Action cameras are designed for remote operation, so they do not offer the facility for manual focus. Both of these technologies rely on the content to drive the quality of a recording.

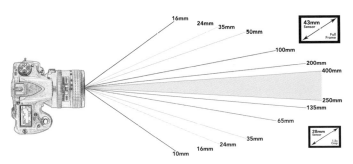

Figure 7 *Sensor type with corresponding lens sizes, indicating the angle of view created with each lens*

4. Zoom, shot size and lenses

Moving between different shot sizes using a single lens is called zooming. Shot size is fixed on a prime lens but most camcorders and smartphones, and some DSLR and mirrorless cameras aimed at video make use of a zoom lens. When using zoom lenses do not rely on adopting a static position away from the main action. Instead 'zoom with your legs' and move yourself nearer to a subject, and use the optical zoom only to refine your framing. There are a number of reasons for this. Shooting with a wide angle allows you to bring the microphone closer to the action to record a more focused and compelling sound. This creates intimacy with a subject and introduces accountability through proximity, which is why the technique has become a trademark feature of the observational method. It is easier to handhold a close-up shot steady using a wide angle lens than it is with a fully zoomed narrow lens. More light can enter the camera with the wider apertures that are available on a wide angle lens and this will allow you to operate in darker conditions. The drawback here is that depth of field is reduced with a wide aperture so it becomes more difficult to maintain critical focus in a wide-angled image. This can be a significant issue for full-frame DSLR cameras when exploring moving subjects. Most zoom lenses allow something like f/3.5 at their widest angle but close down to f/5.6 at the tele end, resulting in darker images. The best lenses feature constant aperture, which means that when you zoom in the lens will not automatically close down the iris.

If you are shooting with a hybrid camera, DSLR or mirrorless then a prime lens is a useful addition to your kit bag. A 50 mm lens on a full frame is considered the most natural representation of the field of human vision. These lenses have large apertures, which help to create images with a shallow depth of field that can greatly enhance the look of your interview material, in particular by blurring backgrounds and drawing the focus to the eyes and face of the speaker. It is harder to achieve this look on the smaller 'crop' sensor sizes, but then again it is much easier to follow focus in most other applications, especially when working handheld. For those in need of something even more compact, the miniscule 'pancake' lenses come in a zoom variety. If you change lenses, think about how this can alter the ways that shots will match in colour, contrast and sharpness. The key is again to experiment before you begin shooting your film.

5. ISO and digital gain

ISO stands for the 'International Organisation for Standards'. This replaces the American Standards Association (ASA) which established agreement over categories about sensitivity, or 'speed', of celluloid film. Old terminology has remained as the technology turned digital, and ISO now refers to the sensitivity setting of the sensor or chip. High ISO numbers are more sensitive to light

Native ISO

| ISO 100 | ISO 400 GAIN +0dB | ISO 800 GAIN +3dB | ISO 3200 GAIN +9dB | ISO 12800 GAIN +18dB |

Figure 8 *Most cameras will allow you to alter the sensitivity of the digital sensor above or below its native factory setting, to help deal with light and dark situations*

and indicate an increase of grain size in the image. Numbers are doubled, corresponding incrementally to a movement in iris stops or shutter speeds. Thus a sensitivity of 800 is three times as fast, or sensitive to light, as a speed of 100. So depending on your camera, the ISO value you choose will have a subjective upper limit of image degradation. For example, on a small MFT sensor video shooters rarely go beyond 3200 ISO, but with a full-frame sensor you can push this much further, to 26000 ISO for example.

If you are a camcorder shooter then you will encounter light sensitivity as a manual setting called 'gain'. This is measured in dB to indicate the intensity of picture noise that enters a scene as you move beyond the native ISO of the sensor and add digital light enhancement, or gain. As a rule, avoid adding digital gain unless there is no possibility for lighting the scene adequately. Some degree of contrast within dark areas is vital if an image is to be improved in post-production, so you may need to make use of gain occasionally. Try to preserve the overall contrast between dark and light areas, to create atmosphere with limited or focused light. Most cameras will add lightness in auto-mode even if the image becomes marginally too dark, so ensure that you disable this function.

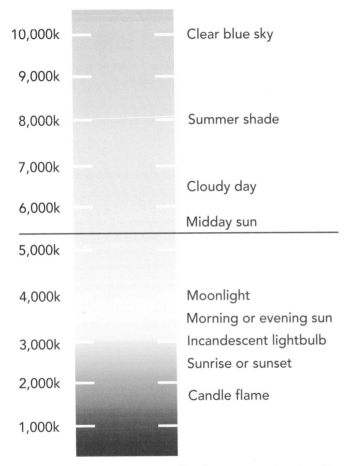

10,000k	Clear blue sky
9,000k	
8,000k	Summer shade
7,000k	
6,000k	Cloudy day
5,000k	Midday sun
4,000k	Moonlight
	Morning or evening sun
3,000k	Incandescent lightbulb
	Sunrise or sunset
2,000k	
	Candle flame
1,000k	

6. Colour and white balance

A camera must be instructed how to read colour in order to create what we see and understand as white. The camera will use this information as a basis to achieve natural and consistent representation of skin tones and other important shades. The sophistication of automatic white balance has developed in recent years but it is still unreliable when natural and artificial light are mixed, or when shadows change colour on a cloudy day. Auto balancing can give inconsistent results, creating more corrective work for you to do in post-production. Light is measured in degrees kelvin (k) according to its 'temperature' (see Figure 9, left) – higher in number but cooler in tone as we progress across the spectrum, from dim orange candlelight at 2000 k to daylight with its strong bluish tones that can be as much as 10,000 k. It is necessary to re-establish white balance with each scene change, when there has been a change in light temperature – for example, moving between indoors and outdoors or switching an electrical light source on or off. Do not alter the white balance within a scene, even if clouds force a change in the ambient light temperature, as it is preferable to demonstrate such changes as accurately as possible in relation to a protagonist's experience.

To establish white balance, hold a white card in front of your subject or protagonist, so that the camera can accurately record the colour of the incident light. It is not strictly necessary to carry a bespoke white card for this purpose, as one can balance on a wall or other non-reflective white surface. However, be careful in a room with mixed lighting – for instance, natural light through windows as well as electrical lights – to select a surface that is

Figure 9 *Colour temperature. Engage ND filters for temperatures above the red line*   Mari Korpela (camera) and Devrim Aslan (sound) working in unison

receiving similar light to that falling onto your subject. Camera systems vary in their functionality but commonly a selection button allows you to lock a setting in place. Most modern camera systems that make use of a colour screen to monitor images offer precise balancing in degrees kelvin, which is easier to set without the use of a white card in situations of mixed lighting, and therefore less intrusive to the action.

Connecting sound to the camera

When operating as a two-person team the sound recordist is usually umbilically connected to the camera operator. Connection is made via a cable loom connecting the field mixer or recorder to the camera, or by two cables running separately from headphones and microphone directly into the audio interface of the camera. Wireless systems are available for experienced users. If you are working alone then the connections are the same but the cables will be significantly shorter. XLR adapters and field mixers use switchable controls to accept a variety of input types, so ensure that you have selected these correctly,

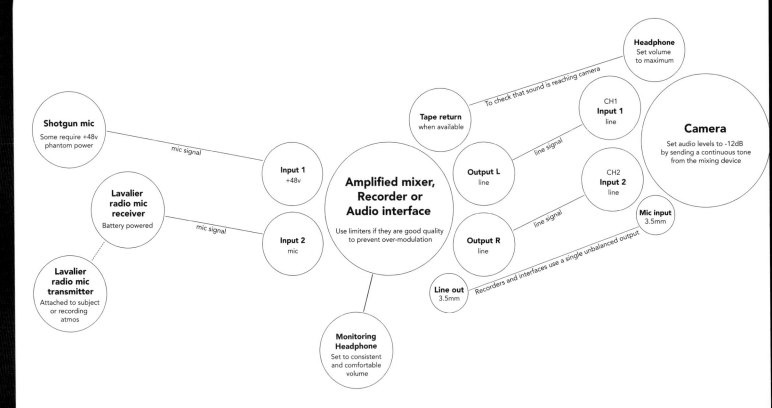

Shotgun mic
Some require +48v
phantom power

**Lavalier
radio mic
receiver**
Battery powered

**Lavalier
radio mic
transmitter**
Attached to subject
or recording
atmos

mic signal

mic signal

Input 1
+48v

Input 2
mic

**Amplified mixer,
Recorder or
Audio interface**
Use limiters if they are good quality
to prevent over-modulation

**Monitoring
Headphone**
Set to consistent
and comfortable
volume

Tape return
when available

Output L
line

Output R
line

Line out
3.5mm

To check that sound is reaching camera

line signal

line signal

Recorders and interfaces use a single unbalanced output

Headphone
Set volume
to maximum

CH1
Input 1
line

CH2
Input 2
line

Mic input
3.5mm

Camera
Set audio levels to -12dB
by sending a continuous tone
from the mixing device

Figure 10 *Common audio connections and settings*

otherwise your audio signal may become distorted. 'Mic' is for a powered microphone that uses its own battery and '+48V' is for a microphone that requires phantom (PH) power via the XLR input, while 'Line' is for an input from a powerful amplified source such as a field mixer or recording desk.

Audio mixers send a powerful signal to the camera at 'line' level, so it is a good idea to check if your camera interface can accept this type of input. If it does not then there may be an unbalanced output from your field mixer that can be connected via a 3.5 mm jack for input into a mixer at microphone level. Either way, mixers and recorders that are controlled separately from the camera must be allowed to control the recording level of the sound. To achieve this a reference signal is sent from the mixer that is established at -12 dBFS (meaning decibels relative to the full scale, where the scale ends at '0' and extends negatively to minus infinity; see Figure 14, p. 108) using manual controls on your camera. If you neglect to do this, the camera will use its automatic settings to override the decisions made by your sound recordist. More about that in Section 3.

Signal-to-noise ratio

Microphones turn air pressure into electrical signals. A microphone needs to have enough power to transmit a strong signal. A weak recording will result in the desired sound, such as a human voice, becoming buried amongst internal electronic static noise in your recording or general environmental sounds. To achieve clear and detailed audio recordings one therefore needs a good signal-to-noise ratio (SNR). Pre-amplification inside

Channel inputs (left) and selection switches (above)

cameras, recording devices and audio mixers increases the power of an audio signal. We aim to achieve a good dynamic range between loud and quiet sounds in our recordings, comparable to contrast in a well-exposed image. If a signal is too loud, it may be clipped by limiters or destroyed completely as it tries to break out of the upper limits of the recording. If it is too quiet then it will be indistinguishable from the 'noise floor' of the recording or other background sounds, as these are lifted together with the desired sound in post-production to achieve broadcast levels. It is recommended that you record the strongest signal possible (allowing 12db of 'headroom' beyond the loudest sounds before clipping occurs) to avoid these problems.

Microphones lose their ability to transform audible sound into an electronic signal as their power supply diminishes, so make sure you change batteries inside microphones, or those on cameras and mixers that supply phantom power, when they are two-thirds spent and do not wait until they are completely drained. Very few microphones and mixers give noticeable warnings when a battery starts to fade and it can be difficult to perceive a weakening signal or the gradual rise of electronic noise. Inexperienced sound recordists who attempt to get every last drop of energy from a battery tend to compensate for the loss of microphone power by increasing the audio recording volume on the camera or mixer. Do not do this as it will result in noisy recordings. Some microphones, such as those designed specifically for use with DSLR and mirrorless cameras, include a +20 dB boost to ensure that a strong electronic signal reaches the camera.

Audio format and quality

Camcorder, DSLR and mirrorless cameras now offer the option to choose linear pulse code modulation (LPCM) options and the ability to add a high-quality audio interface, usually purchased separately. When using XLR interfacing, select 48 kHz, 16 bit or 24 bit audio, which will give the highest quality recordings perceptible to the human ear.

Inputs, channels and tracks

The varying ways that people experience sound and image in different circumstances are well illustrated on an editing timeline. One track of video, perhaps with the occasional overlay, subtitle or graphic, is used alongside many audio tracks, containing all the types of sound that contribute to an audioscape. In our everyday lives we frame images individually and progressively in the blink of an eye and they do not become merged unless there is something wrong. Audio, on the other hand, has no border and we perceive it all around us from a multitude of sources in varying intensities. Before you can recreate such an audioscape it is important to understand how an electronic signal from a microphone is inputted and then channelled to a specific track on a data-recording card.

Inputs are where you connect your microphones to the camera or audio interface. Be consistent when selecting inputs for your microphones. Always choose input 1 for your principal directional microphone and input 2 for your secondary microphone. Input 1 is equivalent to the left input on your mixer or other devices that use 'L and R' instead of '1 and 2', and to the green colour coding for cables that use green and red to indicate L/1 and R/2. This is confusing, but a simple mantra helps – **Red 2 Right**, which then implies the less figurative **Green 1 Left**. It is important to be consistent with your input selection so that you can become aware of the quality of the sound in each ear and know which volume control on your mixer has control over each input. If you are unsure which ear a microphone is targeting, you can identify it by scratching the end of the microphone and removing one side of your headphones in order to hear more clearly the specific sound from that microphone. You can then use this method to check that you have set the system up correctly. Once you have established the system do not vary it, but do occasionally identify each of the microphones to check that you are being consistent.

Most audio interfaces, whether integral to a camcorder or a separate device, will allow you to split one input across two channels. This is useful if you need to record a safety track from the same microphone at a lower or higher level, usually 12 dB of difference. It will also allow you to configure inputs to either the left or right track, so you must be careful to have these switches set correctly. If you do not hear the correct microphone in either ear and your inputs are accurate, check the selection switches on the camera audio interface.

A Mid-Side (MS) stereo system uses two separate channels to record a mono signal and one side of a stereo pattern, which is then reversed onto an extra track at the editing stage. This process of matrixing the audio tracks enables a single microphone to record both stereo and mono, and for advanced practitioners it is the most versatile option. An ambiasonic system adopts the same principles through four separate channels, via four inputs, which will end up as four individual tracks on your editing timeline.

Principal mic	= **Input 1** on camera or **Left** input on a mixer via the **Green** coded cable
	= Input 1 or Left channel display on peak level meter
	= left ear monitoring microphone
	= **Audio track 1** on your editing timeline.
Secondary mic	= **Input 2** on camera or **Right** input on a mixer via the **Red** coded cable
	= Input 2 or Right channel display on peak level meter
	= Right ear monitoring microphone
	= **Audio track 2** on your editing timeline.

Kelly Johnson (left) and Vik Pengilly-Johnson (right) working late into the evening for *One Long Journey*

Lighting

In the midst of darkness, light persists.

Mahatma Gandhi
social reformer and revolutionary

Without illumination image does not exist, so even in the darkest scenes we must think about light. Light adds colour to pigmented objects regardless of where it comes from. A broad distinction can be made between bluish light, which occurs outside as part of the natural environment, and orange or green artificial light, which is imposed by flame or electricity when natural light is not available. Variations in colour are assessed in terms of temperature by their measurement in degrees kelvin (see Figure 9, p. 72). The human eye adjusts to the colour of light naturally but a camera needs help from us to perform this function. The correct 'white balance' setting can be applied using a white card or similar surface, together with camera functions designed specifically for this purpose, or by adding coloured filters to artificial lights and windows.

Natural light

Daylight is bluish in colour and it has a temperature range of between 5,000 kelvins for shady areas and 10,000 kelvins for the brightest sunlight. Whenever possible it is preferable to operate in good natural daylight, as this increases our ability to focus a camera and produces rich tones across a range of colours. However, if the light is too bright then the opposite will happen: colours will be washed out and faded, or details might even be obliterated in the white-out of total overexposure.

There are two main problems with light: too much and too little. When dealing with excessive light, which can overexpose an image, we do not want to increase the shutter speed to reduce the amount of light entering the camera, as this will develop detail in a moving image that appears unnatural to the human eye (see Figure 5, p. 68). We can reduce the exposure to its highest f-stop and smallest aperture, but this may not be enough to eliminate overexposure (see Figure 4, p. 67). We therefore need another way to limit bright light from entering the camera. When the sun is at its brightest, the best option, if possible, is to seek shade or opt to record early in the morning or late in the day, when the sun is lower and the shadows are longer. Unappealing backlighting can occur if a subject is recorded in the shade and the peripheral light is stronger – the overall exposure is reduced, making the main subject of your image too dark. A common example of this can be seen when interviewees are recorded in front of a window, or similarly illuminous background. To avoid this problem, position a subject or protagonist away from bright backgrounds or reflect light onto the dark area to reduce the overall contrast. If this is not possible, set the exposure according to the requirements of the subject and allow the background to be slightly overexposed.

Neutral density (ND) filters work in a similar fashion to sunglasses for your camera. They reduce the intensity of ultraviolet light when operating in consistently bright conditions and help to mitigate the problem of overexposure. Camcorder menus produce a flashing indication in the monitor screen when they think it is necessary to implement inbuilt filters via the mechanical ND switch. Many semi-professional cameras will suggest that you engage the first level of ND at iris apertures greater in number and smaller in aperture than f/5.6. This will increase sharpness

and reduce depth of field, and thus allow you to create more interesting shots. Most outdoor conditions require filtering, so as a rule look to the environment in which you are recording to suggest whether an ND filter should be engaged or not (see Figure 9, p. 72). NDs add a particular kind of grey cast to the picture so it is important to use them consistently when gathering material for a single scene, especially when including shots of the sky or sea. A common mistake is to leave the ND engaged after you have moved on to a new scene where the ambient light is darker, which is akin to wearing sunglasses inside or after dusk. In a situation such as this the camera will suggest that you add digital gain beyond the maximum optical exposure, which results in dark and grainy pictures that lack contrast. If you choose not to add gain then artificial light must be added to recover brightness, so do not forget to remove the ND before continuing to film. Other filters that you may want to consider include a UV or skylight, which both reduce excessive blue tones caused by daylight exposures, or a circular-polarising filter that will help control excess glare and unwanted reflections through a variety of degree settings (see also p. 54).

The biggest challenge arrives when light begins to fade rapidly, because it is late in the day or clouds have gathered overhead. For most documentarists this represents an actuality worth filming but for some scenes you may require consistency with images recorded in brighter conditions. Apart from adding a degree of artificial light, which is difficult to achieve, the best solution is to record a variety of shots that can be used in editing to demonstrate the effect the change is having on the protagonists of your story.

Fading light on the set of *Curse of the Inca* during filming for *Horror in the Andes*

Artificial light

If you are forced to work in relative darkness then you must find ways to increase the amount of light that reaches your subject. One way is to adjust the potential of the camera. This can be done either by increasing the exposure with a widening of the f-stop, which can make focusing difficult, or by increasing the ISO speed on DSLR and mirrorless cameras and adding digital gain on camcorders, which can produce grainy and unappealing images. When a scene is poorly lit and you have exhausted the options of repositioning your subject, by far the best way to get good-quality images is to add more light.

Artificial light is mainly orange or green in colour, with a temperature range of 1,800 kelvins for candles to 5,600 kelvins for a bright LED cluster, or more for lights that mimic full daylight. It is unlikely that you will have brought a professional lighting set-up with you to the field; however, we can consider the principles of three-point lighting in order to find other ways to achieve a similar outcome. The 'key' light is the point that raises the overall brightness of a scene, with an effect similar to sunlight. A 'fill' light is added with less intensity and at a slight tangent to the subject to reduce harsh shadows caused by the key light. And the third point is a 'back' light, sometimes called a 'kicker' or 'hair light', which is used to separate a subject from the background. A way to replicate three-point lighting can usually be found on location using a combination of improvised artificial lights, such as desk lamps and spotlights, reflected natural light and the careful positioning of a subject or protagonist (see also Figure 15, p. 116).

In-built camera lights and head torches are useful in extreme circumstances when they can be established as a feature in your ethnographic story, but for general use they are too weak. LED clusters are good if they can be introduced subtly and balanced to the correct degree of warmth. In ethnographic and documentary work it is preferable to operate with the temperature and intensity of light that exists naturally in a scene and add to this incrementally wherever necessary. You do not need to fill the whole scene with light – highlight certain parts of the image that you find interesting and leave other parts in shade. For instance, if you are shooting, as I was, in a dark cremation ground in India with no mains power supply then it would be inappropriate to flood the scene with strong battery-powered LED light. Instead I chose to purchase candles from a local market, similar to those used by tantric practitioners in their prayers. This enabled me to light faces and key actions but leave the edges of the frame in evocative shadow (see p. 159). If you are in doubt about how to light a scene, ask your fieldwork participants how they perform their activities in low light. It is not usually a viable option to record in total darkness, as an audience geared for a visual display might find this distracting. Similarly, if you do not introduce enough light then your images will lack appeal as the camera increases ISO or gain to compensate for the lack of light.

Mixed lighting can create problems for a camera that the human eye does not experience. For instance, if you are recording in a room with large windows then your principal light source is likely to be bluish. If you decide to increase the lighting by switching on the room lights, or by adding in some of your own, you will be contributing an orange colour into the scene. A camera can only balance for one temperature, so a wide angle here will produce areas of your picture with an undesirable colour cast that is hard to fix in post-production. Again, the solution is to move position if possible, or if not then work with one light source or the other – perhaps by curtaining off a window and increasing only the artificial light. A professional crew will carry large rolls of orange, blue or green plastic that can be used to cover windows or lights, but it is unlikely that you will have that possibility in the field.

If you are operating with lights then allow enough time to set this up. I recommend giving yourself two hours before you start recording with a full lighting set-up

The scene pictured right shows a lighting scenario used to record single person interviews for a film of memory about England's worst mining disaster (see pp. 123-4). We established one lighting scenario and exchanged the banners in the background between interviews. Interviewees sat in the chair shown directly in front of the camera. This was faced alternately left or right for each interview, so that the resulting material could be edited as a dialogue.

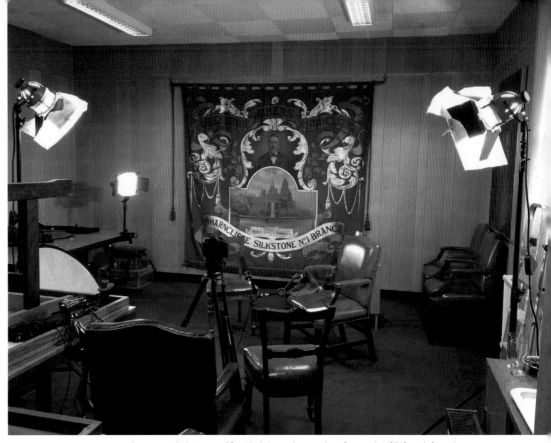

Three-point lighting used for *Black Snow* showing key (front right), fill (front left) and kicker (back left). A reflector can be seen beneath the fill light. Additional sources of light were provided by an external window (right, edge of frame) and room lights (seen above).

Overleaf Rajive McMullen during his journey into Tantra

SECTION 3
Recording

Human life cannot be reduced to the conceptual language with which we render it intelligible or manageable.

Michael Jackson
anthropologist and author of **Lifeworlds** (2013: 7)

There is a fundamental problem for ethnographers when attempting to understand moments of fieldwork that are marked by confusion, ambiguity or uncertainty. How do we attempt to understand something that extends beyond the boundaries of rationality using academic methods that are built on reason? If researchers grow remote from the experiences that colour their fieldwork then a further problem develops in how to express subjectivity in ways that will connect an audience to the lifeworlds of other people. Filmmaking mitigates this problem by employing artistic techniques for data gathering, which can carry us beyond moments of disbelief in the field and prepare us for a more forensic examination at the editing stage. The tantric practitioners I worked with also use a direct and physical engagement with the object of their confusion or uncertainty to seek more coherent expressions. Their solution is to think differently about a situation and act in ways that may be contrary to, or the reverse of what is expected. By doing so, the seeker begins to understand how matter can be shaped by human fear, expectation and desire. It is not that tantric practitioners want to stop making sense of any sort, but rather that they intend to transcend common human limitations in order to reach a deeper understanding of a wider cosmic order.

Similarly, filmmaking uses the intersubjective and performative arena of a documentary film, where acting and thinking are expressed through moments of recorded action. These moments have the potential to evoke an evolving sense of their becoming, rather than rely on retrospective statements about their being. The triangle of action that I outlined in Section 1 of this handbook is a technique for the close examination of situations that unfold in real time and space, and a way to gather the grammatical material for a film. If we are careful to collect all the necessary parts then we can revisit the circumstances of our experiences through the recorded material when we edit. Filmmaking is both experience-led research and experience-led expression. The 'sentences' that constitute our films are 'written' with this experience at the time of recording and we cannot separate our own feelings and actions from those of the people we are working with, so it is important to record them with care and precision. These aesthetics of ambiguity and uncertainty allow us to experiment with the order of processes, by eliminating or truncating action, or searching for subtle motivations in our protagonists, and this can be used to radically improve the ways we understand our fieldwork, leading to new ideas and theories about a topic.

A research proposal helps us to select equipment and imagine what methods and techniques might be useful in the field but it does not deliver much in the way of practical help as we start to operate recording equipment in real-life situations. It is with actual practice that the technical demands of image and sound recording become less of a hindrance. Instinct and intuition start to influence where we position our camera and microphones, and this in turn extends our filmmaking deeper into the performative and experiential areas that offer something different to a writing method. In this section, we will consider how to move and position the cinema technology to explore core ideas in key fieldwork situations, such as those presented in processes, events, performances, on journeys, around tables, on desktop devices and through conversations. The aim is to go beyond words to explore complex and uncertain realities and then to show, rather than tell, an audience how we did this.

Andy Lawrence (centre) preparing to film with Hari Nath Pagal (left) en route to Kamakhya Devi in Assam for *The Lover and the Beloved*

Fieldwork relationships

Remember that you are developing a three-way relationship between fieldwork participants, yourself and your audience that will extend to your crew if you are working with one. A collaborative and reflexive approach to research can help us to comprehend the expressions of others and also develop a greater understanding of how our own actions can be provoked and perceived by the world around us. Fieldwork relationships are not something to be considered only at the early stages of a project; rather they grow in importance as the work develops and they come to define the overall feel of a documentary film.

Approaching research participants

It appears that the popularity of social media and other modern ways of communicating might have taken us further away from the simple act of speaking person-to-person, which as a consequence has made the job of filmmaking more difficult. Sitting in a classroom, it can seem unfathomable how one might learn to engage with strangers through a camera. When I asked my students what they would like me to include in this book, a surprising number replied that a section on how to develop relationships in the field would be useful.

Initial contact can be by telephone, email or social media, but it is a good idea to meet potential participants in person, as this will give a better sense of how they might contribute, or even appear in your film. Fieldwork relationships start with words but it is actions that come to define them. How to pursue potential contributors

is something for a researcher to decide, but I tend to carry my camera with me on initial meetings, not only to justify my intrusion but also to acquaint potential collaborators with the tools of my trade and my primary objectives as a filmmaker. Relationships develop as participants sense your commitment each time they witness you return to their neighbourhood. Begin by recording scenes that are not central to your imagined narrative, so that you can break from filming if necessary. This will serve to acquaint potential collaborators with your role as a filmmaker, help you to make stylistic and technical decisions based on practical experience and filter out unwanted initial interest about the mechanics of filmmaking. If you can spend some time socialising with co-fieldworkers and listening to their stories then you will be able to build a strong enough relationship to gain significant access when it comes to events that are of more central interest to you. There is a fine balance to strike in these early meetings between gathering useful research and moving too deeply into a subject. Try to understand what your research participants find interesting – but be careful not to provoke their expressions of this until the moment is right. Similarly, take note of your own initial perceptions that occur off-camera, so that you can recreate these later in the edit using your establishing shots. This will help audience members to understand how it feels to arrive at your field site and this will in turn help them settle into your narrative.

It is important that you inform possible fieldwork participants about your work and what making a film with you may involve for them, to whatever degree you consider necessary and appropriate. It would be off-putting to spell out in graphic certainty the need for 'time' and 'patience' but it is a good idea to subtly gesture towards these fundamental requirements. Encourage people to participate in your film by showing your own enthusiasm and avoid boring them at this early stage with too many administrative details and the intricacies of your research, unless they ask. If they agree to work with you then at some point soon you will arrive at the need for informed consent, but this is not necessarily something to be dealt with in the very first meeting. When the time does arrive, structure your approach using a participant information sheet like the one I have included in Appendix 2. If a person is reluctant to be filmed and you progress apprehensively, then this will almost certainly transfer to an awkwardness for the audience. It is best to deal with situations like these early on by offering reassurance or finding an alternative to the situation you have in mind. Relationships are important to our research because alongside a growing awareness of the struggles and successes of others comes an increased understanding of our own position. If we can learn to share these vulnerabilities and recognise how relationships can be mutually beneficial then the research journey will become less fraught with feelings of guilt, betrayal and otherness that can develop if either party becomes adversarial towards the other.

Tom Turner (left) and Vik experiencing a tense moment on location for *One Long Journey*

Participating as a filmmaker

The following is an extract from the author's fieldwork diary for *Born* (2008)

It's July and the wind is blowing strongly through the trees as I shout to find my two young sons who are not giving up a game of hide and seek. My phone rings and I immediately recognise the number as Judith's, the midwife I have been working with for the past three years. 'Andy if you want to see this birth you'd better hurry, Helen just called and she thinks it's on its way, her husband's not there, so she's all alone.' 'Okay', I reply, 'I'll be there as soon as I can. When will you be there?' But she has already gone. I shout louder and threaten to leave without the boys.

Eased by a draft in the wake of passing traffic on a busy main road, the gradually opening door reveals a scene inside very different from that of the exterior. Helen has backed away from the door and she is now on all fours, behind her a line of faeces illustrates her journey from living room to threshold. She is panting rapidly as she urges me to shut out the world, which I do, severing my previous domain from this new interior full of sight and smell.

'No, no, I can't do that, not the film, no!' It wasn't the time to point to release agreements, nor to nine months' labour on my part, so I put down the camera and begin stroking Helen's back. I knew that in the late stages of labour faeces had to be cleared from the birth canal to make way for the new arrival. Usefully, someone had once told me that we are born between piss and shit. Judith wasn't here, so what to do? I would not manage to film with one hand and deliver a baby with the other. I had told my students, 'never get confused as to why you are there; the task of a filmmaker is always to film'. Now here I was, camera in unopened bag, stroking a woman's back at the moment we had both worked so hard to reach. I whisper some calming words

and as my strokes increase, Helen's breathing slows a little. I prepare myself mentally and roll each sleeve an inch or two, trying not to break contact with our expectant mother. We both take a very deep breath at the same time.

The doorbell rings. Helen screams. 'I hope that's Judith, I really hope it is', I'm not sure which one of us actually said that. I unfasten the latch as quick as I can. It is Judith. She squeezes through the half-gap, a vision of relief to us both, reassuringly placing a black bag next to Helen, not dissimilar to my own, but having a quite different effect on our expectant mother. Calming. Judith crouches to speak to Helen, I'm still acting as a backstop expecting a fast delivery, but the situation has changed. Helen is now standing and it seems likely that she will climb the two flights of stairs to the birthing room.

As Helen disappeared with Judith up the stairs, my thoughts returned to our film. I throw open my bag and piece together my Sony camera and microphones. I hit record immediately, dispense with the lens cap and flick the microphones into action.

Judith Kurutaç (left) with Helen Pusey (right), moments after she gave birth

Image

No one arrives in the field with a fully developed plan, so it is important to continuously reassess a strategy for filming along with the recorded material. The direction of your film changes to a lesser or greater extent with each new encounter, so think about how you might edit the film while you are still in the field. You are not expected to know how each scene will fit together in the final cut of your film but you should consider how shots will cut together on a particular day of your fieldwork. For this reason take care with camera movement, vary shot size and try to become aware of cutting points as you are filming. Make sure that shots are of a useable length – this is commonly a minimum of three seconds but I would suggest allowing the camera to linger for longer than that, as the most important discoveries often happen after the shot you planned has ended. Ensure that your shots are stable and clear, as it is difficult to edit one shot with another when they are unsteady or searching for focus.

Moving and positioning the camera

An audience engages with a film through the lens of a camera and at the periphery of a microphone, and it is the filmmaker's management of these that creates the cinematic experience. To enhance this you may consider operating your camera handheld or with the aid of a rig, tripod, monopod or even an airborne drone.

Handheld

Most ethnographic documentary encourages handheld recording whenever possible because it is both responsive to fast-moving fieldwork situations and an unpretentious way to express relationships between the filmmaker and protagonists. The handheld camera is considered more reflexive than one constrained by a tripod.

When operating handheld, try to move confidently from one steady shot to another and avoid searching with the camera. Once you have found something of interest to frame, hold your nerve and hold the shot for a useable length of time. It can be an arduous task to support a camera made extra heavy by high-capacity batteries, pre-amplifiers, microphones and perhaps also a light. The first evidence of tiredness becomes apparent when skylines start to tilt to the left as your camera hand becomes weary and the rigidity of your wrist gradually loosens. Camera 'droop' is the second feature of user fatigue. Here the frame gradually nods forward, heads disappear and then jerkily reappear as the cameraperson realises their mistake. Holding a camera in two hands creates a stable image and it encourages slower cinematic movements. For this reason camera rigs have become popular, especially when working with DSLR and mirrorless systems. However, these can be bulky and expensive and not always suitable for discreet recording. In the late 1990s I began filming a lengthy project called *Veldpost* for the Dutch television company VPRO. This was an observational documentary series about social inequality, set in five locations throughout Europe. The house style favoured long camera takes from a position close to the protagonists and its success relied on unique material developed through strong fieldwork relationships and many hours holding a camera at the ready. I imposed a limit of no tripods on the films that I made in Manchester, and instead used an L-arm bracket that was originally designed to support the flash unit on a stills camera. This was a cheap solution that helped me hold my shots steady, preventing camera droop and wonky skylines at the same time as limiting the tiredness that can be a problem when operating in this way.

Martha-Cecilia Dietrich using an L-arm bracket to steady her handheld camera

You may think that handholding a camera in a car helps to compensate for a bumpy road, but in fact the opposite is true – it exaggerates the movement. To avoid excessive camera shake clamp the camera to the body of the vehicle, either by hand or with a magic arm or Dinkum Systems clamp. When filming movement from a static position brace yourself against a tree or doorframe, or rest your elbows on a table if necessary. In all types of handheld camerawork stay relaxed and most importantly breathe deeply and slowly, as it is mainly a lack of oxygen created by constricting breath that leads to tired limbs and shaky cameras. Keep your joints unlocked and your limbs relaxed to move fluidly and tirelessly with the camera along a steady horizontal axis. This takes practice but you can improve quickly if you set yourself tasks such as holding the camera steady while navigating obstacles that have been placed in your path.

Positioning and the 180-degree visual axis

Be careful not to obstruct the protagonists in your film; try to anticipate their movements and position yourself accordingly, and look for camera positions that allow action to flow unhindered. Understand how cutting points are built into a scene and allow this knowledge to inform how you follow a protagonist or subject with your camera and when you allow them or it to leave the frame.

Be aware of continuity issues and the details in your composition that could cause problems – it is easier to address these on location than it is at the editing stage. Certain body parts can claim an unintentional prominence in the frame when one operates the camera in an uncertain or hesitant way, so that the focus rests neither on the hands or the face, for example,

180° axis line

Figure 11 *Recording from either side of the 180-degree axis line will cause an image to swap perspective when presented on a two-dimensional screen*

but instead lingers somewhere in-between. Be prepared to alter your position to reduce shadows that fall across faces or the reflections in spectacles.

Film is a two-dimensional medium that gives an impression of three dimensions. Mostly, this works well until we attempt to cross the 180-degree axis line on which our two-dimensional screen resides. Even if we travel just one degree across this line then the spatial arrangement of subjects in the frame will be changed, so that what was previously on the right will appear on the left and vice versa. This problem is mitigated when a continuous recording take crosses the line, as this movement allows an audience to readjust their perspective in real time and space. If editing is necessary in order to truncate the action, then constant crossing of the line will accumulate confusion in your narrative, especially when filming processions, parades, journeys, dinner parties or other instances where geographical positioning is vital to our understanding of the situation. It is not always easy to correct axis problems with editing tools – 'flopping' an image will not work if protagonists have distinguishing marks on their person or if the scene includes writing of any sort, as this will appear back-to-front when the flop effect is applied.

Tom Turner (left) and Ben Cheetham locking-off a tripod shot on the front of Vik's boat for *One Long Journey*

Ben's camera image

Still shots and establishers

Images that include inanimate objects need an extra degree of steadiness. Use a tripod to record distant skylines, horizons, landscapes, general views and all types of writing. You may also choose to use a tripod when filming human subjects, but be aware how this can desensitise an encounter and also slow down your practice. Pan tripods from left to right (or vice versa) slower than you imagine they should be panned. Look in the direction of the pan before you begin, take a deep breath and then exhale gently through a complete smooth movement of the camera. Allow moving subjects to 'push' the frame and when you are finished panning slow down to allow them to exit the shot. If you want your work to look professional, learn how to pan and tilt through each axis simultaneously, or opt for entirely static shots that are much easier to perform. Avoid jerky, inconsistent and incomplete tripod movements. The key with most tripod work is to move slowly and smoothly. To achieve a continuity of style

for my documentary *One Long Journey* (2016), the same tripod was used to create two distinct styles that were juxtaposed in the narrative to create the desired effect. I asked the two-person crew to shoot from a tripod or stable handheld positions while on land and then lock the camera to the deck of Vik's ballast-deficient boat, with the same tripod, as it was launched. The stability that I perceived in the boatyard where our protagonist gradually prepared for his voyage contrasted with the turbulence of the actual voyage, which generated urgency once his little boat entered the water. Monopods do not replace a tripod, so I would not recommend taking one on location unless you are very tight on space. Monopods can be particularly useful when operating in confined spaces, between tables, in crowds, on uneven ground or where there is a lot of movement, such as parades or long hikes, but most likely you will also need a tripod for architectural shots and interviews, for example.

Andy Lawrence using an improvised dolly to create movement around a commemorative statue during filming for *Black Snow*

Image stabilising

A degree of camera shake is acceptable if the content is compelling: some cinematographers have even sought to generate this for dramatic effect. On the whole, images that wobble are distracting for viewers and most shots are better expressed by holding a camera still, to mimic the ways that the human eye stabilises an unsteady world. You will notice when working at the extreme end of a zoom or with a tele prime lens that the slightest camera movements can create dramatic jerks in the image. It is therefore easier to operate closer to a subject using a wide angle lens, although this can make it harder to achieve critical focus, especially when working with full-frame sensor cameras.

Another way to compensate for excessive camera shake is to use the steady shot function on a camcorder, or the in-built image

stabilisation (IS) in some DSLR and mirrorless camera bodies and most lenses. Stabilising gimbals and drones are used to achieve the steady-cam or dolly shot effect, but unless you have a particular methodological or aesthetic reason to use these then you may find them a technological and physical burden. I have found that wheelchairs, prams and trolleys, are useful when attempting to create smooth moving shots. If you record at an increased frame rate, the speed of a movement can be increased or slowed down and then any residual camera wobble can be eradicated with the 'stabilise' effect that is included in most editing software.

Composition and framing

Your own camera style will develop as you practise but there are conventions that help us to understand why some frames appear to work better than others. Try the 'one shot' exercise (p. 14), where you do not interact with the subject or move the camera significantly. Observe how action develops within the frame and train yourself to look closely at what is actually occurring, rather than search with the camera for something that you imagine should be there. Consider the principles below when reviewing the recording and take note how your own framing acknowledges these ideas.

Rule of thirds

There is a special formula for composing an image that makes use of the magic number three. Leonardo da Vinci thought that an artist who discovered a 'golden section', in both the horizontal and vertical axis of their composition, has the ability to produce

An image composed according to the rule of thirds. Note also how Vik's gaze leads the viewer into real and imagined space

an ultimate and satisfying vision of the world. He based this alchemical idea on the number Pi and its potential for infinite divisions by three. The current proportions of most cinema and device screens conforms roughly to a rule of thirds. In the image above the main subject, Vik, is positioned on the vertical axis in the right third of the composition and the sky, canal and foreground occupy a roughly equal amount of space on the horizontal axis.

Looking space

When framing talking heads allow more space in the direction of sight than behind the person speaking. Similarly, give space to the gaze of a protagonist. In interviews, vary the direction in which the two people address their speech by altering the camera position from right to left and vice versa; this develops a feeling of natural dialogue when the interviews are cut together.

But be sure to remain consistent in the direction of speech for any single contributor. In the image to the left the protagonist is looking into space. Imagine this picture composed differently, with more space given behind him, and consider how that would alter the impact of this image.

Headroom

If you are framing close-up or medium shots of a person, allow only a small amount of space above their head, unless you want to emphasise a particular role or characteristic, such as in the image below. Be consistent in your style of shooting and monitor the edges of the frame to ensure that the microphone is not dipping in from above.

The Assistant Principal of William Hulme Grammar in Manchester, during filming for *British Born Chinese*

Eyeline and level

Experiment by recording a variety of angles from above and below the eye level of the people in your story, and notice how this alters the way they are represented. Adopting a position just below the level of their eyes produces a satisfying sense of presence and therefore it is common practice to angle your camera slightly upwards when recording images of people. A person will be diminished in the eyes of an audience by recording them from above or aggrandised when the camera is looking up from a significantly lower position. You may wish to draw the eyeline more directly into the lens. The documentary filmmaker Errol Morris (in his film, *The Thin Blue Line*, 1988) used this method to render his protagonists accountable to their audience in an eye-to-eye sense. Morris achieves this by positioning an image of himself on a monitor screen just above the camera lens, which has the effect of channelling the gaze of an interviewee directly into the lens. A more conventional framing has the protagonist looking slightly to the left or right of centre, towards an off-camera presence.

Line convergence and foregrounding

Consider how the graphic proportions of an image can be arranged within a single frame to make shots look more interesting. For instance, a path that trails from the lower left corner of an image can guide a viewer's eye to a horizon in the upper third of the same image. The late Russian filmmaker and film theorist Andrey Tarkovsky (1998) refers to a moving subject filmed within a two-dimensional representation of space as 'sculpting in time', where a steady frame is used to accentuate the temporal movement of a subject in space, leading to a feeling of involvement in actuality. This is similar to the way that

Shooting through an object adds interest to the framing and contextual information

Karl Heider (1990) describes 'ethnographicness' in terms of 'whole bodies, actions and interactions', as information that is contextualised in an ethnographic way.

Areas of interest within an image can be emphasised by shooting through objects of relevance that lie in the foreground, such as another person, foliage, items on a table or evidence of a completed task, as pictured above. This way of framing context elaborates a sense of depth, and if there is enough distance between the subject and the foreground one or the other will be out of focus, tempting the operator to pull, or shift the focus, between the two parts of the image.

Shot types

A simple description of 'wide', 'medium' and 'close' covers most possibilities for shot size but it is useful to think about some of the functions that these moving images contribute to your research as well as for your eventual film. Editing is facilitated by the variety of individual descriptive shots and sounds that you gather in the field and their potential to eventually connect in sequence. People who use filmmaking as a research method sometimes forget about the wider context of human action as their interest grows in the nuanced details of their field site. It is important to cover all elements of film grammar for each new scene that you encounter on location, such as the geographical wide shot, illustrative medium, descriptive close-ups and the establishing material that can set the scene. Using the triangle of action technique (see pp. 7–11) will help you understand where to place the camera in order to gather this information. Reality will always appear different in actuality than it does on the imagined horizon of a storyboard or shot list, so try to learn the structural requirements of a filmic sequence but allow flexibility in your recording to respond to what is happening around you. After you have read this section review your favourite films, noting how different shots are used by filmmakers to construct a scene and the impact that these have on the narrative.

Extreme-wide
Geographical shots of landscape or cities help to establish spatial and temporal context at the beginning of a story, or they can signify a change of scene within the narrative. These shots are sometimes referred to as 'general views' but in fact they describe the subjective qualities of a film by expressing perspective, especially when paired with voiced-over narration. The aim is to mimic a sense of arrival – for example, seeing the distant outline or movement of a group of people will encourage viewers to anticipate how they might arrive at the crowd. Wide shots benefit from the use of a tripod, or a very steady hand, and they must be held long enough for an audience to take in the breadth and detail expressed within them.

Wide
Images showing complete bodies and the overview of action will help to establish the relations between people or things from a broad perspective. Frames that include more than one person, animal or object show how ideologies and political postures, as well as personal stories, are enacted in a public context.

Medium
Frame an individual character in the scene to see how they use a particular strategy to cope with an activity or interaction: how they dress, for example. Or demonstrate the nature and extent of your collaboration through your own interaction with the principal protagonist. Getting closer will reveal positionality, drawing a potential audience into the emotional reasoning behind your camera movements.

Close
Close-ups enable a temporal break from continuous action without the need for discontinuity in the editing. They provide indexical material that will help an audience focus on the emotions, strategies and consequences of action. Typical

close-up shots might include a protagonist's face, their hands or the effect of their labour. Point-of-view shots can help an audience feel involved in the overall action from a specific perspective and add an important element of reflexivity to your work (see Figure 1, p. 10). When filming close-up shots try to anticipate action. Line up a shot in a way that allows the action to 'fall' into the frame, in order to avoid chaotic camerawork. Make sure the frame is wide enough to accommodate subtitles, if you are considering using them. When working alone, try to record close-up shots handheld using a wide angle lens, so that you can also record detailed sound from a position close to your subject.

Extreme-close

As its name suggests, this slight variation on the close-up is intended to add emphasis. For example, an extreme close-up shot of a face will highlight a particular emotion. Very close shots are also useful to 'signpost' a story with things that would usually require close inspection, such as written instructions, ingredients or fine tooling. Close-ups should be used judiciously, to mirror the ways that we see in our everyday lives, unless, that is, you are aiming for an unnatural feel in your film in order to highlight the arbitrary nature of an action.

Point-of-view shots can be wide, medium or close, depending on the perspective of a protagonist's gaze. A common use in ethnographic films is to demonstrate detailed actions or information held at arm's length, such as a photograph or diary entry.

Summary tips for shooting

Images that help to truncate a lengthy process, or cover awkward cuts, should also add something significant to the narrative. **Cutaways** are often referred to as 'pick-ups' when they are collected after the main filming has ended. Classic examples of cutaways are a clock to signify the passage of time, a family portrait hanging on a wall or the label on a jar. Try to collect these at the time of recording, as this will help to ensure they are relevant and available. Cutaways contribute to good coverage and they can prove vital in adding signposts to the narrative of your eventual film. Be creative with your choice of cutaway material and don't return to the same shot, unless you are aiming for a monotonous effect.

The minimum length of a useful shot is three seconds, but in slower observational films shots tend to be far longer, especially when the frame includes detail from a wider perspective. Observe how action unfolds from within the shot and time your recordings to suit this. When following close-up action ensure that you arrive at steady shots, held for a minimum of six seconds, unless the motivation from within the shot suggests otherwise. Make sure the framing of a medium shot and a close-up are significantly different. If they are too similar, the scene will appear to jump awkwardly when it is edited together.

When operating using the triangle of action technique, allow your camera to be directed by the movement within the frame and look for natural cutting points, such as the wipe of a hand or the subtle gesture of an eye. These will guide your camera towards the next shot. It is not necessary to terminate the shot at each cutting point – some of the best action happens after the main action has ended. However, once two or three cutting

points have been passed then it is probably time to move on.
Use the camera to explore the scene and at the same time gather
the individual shots that are necessary to build a cinematic
narrative.

Extreme Wide

Wide

Medium

Close

Extreme Close

Point of view

Figure 12 *Framing images in different ways provides useful material for descriptive
film sequences. It also brings variety to analytic decisions when editing these frames
in sequential order*

Sound

Just as 'life takes place' so does sound; thus more and more my experiential accounts of the Kaluli sound world have become acoustic studies of how senses make place and places make sense.

Steven Feld
sound artist and author of **Music Grooves** *(1994: 257)*

Sound is a pressure wave that occurs in air at varying frequency and intensity: we can think about sound as description by vibration. Similar to light, sound is reflected, obscured and altered as it passes through and around objects. Sound is, however, perceived differently to images. We are capable of processing more than one sound at a time, even if they seem unrelated, and it is difficult for the human ear to isolate individual sounds. Images, on the contrary, are progressively framed in the blink of an eye and if we wish to avoid them we can avert our gaze. Sound nearly always grabs our attention first and then we seek to extend the meaning we attribute to this by locating, or imagining, a picture that may be associated with it. The ways in which audio is experienced help to define the work of a person tasked with recording sound for a documentary.

Sarai Ramírez-Payá (right) explaining how to place a microphone to research participants in Tamil Nadu

Synchronous sound

Imagine a sequence of children playing in a schoolyard. Wind is blowing through the trees, cars are passing along a road and an interview with the head teacher of the school is being recorded next to a construction site. In this imaginary scene we see wide, medium and close images which describe visually what I have outlined above, one after another. The audio from each detailed recording, however, runs throughout the entire scene, with the balance in volume changing along with the image. As sounds that we have previously heard become synchronised with images our sense of involvement in the scene increases. It is therefore vital to acquire close and detailed audio recordings from each scenario that you film as well as separate atmospheric recordings from the wider scene. It is also important to record images associated with sounds that cannot be ignored, such as the construction site, which might otherwise not have made it into your film.

Synchronicity gives a film authenticity by evidencing the connection between sound and image in their relationship to cause or effect as a motivation in your storytelling. When recording synchronously the microphone should be placed as close to the source of the sound as possible, so that when the loudness level is adjusted appropriately in the sound mix the signal remains strong and clear. When recording people speaking or other sounds that are contingent to an image, ensure that you have also focused the camera on the source of the sound. Even when people are talking it is possible to consciously pan away to reference something that they have referred to, but you must return to the source of a sound and favour this. Alternatively, stay with the main action and then pick up the reference shots afterwards.

Room tone and atmospheric sound

For scenes that include spoken words, be sure to record one minute of room tone from the perspective of your protagonist but without their voice present. This will help when you come to edit their speech, to overcome the clipping in and out of background sounds, such as air conditioning, traffic noise, a distant aircraft or playground. A portion of tone can also be used to create atmospheric continuity if you need to cut redundant parts from a sentence or add words that are missing or unclear from another section of speech. Room tone is recorded at the same level as the synchronised recording, even if this appears quiet, so that it can be applied to the beginning and end of problematic audio clips without a shift in perspective or loudness. If you have recorded it slightly too loud or quietly then it can be adjusted in the sound mix (see p. 165).

Once you have finished recording the synchronous elements of a scene then turn your attention to the variety of atmospheric sounds that contribute to a wider sound environment. These can be found in birdsong, water moving across a river bed, wind through trees, distant music or in less obviously appealing scenarios, such as building sites, power plants, passing aircraft or road traffic. Aim for recordings that are as clean as possible, so the balance between separate sounds can be adjusted to suit the perspective in scene or shot size changes. This usually means that the sound person needs to move nearer to the source of the sound. If you are working with a sound recordist, it is useful if they keep a log of these sounds, so that you can check you have everything covered and then later import this information into the editing log.

Unwanted sound

There is an important distinction to make between undesirable noise and poorly recorded sound. In his outline to an 'Anthropology of Sound', Rupert Cox (2017: 2) notes that structural theorists can make noise a villain because it gets in the way of communication or is otherwise out of place. Such approaches might prioritise one narrative over another, and in doing so ignore the subjective impact that sound has. Cox, like Feld, advocates the practice of sound recording as a way to explore the ethnographic potential for noise to take its rightful place in a more complete ecology of sound. However, unwanted sounds that arise due to limits in the audio recording technology or because of our inability to use it properly should certainly be avoided.

Wind can present a challenge to recording audio in exterior environments. It produces a low frequency rumble on a microphone that is not perceived by the human ear in the same way, and therefore if it is not well managed it can distort a recording beyond use. Protect your microphones from wind by using a furry windshield(see pp. 45-9), or by positioning yourself in a way that offers shelter to microphones from the strongest gusts, while maintaining focus on the source of the sound. Ethnographic documentary aims at understanding the experience of others, so attempt to record sound as you imagine it exists for protagonists, whatever difficulties this might present.

Other environments, such as those dominated by radios, air-conditioning units, roads, construction sites and aeroplanes, need to be managed so that they do not distort the final presentation, beyond their usual ability to do so. Any sound that is audible to you will also be pre-mixed onto the audio track of your recording device. Radios and other sources of music can cause continuity problems when you come to edit the material and also create rights clearance issues for broadcast. Turn the radio off if you perceive no significant consequence extending from eliminating the problem. However, if these sounds are of vital importance to the protagonists, you must balance the inconvenience that they present with what they offer to our ethnographic understanding of the situation. If you choose not to turn off disruptive sounds, you should reference the source of the sound with images recorded on location that can help you to build a narrative around such noise. If you are forced to record someone talking near a busy road and you need this information to drive your narrative, then ensure that the speaker is facing the traffic, so that you can direct the microphone towards them and away from the road noise. However, if you are exploring the ecology of road noise then you may do the opposite. A directional microphone will allow you some ability to shield a recording if the road sound is unwanted. It is inappropriate to try – and most unlikely that you will succeed – to shut down construction sites, airports or playgrounds while you film. If the noise created by them interferes with otherwise clean interview recordings they can be referenced with a 'glance from the window'-style shot that can also help to contextualise your narrative.

Switchable high-pass filters, sometimes called bass-cut, can be engaged on directional microphones at the time of recording to reduce unwanted low frequencies created by wind, traffic and shock-mount movement or boom handling. Similarly, high-pass filters can be added later at the editing stage, as can low-pass filters to limit the effect of high-pitched sounds such as mobile phone interference. In removing a frequency, such filters can have an adverse effect on the tonal range of voices and alter the way they are perceived. A better solution is therefore to turn off mobile phones, attend to boom handling issues and move away from distracting sounds.

Sound bounces off walls and hard surfaces and these reflections can create echoes or excessive low frequencies. To mitigate this problem make sure your microphone is at least three times nearer to the source of the sound than it is to the reflective surface.

Microphone placement

Some of the ideas we have discussed in terms of operating a camera can also be applied to sound recording. Audio becomes focused by placing the microphone within a frame, the edges of which are defined by how a sound becomes more or less clear at its peripheries, or where it crosses over with other sounds. An important difference between framing sounds and images is that there is no clearly defined edge to the framing of audio. It is therefore important to get a microphone close enough to the source of a sound, and at the correct angle, to achieve a good signal-to-noise ratio (SNR) (see pp. 75–6). Images tend to drive most film narratives, but do try to avoid occularcentrism if your aim is to properly explore the relationship between perception and expression. It is possible for an image to be compromised in order to achieve closer sound: for example, you may want a wide shot but the sound is too general so you need to move nearer to the action to find audible clarity. This may have the unintended effect of intensifying the action and lead to key moments in narrative development.

Commonly a boomed microphone is placed just above the image as it is framed by the camera because this is where there is the least amount of space between the edge of frame and the source of a sound, which in documentary is disproportionally represented by the human voice. When you are operating a boom do not wear rings or other objects that might clatter on the pole and consequently disrupt your recording. Also ensure that you have wrapped the cable that joins your microphone to the camera or mixer around the boom pole, allowing just enough slack to adjust the angle of the microphone. If you leave too much slack, wind will crash the cable against the pole.

A microphone can be moved nearer or further away from the source of sound to adjust the audio recording level up or down. It can in fact be withdrawn quite quickly from an unexpected loud sound, such as a passing siren, to prevent it overwhelming the recording. As the microphone creeps forward or recoils from a sound it mimics your own reactions, and thus it must be treated with tenderness and care. When operating solo you may need to fix the microphone to your camera. The downside of this is that it prevents movements such as those just mentioned, and on the whole distracts you from considering microphone placement at all. The perfect camera placement for the shot you need can be several metres away from your subject but the best place for your microphone is usually nearer. Camera-mounted microphones are also subject to unwanted handling noise as assign buttons are selected or focus rings and iris dials are manipulated. Think about how you can position your camera for the best audio – or

better yet, run the mic on a longer cable to a boom pole or stand closer to your subject.

Solo shooters may find wireless microphone systems a convenient way to record a subject or protagonist. Attach the microphone in a discreet way to clothing within 30 cm of a person's mouth. Because these microphones are omni-directional they can be placed wherever is convenient, rather than necessarily being directed at the mouth. Participants often forget to mute their microphones when they have finished filming a scene, or break to go to the toilet. Such moments may well increase your understanding of a person or situation but it would not be considered part of an ethically informed project to deliberately exploit this potential, or to capitalise on the drama of such an encounter by including it in your film. A radio microphone can also be used to record atmospheric sound, either alongside the directional microphone on top of your camera, or in a static position when you are recording within a single room, for example. A useful exercise to help you understand microphone placement, especially if you are considering using remote microphones, is to record a one-shot with your mobile phone or other device using an integrated microphone. Allow the sound to guide your movements and try to recognise how the requirements of sound affect the framing and proximity of images.

Ambiasonic microphones are designed to record sound in 360 degrees. They can be configured in multiple ways, as directional microphones to record far away or as near field omni-directional mics. They have purposes beyond the individualised VR experience that they have become associated with and their use for documentary is set to grow as they reduce in price. If you are

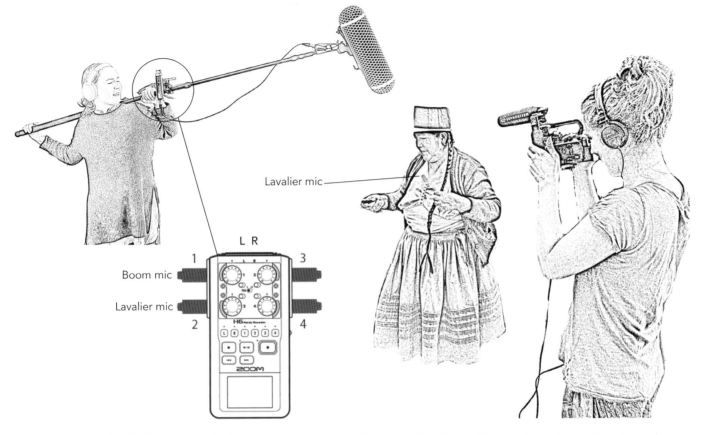

Lavalier mic

L R

Boom mic

Lavalier mic

1   3
2   4

Figure 13 *Recording solo and with a sound recordist. Solo operators must move themselves nearer to the action to achieve a good microphone position whereas a boom operator can place a mic independantly from the camera. Both have the option to use a remote lavalier microphone to gain a closer perspective.*

Audio recording interfaces, such as the Zoom H6, have six independent audio channels. Channel 1 is reserved for the principal microphone and Channel 2 is occupied by a secondary microphone, as in this illustration where an omnidirectional lavalier mic is used. Channels 3 and 4 are useful for recording additional atmosphere tracks but they are commonly left unoccupied. Alternatively, all four audio channels can be used to configure an ambiasonic microphone. The two remaining audio channels (L R) are reserved for a bespoke MS or stereo microphone that is attached directly to the unit, allowing further audio perspectives or the option to use the recorder in a low profile way without additional microphones and cables.

using a 250-degree or 360-degree camera in a vérité style, you may prefer to wear in-ear binaural microphones to represent sounds from an embodied as well as a 360-degree perspective. But this does not allow for much decision making on the part of those experiencing the VR, where ambiasonic offers far more possibilities. It is important to consider how the position and movement of a single microphone used for multiple sources of audio can impact the sound environment created in your film, so test the system before applying it in your field site.

Recording level and monitoring volume

Learning how to record sound begins by listening out for important changes in the texture and presence of audio as you move the microphone. To do this successfully it is vital that you understand the difference between the level at which a sound is recorded and the volume at which it is listened to during recording. Recording level is the balance between microphone signal and other noise. An appropriate level ensures a good signal-to-noise ratio (SNR) at all times. Volume determines how loudly you listen to that recording or how high you set the overall loudness in post-production. Changing the volume does not alter the SNR, which is the most important technical aspect of sound recording. It is tempting to let your camera make these difficult decisions about how your sound is recorded but you should in fact avoid automatic gain control (AGC), which produces flat and uninteresting recordings by reducing the level of loud sounds and increasing quiet ones. Using AGC mode in unpredictable audio environments also causes the camera to hunt for optimal recording volumes, giving you an added

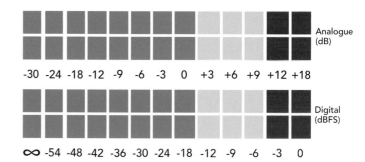

Figure 14 *Analogue and digital audio scales with their corresponding measurements*

headache in post-production as you attempt to remove these level changes. For this reason, it is best to control both your recording and listening levels manually.

Recording level

To understand this next section properly you will need to refer to the specifics of your equipment, so do not worry for now if you cannot follow everything. The recording level is the power at which a sound, measured in decibels (dB), is saved digitally onto a data card. Level is controlled separately from the volume at which you monitor your recordings and it is important to understand the impact that confusing levels and volume will have on your recordings. If you raise the listening volume of a sound that is being recorded at too low a level, you may hear it clearly in the field but it will be too quiet to use in post-production. Conversely, if the monitoring volume is set too low and you increase the recording level to compensate for this then you risk distorting the sound, also beyond use. As a rule, it is easier to raise a sound that has been recorded slightly too low in level than to correct a sound that is distorted – but both mistakes should be avoided.

Modern digital equipment uses a measurement system so that you can accurately assess the level of your recording. This is calibrated in dBFS, meaning **d**eci**b**els relative to the **f**ull **s**cale, where the scale ends at '0' and extends negatively to minus infinity. Any sound recorded above '0' is distorted, so all of your recordings will be in the minus (-) region. Some professional sound recording equipment, such as the Sound Devices Mix-PreD, uses a scale that derives from the days of analogue recording, so you will see that this scale also extends into the positive region (+). When a mixer like this is used it is important to send a reference tone from the mixer to the camera at line level (see Figure 10, p. 74). This will enable you to lock the camera in manual audio recording mode, so that you can control the recording levels through the superior technology of the field mixer. Because of the difference in these two scales, setting the tone at -12 dBFS on the camera means that your sound will peak at this number despite the fact that it is shown as peaking at 0 dB on the mixer. You will therefore have 12 dB of 'headroom' on both systems before distortion will occur, in case loud sounds enter your recording.

Setting the recording level too high or too low will have an adverse effect on your audio recordings. If a level is set above its upper limit then distortion will occur, and if it is too low the signal will be weak and need to be boosted in post-production, also increasing less desirable noise. Voices occupy the most present space in your audio environment so these can be recorded at -12 dBFS (0 dB), allowing a further reach to -6 dBFS (+6 dB) as

an absolute upper limit for the loudest parts of that speech. This allows a further 6 dB of 'headroom' before distortion will occur. If sounds reach above this upper limit they may distort and become unusable. If it is likely that the sound you are recording will become much louder, then work further down the scale, always ensuring there is enough headroom to avoid distortion. Atmospheric sounds such as distant music, birds or passing traffic are recorded at an appropriate level beneath voices, with a lower limit of -20 dBFS. Do not record these too quietly because then the focused audio can become lost amongst recording noise. Loudness can be adjusted to suit a narrative at the editing stage, where it is far better to reduce rather than attempt to boost it.

The most common culprits for poor-quality audio recordings are a weak SNR caused by a lack of microphone power due to spent batteries, poor-quality pre-amplification in camera equipment or excessively low or high recording levels.

Manual control of recording level

Human response can be slower than the automatic settings in your camera so you will need to learn how to compensate for loud sounds when you are in the midst of a recording in the following ways:

Jon Tipler recording stereo and surround sound for *The Lover and The Beloved* with a Roland Edirol and Sound Devices field mixer

1 Draw back the microphone. This is equivalent to turning the level down for a specific sound and it mimics the way that a person might recoil from a loud sound to reduce its intensity.

2 Lower the recording level. It can be difficult to do this fast enough and then go back to the original level when regular sound resumes, especially if you are a solo shooter. This method is the right one to choose if the new level will remain appropriate for a significant amount of time and when the level change can be undertaken smoothly. Do not reduce the headphone volume as this will have no impact on your recordings.

3 Use the in-built limiters of your audio interface, mixer or recorder. The analogue limiters included with the Mix Pre-D are very good and these can be permanently engaged, but those on cheaper pre-amplifiers, recorders, interfaces and cameras are rudimentary and they can distort your sound.

4 Set each channel independently to compensate for loud or quiet sounds. Most audio interfaces allow you to select how you target each recording channel with two independent microphones, or in this case one quality microphone split across two recording channels set at different levels. Move up or down in increments of at least 3 dB and it is recommended that you record safety tracks at + or -12 dB and make finer adjustments in post-production.

5 If your audio interface does not allow you to split a single microphone across two independently controlled channels then use two microphones each set at different recording levels.

Audio monitoring

Each time you set up your equipment check that you are receiving sound through your headphones and also onto the data card in your camera or recorder. The best way to do this is to identify each microphone in turn by giving them a scratch, note the headphone ear where each scratch appears and also look at the left and right channels of the visual scale to see if this tallies with what you are hearing. While you are doing this it is best to monitor the sound directly from the camera or recorder using the 'tape return' facility, so that you can check that something is actually being recorded, even if you intend to listen to the audio via the more responsive interface for the majority of your recording (see Figure 10, p. 74).

Once you have connected your camera and audio interface and set the correct level, using tone if necessary, then you must establish your listening volume. Do this by recording a voice, or other noise that is easy to distinguish, at an appropriate level (see above) using the LED display. Then adjust the listening volume to a loud but comfortable position; keep this consistent throughout your recordings to avoid the problems associated with confusing recording level and listening volume. Immerse yourself in the sound that you are recording to the fullest extent possible by using a good-quality set of closed-back headphones with a flat response. If you are recording in mono and find it difficult to negotiate your surroundings, you can keep one ear enclosed in one side of the headphones, pointed in the direction of your microphone and leave the other ear free to listen to what is occurring outside of the recording.

Recording levels can be monitored visually using LED or digitally displayed meters. However, visual monitoring gives no indication as to the quality of a recording, so once you have established

Martha-Cecilia Dietrich showing research participants how to monitor sound

an appropriate level using a peak meter turn your attention back to how you hear the audio through the headphones. Careful listening alerts us when the power of a signal becomes diminished or absent, perhaps because of weak batteries or poor microphone positioning. Or when unwanted noise is present in the recording, such as boom handling or wind distortion. Or if we lose concentration and move the microphone away from the axis of a sound. Pay particular attention to noisy jewellery, fidgeting hands, squeaky chairs and passing vehicles as these can render recordings unusable if they are not eliminated, or referenced by visual imagery.

Operating in key situations

Certain activities feature frequently during fieldwork – these present you with a good opportunity to explore core ideas using the techniques mentioned earlier in this book in social situations that research participants are familiar with. People working, playing, meeting, speaking, reflecting, travelling, walking, eating, texting and performing are common scenes in documentary films because they give us an insight into the day-to-day life of protagonists and audience members can relate to these situations because of their experience with similar activities in their own cultural settings. Such scenarios can therefore become crucial during an edit as you attempt to develop character, construct or bridge between scenes, move your story forward and to signpost important narrative developments. You can refer to Section 4, *Rough cutting to find a story*, to see how the situations covered in the subsections below are positioned in the edit for various modes of documentary. This section aims to guide you through some of the possibilities and challenges when recording in such situations.

Processes and events

Processes involve sequences of actions that have a strategic impact on a person's life and for this reason they will probably provide the central scenes in your film. This is also why the triangle of action technique is the cornerstone of a method of filmmaking for fieldwork. An event is the extension of a process, usually involving more than one person and taking place over a longer period of time. Anthropologists have used events as

an empirical lens through which to see and understand the beliefs and mechanisms of wider society. Ritualised behaviour that supports the status quo or critical happenings that disturb it are culturally embedded and so they can be compared across cultures to see how people act in similar or different ways.

Processes and their extension into events happen in real time and space, so they provide a rich resource for narrative storytelling and analysis. In order to see how experience unfolds temporally we must keep up with fast-moving processes and not ask protagonists to repeat actions, so your own speed of movement and spatial positioning are both important. If we are to examine the details of a scene later at the editing stage, we must gather a variety of shot types that will allow us to experiment with their arrangement. Wide exterior establishing shots demonstrate the time of day that an activity takes place, where in the world it is located and what type of infrastructure is required. Medium, interior or geographical shots help us to understand the arrangement of a room and how the people in the room relate to each other. Close-ups tend to focus on emotion, usually expressed by a face telling us if a task is pleasant, difficult or boring. Let us take the process of bread making for example, and apply the triangle of action technique outlined in Section 1. Shots of hands kneading dough, packing baking tins or switching on an oven will help us understand the procedures required to make bread. By observing risen or fully baked loaves we can then start to understand the impact that these strategies have had.

We can continue this chain of cause and effect in any direction that our research demands. The activity of making a loaf of bread may take three hours to complete in real time but a film sequence of the process might only be five minutes long. To edit a sequence like this you need to be selective and eliminate certain parts of the process. By looking closely at your material and considering carefully which parts are important to include, one becomes an expert in bread making. Someone viewing your film, if they have the correct ingredients and equipment, should be able to make a successful loaf of bread. If we extend this example into the realm of an event film, on the subject of food for example, we might also record subsequent processes involving transporting the bread and selling it at market. Each time we begin a new process or change location, the same variety of shots is required to build a new sequence. The example I have used here can be seen to good effect in Yasmin Fedda's short film *Breadmakers* (2007).

Interviews, testimonies and conversations

There are three common scenarios for recording words that are spoken in films. Interviews recorded in a controlled setting place an emphasis on adequate lighting and sound quality so that segments of the recording can be placed anywhere in a narrative, as voice-over or in sync. Such recordings might focus on the present or they can be forward thinking or reflective. Oral testimonies that situate a protagonist in their environment are immediate, responsive and defined by extraneous and contextualising sounds and images. Their use is more specific to the scenes they have been recorded in. Conversations that occur between fieldwork collaborators or in dialogues with the filmmaker can be a useful way to discover things that may not be included in a list of interview questions. A testimony is different

to an interview because it is open-ended and it is directed by the protagonist who is speaking, rather than the interviewer. Usually some sort of compromise results where the filmmaker uses a semi-structured mode of questioning to cover established topics of interest, but at the same time they leave ample scope for elaboration and divergence by the protagonist, which might uncover new and exciting things.

It is useful to record words spoken by your principal protagonists at the start and/or the end of your fieldwork. The benefit of recording an interview or testimony at the beginning, when things are uncertain, is that it can be used later to establish a story. The drawback is that this can set a precedent for explanations rather than the more explorative technique of 'asking' searching questions with the camera and microphones and then following action as it unfolds. If this is your priority, then conduct an interview after you have finished recording the main action. Either way, a stock of information is a great help when you need to signpost a narrative or develop how a central character is positioned in your story. Take care with both the picture and the sound, so the material can be used in various ways to suit the final production. Images that are synchronised with spoken words need to be composed well, and sound that is used as overlay must be recorded without background noise.

Tips on recording testimony

1 **Ask open-ended questions** that promote more than a single word response. Touch on issues that you know your protagonists care about and develop a structure to your questioning, so that you cover everything you hope to talk about.

2 Think of **testimony as a performance.** Use the triangle of action method (pp. 7–11) to focus primarily on the face of the person speaking, but become aware of how hands can also express emotion and the way that words affect other people who are present. Try following a protagonist's line of sight or hand gesture with your camera to see what they are referring to before returning to their face. In a formal interview one should always focus on the interviewee's face and pick these shots up later.

3 Position **microphones close** to the person speaking in order to reduce background sound, but make sure these are outside of the frame and not a distraction to your interviewee (pp. 105–8).

4 Train yourself to use facial gestures to **respond to questions** rather than verbal affirmations. But if you nod, make sure you do not also nod the camera.

5 When filming **testimony while walking**, use a radio microphone to get consistent sound and stay slightly ahead of your protagonist with your camera, so that you can record the expression on their face and your directional microphone remains within its axis of recording.

6 Be aware that some **interviewees will scratch** themselves, tap their feet or fingers and generally fidget. Be gentle when you ask them not to do this. Watch out for clothing that will impede or distort the signal from a radio microphone.

7 Listen out for **low-level unwanted sounds** such as air conditioning or computer fans. If they cannot be turned off then record a full minute of room tone from the perspective of your subject (pp. 104–5). This is especially important if you hope to use testimony as voice-over.

8 Avoid recording interviews, testimonies or conversations next to a **busy main road**. Be aware of external noise when selecting rooms for controlled interviews. Nearby kitchens, roads, building sites and school playgrounds are all common problems.

9 **Turn off radios** and other distracting narrative sounds wherever possible as these will cause you problems when you attempt to edit the material. You may also have to clear the intellectual rights for background music.

10 Think about the requirements for **getting a good picture**. Light your subject well and position them away from **distracting backgrounds**. The positioning of a tripod should allow you to get distinct wide, medium and close shots.

11 Be aware of **eyeline** and think about where the interviewer and interviewee can be positioned to get this right. Unless the sound recordist is conducting the interview they should not engage visually with the interviewee, or the eyeline will be diverted from its established direction.

12 Think about how **your own role** can provide narrative context to the responses you receive from an interviewee. You may need to record the interviewer's questions again after the interview has ended, if you hope to also include them in your film.

13 Ensure that you get a handful of **good establishers** for each location, to help develop a creative way into the scene. Also record **room tone** for each location to assist with the editing of spoken words (p. 104).

14 **Cover the scene**. For example, even if you imagine your eventual film will only include voice with non-synchronous overlaid images, shoot your interview with well-recorded images, as you may discover that you need this material in the edit to better express your ideas.

15 **Cutaways** (p. 100) help to patch over bad cuts at the same time as developing character or situation, so be creative and make sure they are relevant to the scene you are recording. Avoid repeating the same cutaway in your film.

Kieran Hanson (recording sound) and Andy Lawrence (camera) with Dr Elena Barabantseva (centre) interviewing Daniel He (far left) and Kevin But for *British Born Chinese*

Andy's camera image

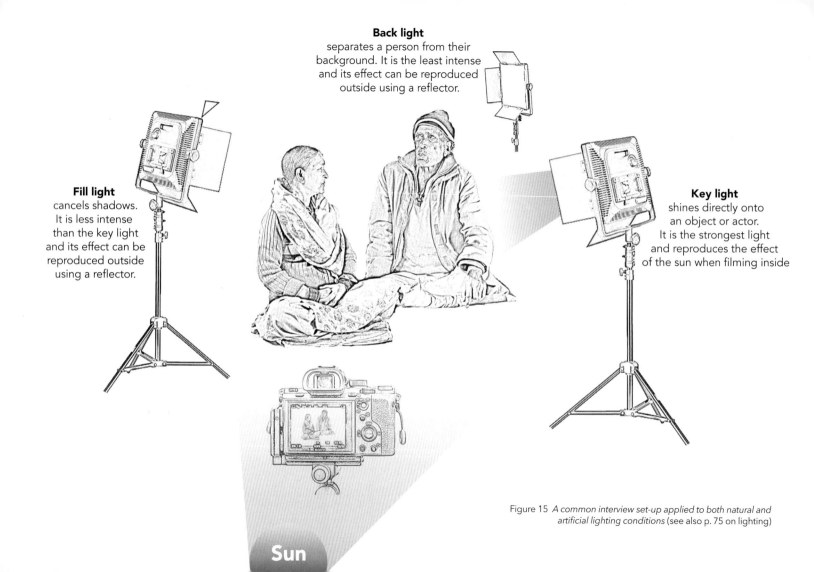

Back light
separates a person from their background. It is the least intense and its effect can be reproduced outside using a reflector.

Fill light
cancels shadows. It is less intense than the key light and its effect can be reproduced outside using a reflector.

Key light
shines directly onto an object or actor. It is the strongest light and reproduces the effect of the sun when filming inside

Sun

Figure 15 *A common interview set-up applied to both natural and artificial lighting conditions* (see also p. 75 on lighting)

Yourself and others

There are varying degrees by which a filmmaker enters their own film as a protagonist. In some narratives the presence of a filmmaker is palpable but not visible. For example, in the image below (*Objects of Resistance*, 2017) Kate Blackmore is returning the work to its co-creators. She has retained the edge of her laptop computer in the lower portion of the frame and chosen a classic portrait composition, to subtly acknowledge her own position in the scene without distracting from the main action.

If you wish to play a more explicit role in your film you can turn the camera or microphones directly towards yourself. This technique was made popular by the English documentarian, Nick Broomfield, who assumed the role of a charming but uninvited guest in the guise of a location sound recordist. In *The Leader, His Driver and the Driver's Wife* (1991) Broomfield provokes his hosts to express thoughts and activities associated with the apartheid regime that existed in South Africa at the time – they may not have done had they known the full extent of Broomfield's intentions. His film about a convicted female serial killer of seemingly unsound mind, *Aileen: Life and Death of a Serial Killer* (2003), is a haunting and complex journey through mixed emotions of judgement and sympathy. Broomfield navigates this ethically difficult terrain by also putting his own emotions on trial.

The filmmaker as protagonist approach allows for disparate elements of a film to be brought together, often by assuming the role of the viewer who is discovering what is happening in front of the lens for the first time. A more subtle approach can be achieved with a reflection in a mirror, a shadow or through the use of one's own voice as narrator. It is important to ensure consistency of coverage when recording reflexive moments, so they can be used throughout a narrative that may eventually be cut from only a small section of the material that has been recorded.

Rodney Kelly and his family watching Kate Blackmore's film, *Objects of Resistance*

Planes, trains and automobiles

Filming out of a window, sunroof or the open boot of a moving car, from a rickshaw, bus, train, aeroplane or boat, or from the back of a motorbike or bicycle can all produce useful material that will help to bridge sequences and connect scenes. Material of this sort can also be used to explain geography, elaborate on the experience of a traveller, or used with voice-over to recount some other aspect of your story.

Many documentary filmmakers record from a moving car by leaning out of an open window with the camera handheld and directed 60 degrees forward. You will get better results if you use a device such as a magic arm to clamp the camera firmly to the body of the car. Make sure you shoot consistently from the same side of the vehicle to avoid problems when crossing the 180-degree line (pp. 93–4), unless you also want to record material useful for a return journey. Lock the manual controls on your camera to avoid problems created by shifts in focus, colour balance, shutter speed and exposure. To cover a scene of this sort you will need a medium and a close-up shot of the driver. Try to include them glancing towards the window from which you have recorded the moving wide shot, as this will help to motivate your cuts to the general view from the car when you come to edit the sequence. You will also need a cutaway of the driver's hands on the steering wheel and perhaps one where their hand enters the frame to change gear. These cutaways will be of great help if you need to truncate the driver's words, or reference changes in engine sound while someone is speaking, or literally alter the tempo of your edit by shifting it up or down a gear. If there are two people seated in a car and you would like to describe their relationship, sit in the back seats and push the microphones forward. In this way you can use

the camera to catch a visually exciting angle of the driver's face in the rear-view mirror and record side-angled shots of the driver and the passenger that can be cut together to express their dialogue. Once the main action has ended, record wide shots of the exterior of the vehicle, both static and moving, that can be used as a way to enter or leave the scene. The triangle of action method can be applied to any vehicle to see how actions and emotions extend from and towards the driver or passengers.

An ARRI magic arm used to record close-up shots of Kevin riding his bicycle.

Guided tours and walking

Museum curators help us understand an exhibition through their knowledge of the artefacts and familiarity with the ideas that inform the ways they are exhibited. Similarly, someone who acts as a guide in a film narrative can help viewers to navigate the geography of a scene and understand strange things they encounter on screen. Such a person has expert knowledge of processes and events and they usually occupy a leading role in the film. Guided tours work especially well when the camera is handheld, with the ability to respond quickly to glances and hand gestures. Roger Canals uses the technique to good effect in his film *The Man who Loved Books* (2015), about a Catalan anthropologist who worked at a London University for forty years before his untimely death. Canals invited friends, colleagues and relatives to wander through the man's library and comment about him by referring to the books that he loved and remarking on the logics by which he arranged them. In his use of this technique Canals manages to include in his film the presence of a person who is otherwise physically absent.

When filming guided tours aim to find a position slightly ahead of your protagonist, so that you can see a good portion of their face. A common mistake is to film from slightly behind, so that the person cannot be recognised and is away from the recording axis of the microphone – both of which work against the development of a narrative. It is not easy to hold a backwards walking shot, but a minimum of five seconds is all that is needed for it to be of use in the edit. To avoid uneven camera movement and tiredness, breathe easily and keep your arm and leg joints slightly bent and relaxed. As you move out of this walking backwards position you can revert to a 'behind the head' shot, which will give you a reverse angle that shows the direction your protagonist is heading. The synchronised sound that you recorded in front of your protagonist can later be trailed over the reverse angle shot – which is off-mic, and the movement of the mouth cannot be seen – to give an impression of continuity.

Be aware of the 180-degree axis rule when recording processions or other activities that have a particular spatial trajectory (see Figure 11, p. 94). If the line is crossed, then it will appear as if the parade has changed direction or is on its way home. To avoid this, look for camera positions that allow participants to enter consistently from the same side of the frame, or shoot from directly in front of or behind the procession. Another solution is to pan your camera with the parade as it passes and then allow it to snake off into the distance before running to catch up with it again to repeat a similar shot or take up a new static position.

119

Lloyd Belcher using a gimbal to record smooth walking shots of himself as the principal narrator of his film *Nepalese Drug Users in Hong Kong* (2017)

Tables and desktops

Some research encounters happen around a table at breakfast, lunch or dinner. This may not present you with the most exciting scenes in your film, but it does offer a creative way to show how certain rituals, like sharing food, are performed. Steffen Köhn (2020) points out that, in the light of internet-based forms of communication and the rise of social media, the screens of our computers, mobile phones and tablets have become primary sites for worldly interaction. As a result, the desktops on which such devices rest have also become important locations for ethnographic documentaries that seek to explore the poetics of digital culture.

When filming people sitting around a table it is best to establish a 180-degree axis and choose your camera positions from one side or the other. If you cross this line, by circling around the outside of the table for example, then the people in your film who may have previously been on the left of screen will swap to the right or vice versa, resulting in spatial confusion (see Figure 11, p. 94). The same disorientation does not occur if you include the moment of camera movement at which the line is crossed. When framing table groups interest can be developed in the shot by foregrounding the back of someone's head in soft focus while focusing sharply on the person that they are conversing with in the background. When someone is operating a desktop device alone, you will need a variety of shots from different angles that will cut together into a single sequence and allow options for narrating the scene. Adopting a position at either of these types of table yourself will add a point of view that can introduce a moment of reflexivity to your story or evoke the embodied perspective of a protagonist. Screencasts, or the

Jón Bjarki Magnússon filming his grandfather eating lunch

feed from a webcam, are useful resources if the emphasis in the editing is online communication.

To get good images, ensure that there is enough light emanating from a screen to light the user's face, or position available lighting strategically when attempting to illuminate a dimly lit dinner party. You can increase the key lighting on faces by carefully adding an up-light, or by introducing something more atmospherically appropriate, like candles. As far as sound is concerned, a directional microphone is adequate for recording a table scene if it is manually operated and well positioned. If you are working solo and the camera needs to change position frequently because of the constraints in space, then you risk conversation being recorded off-axis of the microphone, so in this instance it is better to place an omni-directional microphone in the centre of the table, perhaps hidden between condiments or attached to a vase of flowers. Make sure the microphone is suspended in some way, so it is not susceptible to the bangs and taps that a table frequently receives.

Performances

All knowledge is performed, but some activities are more consciously acted out and these may require you to adapt your equipment and approach to suit special circumstances. For example, a monopod might be useful if you want to record the involved perspective of an audience member. For situations such as music concerts, theatre plays, political campaigns and so on you will need to practise operating the equipment with technical accuracy in a busy environment, while looking after fieldwork relationships and diverting unwanted interest away from your filmmaking activities.

When recording an entire theatrical or musical performance, ensure that SD cards have enough space on them and the camera you are using does not impose a file limit on single-take recordings. Also make sure there is enough capacity left in camera, mixer, recorder and microphone batteries to last the show. A continuous recording will produce an uninterrupted audio track that can be unlinked at the editing stage and cut to a variety of appropriate wide, medium and close shots. When filming, hold each new frame for at least six seconds so that your material is of a useable length and you are not continuously roaming with the camera. It is useful to record the reactions of audience members after the main performance has ended, or during a part that you do not intend to use. This will help to overcome the awkward cuts that you will encounter during editing and to develop the sort of intersubjective details that may be of use in your research. When recording music, think about how repeats in a chorus or verses provide an opportunity to truncate the performance to suit the length of a sequence or film. Such repetition will also allow you to record the variety of

shots necessary for your story to retain interest for viewers. Like any event, it is not always the central performance that is the most interesting aspect. Think about how preparations, or the aftermath better describe the emotion, strategy and impact for those involved. Remember to record a handful of exterior shots, to establish the location of a performance in your story.

Sound can become a problem when recording an amplified performance. You may be able to receive a line level feed from a recording desk directly into your camera or separate recorder. If you do this, remember to switch from 'mic' to 'line' on the audio input setting of your camera or device (see Figure 10, p. 74); otherwise the sound will be over-modulated and distorted. A recording of this type is of limited use, as it lacks general ambience from an involved audience perspective and the individual elements of the performance are permanently mixed according to the skill and preference of the person operating the sound desk, which will reduce the scope you have to imprint your own interpretation onto the scene. I find it useful to record this feed to a separate device, like a Zoom recorder, and then use the two tracks available on my camera for a directional and omni-directional microphone for ambient sounds. If you are operating solo then consider using a radio-controlled microphone attached to a principal protagonist, together with a top-mounted directional microphone to record the sound of near field action.

Two 800 watt halogen lights were used to record images from the National Union of Mineworkers archive in Barnsley, for *Black Snow* (also see overleaf)

Archive

So far, our discussion of cinema craft has concentrated on recording images and sounds that unfold through contemporary events, in real time and space. If we want to understand a field site in the ways it existed before we arrived, then we must look elsewhere. Under this heading, I will consider some of the practical issues involved in using historical sources to inform and express an ethnographic film project.

Archival material can be discovered in many forms, including edited movies, raw film footage, audio recordings, still photographs, newspaper clippings or web pages. Images of old books, paintings or photos recorded on location – held in a person's hands or projected onto a wall for example – are not considered to be archive as they are involved in the contemporary enactment of fieldwork. Archive, on the other hand, is usually held in a library or specialist service, or sometimes locked up in a government repository away from public use. However it is discovered, finding such a rich resource can link us to the past and help us to decipher the present.

Filmmakers vary in their advice about how to integrate archival material in a film. Some delineate the sources, carefully indicating with title or editing style how the materials differ from one another. I prefer to treat archive in the same way as my own recordings, matching action and looking for textures that can build bridges between the convergent forces of past, present and future. I worked in this way recently on a research film directed by a professor of management humanities, Stephen Linstead. *Black Snow* (2017) is about a mining disaster in the mid-Victorian era that eradicated two generations of men and boys from three English villages. In order to recreate these terrible circumstances and underline the critical nature of this event, we used archive materials cut in a continuity style along with virtual reality scenes of the explosion and contemporary reconstructions. Linstead (2018) notes how he innovated a non-formalistic approach to organisation, using art and affect as a route to understanding what he termed 'casual' (as distinct from formal) organisation and the emergent roles of non-official, fluid and subaltern groups. *Black Snow* represents a reconsideration of how past events are narrated and at the same time demonstrates their contemporary legacy in South Yorkshire. This film won the 2018 Arts and Humanities Research Council (AHRC) award for Best Research Film of The Year.

Archive material should be credited to its original authors. This not only adds historicity but it is part of an ethical approach that acknowledges the labours of others. Before committing to using such materials in your film, consider whether you will need to clear the artistic rights, so that you can broadcast your film without the risk of legal prosecution. It is likely that you will use the recordings in a different way from their authors' original intentions – this adds a further ethical imperative to explore their genealogy. If the material is not from a personal archive you may need to gain permission to use it from elsewhere. Libraries and other repositories tend to inherit the right to grant use according to a published set of criteria, including costs, but sometimes it is necessary to track down the people who generated the material. Broadcasters, distributors and some festivals expect you to have all the relevant clearance documents in place if you are submitting your film for their consideration.

A gift from the Miners Federation of Great Britain to the MP for Barnsley during the 'Great Lock-Out' of 1893

An ethnographer may decide to include archive material in their eventual film, or may simply consult it to gain a better understanding of an aspect of the project that they will later reconstruct or refer to in contemporary settings. Until you know exactly how you will use the material it is a good idea to acquire recordings or reproduce photographs to a standard that is high enough to suit all eventualities. Film clips can be converted to the format you are working in and then imported into an editing project in a similar fashion to the other recordings you have made. The same is true for archival audio recordings. It is important that scanned photographs are of high enough quality, which is at least the pixel ratio of your video production (3840 x 2160 pixels for a 4k image). However, I recommend that you make them significantly larger as this will allow you to zoom into sections of the picture or create a 'Ken Burns effect' moving path through it and retain the overall pixel ratio for any section that you choose. For example, if you wish to zoom into a portion of the picture that occupies an eighth of the total area of the frame and you are exporting your film in 4k, then you will need to record your image eight times larger than 3840 x 2160 pixels. Lastly, make sure that you log and back up this material in the same way as other recordings (see pp. 128–31), so you can access it quickly during the edit and not lose those long hours of labour spent on the internet and in libraries.

SECTION 4
Editing

Freed from the boundaries of time and space, I co-ordinate any and all points of the universe, wherever I want them to be. My way leads towards the creation of a fresh perception of the world. Thus I explain in a new way the world unknown to you.

Dziga Vertov
Soviet filmmaker and film theorist (Vertov 1923, quoted in Berger 1977: 17)

Our task as video editor is to recognise the potential in recordings to clarify and challenge research ideas. It is also to create meaningful allusions to these ideas through a coherent and engaging story using moments of actuality. A documentary film can only communicate directly through two of the five senses: hearing and sight. Its possibilities are not boundless as they are in the real world where touch, smell and taste contribute towards experience. Laura Marks (2000) has argued that the haptic potential of a film is extended as sights and sounds activate emotions that are connected to the other senses. These combine to trigger physical memories related to cultural experience that go beyond the realms of seeing and hearing. Whatever their eventual reach, images and sounds must first be wrestled into some sort of order by a process of editing, which will undoubtedly force us to look closer into the experience of our fieldwork participants and also of ourselves.

Editing is a repetitive process of organising and attempting to understand many hours of recorded material until it can be distilled and shaped into a coherent narrative, using computer software and technology designed specifically for the purpose. By referencing experiences recorded on location the researcher can develop and test theories about their field site. During fieldwork for two of my films I spent time in the jungles of north-eastern India. In this dense forest, yogic practitioners sit motionless in small cabins for extended periods of time, concentrating on two-dimensional diagrams they call 'yantra' – a Sanskrit word for 'machine'. Such drawings depict a deity of the Hindu pantheon and their purpose is to inspire a three-dimensional form that will eventually appear to enlighten the seeker. The form in which this godly figure arrives is an expression of the thought patterns of the practitioner, so unless these ideas are somehow rooted in a broader reality the results can otherwise be surprising. Whereas the two processes are materially different, I was struck by a similarity in intent between this and video editing, which also relies on textures of engagement to develop a route towards the final expression. Using video editing as a method to understand fieldwork reminds us that in ethnography, theory and structure are more comfortable when they arise through our experience of a location rather than when they are imposed onto it from a distance.

In order to analyse material thoroughly and arrive at new and original ideas about a field site, one must struggle with how the parts of a film connect. In the tantric aghori tradition, Indian seekers purposefully invert meaning to experiment with perceived order and authority. In a similar way, video montage is aimed at disjuncture as well as continuity, and the researcher should avoid becoming attached to neatness before various iterations of a story can be tested. A professional editor can help find a better cinematic expression for the material but only you

Rajive McMullen visiting the cabin of a tantric yogi in the Assamese Jungle during filming for *The Lover and the Beloved*. A yantra can be seen painted in white

...an discover where the important aspects of your research lie. If you do choose to work with an editor, then deciding when to engage them is important. In mainstream documentary projects an editor often joins a project before the shooting begins, to alert the director to the variety of material that may be needed to develop the story. This information is then turned into a scripted storyboard, which in turn becomes a list of required shots and sounds for the crew to gather on location. Due to budget constraints and academic sensibilities, in ethnographic work it is common for the lead researcher to act alone until the rough cutting is complete. At this point, many researchers choose to bring an editor onboard to help them tidy up the work and/or technical finishing. Even at this stage a professional editor will need to look creatively and deeply into the material to find the shots they need to build scenes, connect sequences and signpost the story so that other people can understand it.

The majority of this section concerns the practical stages in a post-production workflow for file-based digital video and audio. Certain stages in post-production act overtly as tools for analysis, such as logging shots and transcribing spoken words, rough cutting to find a story, selecting styles and applying techniques, and feedback screenings. Other parts of the process, such as the management of media, colour correction, sound mixing and mastering, have less to offer directly in terms of analysis but nevertheless are essential to the overall outcome. Imagine your film like a house-building project, where the refinements must be built on firm foundations. It is important not to skip a stage as each one is dependent on those that came before it.

Information about editing software and the relative merits of different programs can be found in Section 2. In this part of the book the aim is to avoid terminology associated with any particular program, in the hope that readers can find the relevant ideas in whatever software they choose. The best way to learn the craft of video editing and the specifics of an interface is by working with your own material. Fortunately, most software companies offer a free download for a trial period to tempt you with their product. Comprehensive help is available from in-program guides, and useful video explainers are easy to find using a subject search on the internet.

Preparation for an edit

Organising media will help to ensure that all the possibilities contained within it are explored and you do not inadvertently overlook certain parts. Professional video editors need a detailed log and transcript to assist them in communicating ideas with a director. For a researcher, logs and transcripts are a vital resource to complement and sometimes contradict their mental recollection of the fieldwork. Before starting to look at the material, ensure that you have backed up the whole of it in three separate places.

Media management

Backing up material will help to ensure that your endeavours during the production of your film are not wasted if a hard drive fails or goes missing. As you enter the editing stage it becomes necessary to expand the file structure on the hard drives to include the time and labour spent in post-production. These new folders are replicated on each hard drive, so that you end up with three copies of all the work relating to your research project. The following are suggestions for folder names, along with an indication of the type of material you might place in them. You may need to adapt these to the specifics of your own project.

Original material

A place to store the audiovisual recordings that you created during fieldwork. If you have not already done so in the field, firstly download this material into the 'original material' folder on one hard drive. Then create a subfolder with a name that refers to a specific day of the shoot and put everything you recorded on that day into this folder. Do not rename individual clips as the computer sometimes uses the original file names to decode them. If you have two or more clips called the same thing then create folders with suffixes of A, B, C and so on. Repeat this process for each day of your entire shoot. You can make changes to the file names and place these into category bins from within the editing software. Check that the entirety of your material has transferred by randomly selecting clips and watching short sections of them. Make certain that you check the first and last clip and recall whether or not these were indeed the first and last things you recorded on that day. When you have done this, you can then back up the media from this hard drive in two other places. It is impractical and generally considered unethical to store recorded material on the cloud, which is susceptible to hacking. If you are working with sensitive material then you can encrypt your hard drives, so they cannot be accessed without your authorisation.

Proxies

These are lower quality reference files that link to ultra-high definition material, for use on a computer that has inadequate graphics support to play the large files smoothly. Images are transcoded into lower quality, smaller sized files for the purposes of editing. Once the editing is complete these files reference the original files for export at full quality.

Project files

A place to store the editing software 'project' file that contains the decisions you have made in terms of arranging and manipulating your original material. The project file is like a recipe used by the computer to prepare the raw material of your film. It represents the sum total of your labours during the entire editing process, so take good care of it. If you choose not to import your recordings into the project but instead reference them from their stored location (which is recommended), then you can store a back-up copy of this small file on the Cloud, as it does not contain material that could infringe data regulations. You should save your project frequently and back it up somewhere safe at the end of each editing day.

Audio

A place to store sounds that you have gathered during post-production. Create subfolders for 'music', another for 'sound fx' (meaning sounds that you have downloaded from the internet) and another for 'foley' (meaning the sounds you have recorded yourself to enrich your soundtrack).

Stills

This folder contains all types of photographs and exported still frames – for example, production stills or iconic images for publicising your film and scans of archive pictures, newspapers or other third-party material.

Graphics

Artwork for titles, credits, funding logos that appear in your film, print materials and websites.

Exports

This folder holds rough cut versions of your film as work in progress (WIP), teasers, trailers and final cuts.

Deliverables

For your master export files, so that you don't get them confused with other versions of your film.

Admin

A folder designated for release forms, participant information sheets, ethics clearance documents, equipment inventories, budgets, hire agreements, funding applications and so on.

Writing

A place to store your research proposal, 10-word log line, synopses, statements and even conference papers and journal articles that relate to the film project.

Tip Aim to maintain a **constant back-up** of all materials associated with your film on each of the three hard drives. By following this procedure, if one drive is lost or damaged then you can link your project file to a back-up drive and continue your work without disruption.

Log

As well as closeness to a subject, filmmaking for fieldwork also requires distance. To understand the recorded material and find clips more easily once you start cutting, it is advisable to make a written record of all the images and sounds that you have recorded. This process will help you to make the transition from fieldworker to editor by balancing your reactions to certain material and helping you to see its potential within the broader story you are exploring. Individual sounds and images take on a wider metaphorical importance as they are joined together into sequences. This is hard to comprehend at first glance, so it is necessary to consider all the material and not discount sections of it before it can be subjected to the editing process. I have made significant discoveries in material that I would rather have forgotten about because of its compromised quality or the way it evidenced my own moments of awkwardness in the field. A detailed log can therefore increase your understanding of the materials and improve the efficiency of your editing.

At its most basic, the information you need for this is:

- Folder (labelled according to your media management with the date the recording took place).
- Clip name and/or number (also labelled according to your media management).
- Description of image – shot type, length and movement, together with an indication of what occurs in the frame.
- Description of audio – microphones used or mute.

Try to avoid making pejorative statements about the material, such as 'bad shot', 'rough sound' and so on, as this will encourage you to discount it from the editing process. Equally, do not congratulate yourself on material that you consider to be of high quality, as this may prompt you to force it into the narrative even if it has no useful role to play.

Transcript

It is difficult to edit an interview or testimony without consulting a written version of the words spoken in your recordings. In addition to helping the cutting process, transcripts draw your attention to what was actually said and how it was spoken, beyond what you can recall. Transcripts also assist in reducing the length of an interview to a minimum by avoiding repetition and redundancy, and they develop a useful ethnographic archive that can be referenced later in written work.

Every word that is spoken must be transcribed, especially if the language is not one that you understand fluently. In this instance you will need to employ someone who can translate the audio as part of the transcribing process. Rough translations can be gathered in the field, either in 'real time' during filming or after shooting but while you are still in the field. This is a cost-effective and useful means to translate if you have recorded a large amount of material, or if the language is not widely spoken. At some point you may need to gain a more precise translation, especially for sections that you are considering using in your film, but an initial translation is usually adequate to begin rough cutting.

There is software that is designed to turn audio into text, but be aware that machines may transcribe inaccurately when sound quality is poor or the language is spoken in a dialect. The primary reason for transcribing is to develop a deeper understanding of the recorded material – there is no better way to do this than to write down each word yourself. You can either expand the audio section of a log or create a separate document to house this information. Once the work is complete, sections of dialogue can be highlighted to indicate parts that may be useful to the narrative of your film. When these are cross-referenced with the shot descriptions in your log, it becomes easier to see how those sections will cut together into an effective sequence. Logging and transcribing for broadcast media purposes requires a strategy that will be universally understood because the material is passed between different editors and people working on the post-production of a film.

The key to preparation is organisation

Designing your film

A designer knows he has achieved perfection not when there is nothing left to add, but when there is nothing left to take away.
Antoine de Saint-Exupéry
aviator, poet and author of **The Little Prince**

Filmmakers tend to agree on the stages necessary for an effective editing workflow and in what order they should be implemented. Less unanimous is how they place emphasis on these stages, which varies according to the personality of the filmmaker. Broadly speaking there are two categories of editor, which we will refer to as 'architects' and 'alchemists'. A person who plans extensively before they begin any sort of construction project can arrive quickly at their anticipated destination because they are less likely to encounter the unexpected problems that can delay proceedings – these are the architects. Someone who uses texture to influence their progression can understand a great deal about the materials, as they stir the ingredients with varying intensity, but this does not guarantee that solid form will be achieved – these are the alchemists. The good news is that narrative develops on this journey regardless of whether a route is set early on or we prefer to commit ourselves to chance.

Vik Pengilly-Johnson at his workbench

The length of a film is best directed by the attention span of an audience and the suitability of the material, so whereas it is a good idea to set initial targets it is equally important to keep these flexible until you have tested the material. Ethnographic films that are directed solely by optimism tend to be too long, so try to be realistic and seek editorial advice from would-be audience members. You may want to bear in mind the popular categories for festival inclusion. These are often defined by length, such as five-minute shorts, films under twenty-five minutes, and feature-length documentaries of over fifty-six minutes in length. You will find a place for your film if it is between categories but fewer options may be available to you.

Paper edit

Even successful alchemists benefit from organising their ingredients and tools. Try using small pieces of paper to represent individual images, sounds and entire sequences. Arrange these by moving them around a flat surface, as you would the pieces of a puzzle, until you are happy with a potential structure for the whole film. Spoken word testimony and other audio overlays can be treated in the same way, by positioning them under the sequences you have mocked up. When you

have decided how to assemble your images and sound, make a written list of the material you have selected, to help you import the material into a computer-based project. Most editing software includes tools for creating a digital 'paper edit' but I find the physicality of paper and the way it resembles cutting old-fashioned celluloid film contribute to a fun and creative way to begin.

If you have trouble planning a rough assembly of your material because you do not know where to start, try developing an architectural plan for your film. Divide the overall estimated length equally between a beginning, a middle and an end. Then divide each of these again between the number of principal protagonists, or situations that you hope to explore. For example, for a twenty-minute film, after you have taken two minutes for an exciting hook and title at the very start, you will have eighteen minutes remaining in which to tell your story. This breaks down to roughly six minutes each for the beginning, middle and end. If you are collaborating with three main protagonists then you will need only two minutes of introductory material for each person, two minutes of material that expresses your protagonists dealing with the subject of your research and only two minutes of concluding material for each. In this way you can focus your attention around the potential of your best material to serve a basic narrative, and the task will seem more manageable. The most important thing is to arrive somehow at an idea for the assembly cut of your film.

Previous page A publicity poster designed by Ross Phillips for *One Long Journey* that includes a 10-word log line

Working title

If you have written a research proposal then you will already have a title and log line. I prefer to combine academic and artistic ideas, so I use one title and log line for both the research paper and the film; others may want to organise these slightly differently. As an example, if your film is set in a shoe shop and the principal protagonists are two shoemakers then a broad moniker such as 'Shoes' will not give much insight into the metaphorical intentions of the film. A more descriptive title, such as 'How They Fit', will help you to focus the attention of an audience on the relationship between the two shoemakers and also the way they feel about shoes. As a general rule, the simpler the title the better.

10-word log line

One man's dream to build a boat … and sail it home

If you are pursuing any kind of funding for your film then you will need to present your initial ideas in terms of a pithy story. A key feature of this is to choose ten words that express the idea for your film in a snappy and informative way. The AllRitesReversed production team crowd-funded *One Long Journey* and both the title and the log line survived intact for the entire four years that it took us to complete the film. During the cutting process these ten words acted like a poetic puzzle, or *zen koan*, that must be deciphered through the myriad choices involved in editing. Because ten words are brief, they don't constrain your exploration but they do remind you that you need a beginning, a middle and an end.

Beginning an edit

Creating a new project and saving your work

We have now arrived at the stage where the editing software you have selected for cutting your film is required. Information in this section of the book can be applied equally to any software available but you may need to consult the help section for your individual program to understand how different terminology is used to describe its functions.

Opening the software prompts the user to create a new project. Your working title can be used to save this to the 'projects' folder on the hard drive that you are working with. The project file remains relatively small in size throughout the editing process – but it contains all of your post-production work, so do remember to back it up frequently. Next you are asked to select timeline or sequence settings. It is recommended that you edit your material using the same format that you recorded it in, so select settings that match the majority of your recordings. A 'timeline' is a visual representation of your edit and you can mix formats within one timeline, so don't worry if you are using various sources with different resolutions. Your software will have a default setting for a new timeline, so be careful to check that the resolution and frame rate are the same as most of your recorded material. It is important to check that the audio tracks are set correctly for either stereo or dual-mono (see p. 163), which depends on how you have configured your microphones during filming (see pp. 73-7). Ultimately, in order to export your film you must conform all of the material to a unified format called a 'codec'.

Codecs are a way of grouping audio and image data into packages that allow them to be edited and shared. Currently there is not one solution that suits both tasks equally well. It is easier to work with large files where audio and individual image data are processed separately, but it is more efficient and therefore easier to share smaller files where images are grouped together. If in doubt, select a 'same as source' codec for editing and mastering purposes to retain the highest quality and then export different 'transcoded' versions to suit whatever output you want. In other words, if you have recorded your material using the MOV codec at 4K, 25p, 100 Mbps, 48 kHz, 24 bit in dual-mono, then choose these settings for your new sequence.

The workflow for a project using 360-degree media is the same as for two-dimensional films but you can select different effects, titles and viewing options.

Organising bins

On entering the workspace you will see a project frame that includes a place where you can organise the recorded material that you will import into the project in separate 'bins'. It is a good idea to establish a bin structure that will allow you to keep your reference material and cuts well organised throughout the editing process. This involves thinking ahead. You can add bins later but it is best to follow a structure, otherwise you may get confused and lose clips or edits. What follows overleaf is a typical bin structure, with suggested category headings and examples of the sub-bins you might have in each category:

- **Original material** (or 'Proxies' if you are working with them)
  Day 1
  Day 2
  Day 3 (and so on until you have a folder for each shooting day, or if you prefer, organise your material according to type)

- **Edits** (variously called 'timelines', 'sequences' or 'events' in FCPro)
  Assembly cut
  Rough cut 1
  Rough cut 2
  Rough cut 3 and so on …
  Fine cut (you may have more than one of these)
  Final cut with subtitles
  Sound mix only
  Final cut with sound mix
  Final cut with sound mix and subtitles
  Trailer or teaser (depending on whether you intend to use these before or after your project is finished)

- **Audio**
  FX (meaning sound effects)
  Music
  Wild track (audio recorded separately from images; includes 'foley' recordings made during editing)
  Studio voice-over
  Pre-sound mix (to send to a professional in sound mixing, usually as an .AAF or .AIF file)
  Sound mix (the file returned to you by the sound person, usually as a mixed two track stereo .WAV file)

- **Titles**
  Main title
  Inter-titles
  Name tags
  Credits
  Subtitles

- **Graphics**
  Funding or institutional logos
  Title art
  After Effects (if you are including this sort of treatment in your film)

- **Archive**
  Stills
  Movies (including previous films that you have made)

- **Images**
  Original images
  Iconic images (screen grabs from the film)

- **Exports**
  3min teaser (or perhaps a trailer)
  Assembly cut
  Rough 1
  Rough 2, 3 and so on …
  Fine cut test-screening version (WIP)
  Pre-sound mix fine cut
  Reference video for sound mix
  Final cut with subtitles (if you are using in hard subtitles)
  Final cut without subtitles (if you are using in hard subtitles)

Importing recorded material

Importing in this instance means to transport the original recordings into the project, following the list that you created after paper editing. This can be achieved in two ways: either by referencing the original files from their source location or by making a new copy of the material to be stored within the project. To keep the project file small in size and your original material well organised and secure I recommend that you bring the recorded material into the 'media browser' of your editing software by referencing the source folder rather than importing it into the project. The software will reference your material without altering it in any way.

If you are working with high resolutions or fast data rates then you may need to create lower quality proxy versions of your originals using transcoding software. In this case you can reference these new files from their source for the purposes of editing and then change the reference to the higher quality originals before you export the film. If you are using a low-resolution screen it is a good idea to place a watermark on any proxy files, so it is easier to see which files are full quality and which are downgraded proxies. If you decide to import rather than reference your recorded material, then the software will make copies using the sequence settings that you have selected, but this will result in a very large project file.

The assembly cut

If you have organised your material into software bins, you can drag individual files, according to your paper edit, into the source monitor or straight onto the timeline in order to begin editing. The assembly edit is a collection of your best material with linked audiovisual clips and it can be more than twice the length of the running time you are aiming for. This long form represents a starting point not a destination, so it does not need to live up to all the expectations you have for the eventual film. The purpose of working with a complete assembly is to encourage you to think about the possibilities for a narrative arc and whether or not you have enough material to support the beginning, middle and end of an idea. If you have recorded sound and images using separate devices during fieldwork, synchronise this material for each clip and then link the high-quality video and audio tracks together before you start cutting. If you neglect to do this, it will become more difficult to locate and connect these separate recordings further on in the editing, as long takes become cut into smaller sections and scenes are woven together using camera audio.

Once you have roughly assembled the material, move individual shots and whole scenes around that do not fit together well. You can trim rough edges away from each shot and even try cutaways in position as overlays on separate video tracks, but avoid any fine cutting until you have resolved the structure of your film. Finally, watch the assembly cut in its entirety without pause and take time to think about how you will transform this fragile collection of ideas into something capable of carrying your audience on their cinematic adventure.

A close-up of Vik at work

Rough cutting to find a story

The antithesis of the structured is not the truthful, or even the objective, but quite simply the random.

Dai Vaughan
film editor and author of **'The aesthetics of ambiguity'**
(1999: 57)

With the assembly cut as your foundation, the next task is to test how this material works in different iterations of a story. Editing is a research process where we look closely at our recordings and think deeply about their ethnographic significance, in order to better understand the circumstances from which they were made. This works in tandem with the other main job of an editor, which involves selecting the most engaging material and placing it in a narrative order that satisfies you, your collaborators and an eventual audience. Similar to working out an ideal layout for household furniture, it is necessary to start with an imperfect arrangement in order to experiment with what works best in practice. Any material included in a film must contribute to the overall narrative in terms of its content, ability to develop character, establish and bridge scenes or signpost important aspects of the story. Recording in key situations will help to address these requirements. There is no space for useless material and your cutting decisions represent a commitment to eliminate certain recordings, once they have been thoroughly examined. As the pieces of this puzzle begin to connect, old theories are tested and new ones emerge. The concrete nature of a film does not deny the abstract thought that is necessary to work with theory when we consider the process of editing alongside the aim of storytelling. Because video editors are seeking a new order they must work with structure, but this does not imply that editing is simply aimed at developing continuity. Montage is also a tool for the disruption of established order, where space can be created within a film narrative for the application of imaginative theory (Suhr and Willerslev 2013).

Beginnings, endings and narrative arcs

A classic approach to storytelling establishes people, locations and ideas at the beginning, presents a dilemma in the middle and leaves resolutions for the end. The narrative arc is a thread that stretches through the entire story, capable of unifying the various elements so that others can also relate to it. Some ethnographic stories have in-built narrative arcs that follow the chronology of fieldwork. Others make use of journeys, processes and ritual events to summarise wider beliefs and practices in a format that is easy to locate in a processual film narrative. But there are also conceptual ways to organise an ethnographic narrative, for example through a personal diary, a biographical portrait, with dramatic fiction or in a constructed essay.

Beginnings are important because it is here that one secures the attention of an audience. However, there is little point working in detail on a beginning that does not have a middle or an end, so leave titles, fine cutting, colour correction and sound mixing until later. Instead, work equally across all the scenes of a rough narrative until you have established a workable structure. At the end of the rough cutting stage it is a good idea to question each and every shot that you have used, asking it to account for its contribution to an individual scene, or to the greater purpose of your story. If you feel that you have come to the end of your creativity, ask someone else to watch your rough cut and listen carefully to what they say. As you near completion of the rough cutting stage and settle on a narrative structure, look through all of your material once more. With new discoveries you have made along the way and the imperative of a story in need of tightening up, you will certainly see new possibilities in your recorded material to answer lingering questions and solve structural problems.

The following narrative devices give a brief idea of how to structure a documentary story. It is important to think about possible models before shooting, so you can gather the material that will serve these ideas in the edit. It is also necessary to cover the likely possibility that you will use more than one device. For example, an event can open a portrait film that takes us on a journey.

Daytime chronology

This narrative device has the potential to be understood in any cultural setting where the satisfying of human necessities across the structure of a day helps produce order in people's lives. You may have recorded material over a number of weeks or even months, but with an eye for continuity and the judicious use of a sunrise, the crow of a cockerel and a sunset, it can be brought together into the chronology of a day. Robert Gardner's film *Forest of Bliss* (1986) is a good example of how ethnographic ideas are made coherent by the way they are incorporated into the impression of occurring over a single day. Such reordering and poetic license can also, however, become subject to criticisms of manipulation or mis-representation.

Journey

A travelogue usually develops through a narrative order in which arrival follows departure. Journey films are typified by the road movie and commonly involve a search for someone, something or an answer to a lingering question. I used this approach in two of my films, *The Lover and the Beloved: A Journey into Tantra* (2011) and *One Long Journey* (2016), where external events acted as a metaphor for the personal transformation of the protagonists. This is a popular device for those using observational and participatory methods to build a sense of trepidation and excitement into their films, as protagonists struggle with their sense of direction and reflect on personal experiences. Journey narratives can also be driven by your own experiences, where they look and feel more like a diary film – Ross McElwee's *Sherman's March* (1986) is a good example.

Diary

This model is a good way of narrating a documentary story when there is no inherent narrative. A diary provides a reflexive device that can help situate the way that personal experience leads to academic discovery. In her film *Red Earth White Snow* (2018), Christine Moderbacher uses her personal memories and feelings, combined with poetry articulated in the form of voice-over narration, to question the activities and interactions of her Austrian father as they progress together on a trip to Nigeria in support of a Christian humanitarian aid project. The days of their visit and her growing understanding of aspects of their relationship both help to give narrative structure to the film. Similarly, in *News From Home* (1977) Chantal Akerman reads written correspondence with her mother in France as voice-over for her documentary, which explores the circumstances of her own lonely existence in New York.

Portrait

In an attempt to express a wider and more complex world that is difficult to grasp, it is common for ethnographic filmmakers to concentrate on one central protagonist in their storytelling. This can be someone who is adept at what they do, a character of central importance to their community or one who lives on the margins of society. As we get to know this person through the way they are presented in the film, we begin to trust their impressions as evidence and understand what is happening around them through our own emotional connection to them. Daniel Lema's film *Griot* (2015), about a British international artist who explores his African and Jamaican diasporic identity through clay, concentrates on unique and adept aspects of personhood to recount a wider story about migration.

Fictional narratives

Films that deal with past events, or focus on activities deemed too painful to record in a documentary fashion, sometimes use fiction as a narrative device. Fictional or semi-fictional methods are also popular when the experience of fieldwork participants is of specific interest. Choosing a collaborative approach invites you to explore ways of knowing and telling stories through the creativity of others. The genre of indigenous media extends this to the point where people who may once have been the subject of academic study take hold of the means of production, to create their own representations, fictional or otherwise. This model was used to good effect by Kieran Hanson in his graduation film from the Granada Centre for Visual Anthropology, *Shooting Freetown* (2011). This film is an eclectic look at how young people in the capital city of Sierra Leone developed a creative scene in order to better express their hopes, dreams and desires.

Episodes

If you are pursuing a narrative that is created from events that are separated by geography or time, you may need to impose a structure onto your film that can help viewers understand the spatial, temporal or ideological arrangements you have chosen. Filmmakers may deal with this by dividing their films into segments, often with inter-titles that signpost a progression to another part of the story. David MacDougall adopts an episodic approach in his film *To Live With Herds* (1972), about the lives and circumstances of the Jie, a pastoral people living in north-eastern Uganda, who arrange their calendar around activities concerning the care of cattle. MacDougall's film is also divided according to this calendar, in order to express the difficulties that a life built around tradition can present when it conflicts with the movements of a modern nation state.

Essay

This form of documentary narrative uses language or voice as the guiding device to present an academic argument. As the name suggests, the essay film is the mode of documentary most similar to its written version. There are myriad possibilities for assembling an essay film with any kinds of materials, so it is crucial to consider both the protagonists and eventual audience when narrating fieldwork in this way. The international relations scholar William A. Callahan uses his own voice in combination with archival and media footage to link personal experience with international politics. In his film *Great Walls* (2019) he applies humour and artistry to critically rethink the meaning of walls and how they shape people's everyday lives. Callahan has noted that a visual turn in international relations prompted him to use reflexive commentary alongside archive materials and his own contemporary recordings to develop the idea of politics as multisensory performance. Another example is the Dutch anthropologist Mattijs van de Port, who interweaves personal stories with images he encounters along a literal and metaphorical journey through the rainforests and cities of Brazil. The resulting film, *Knots and Holes: An Essay Film on the Life of Nets* (2018) is a playground for exploring ideas about human relations. Beyond the world of research, this storytelling device bears similarities with documentary filmmakers such as Agnès Varda (*The Gleaners and I*, 2000) or Michael Glawogger (*Untitled*, 2017).

Events

Human activities are performed daily and some are ritualised on special occasions. These events become an empirical lens through which to view the wider concerns of a society. They tend to have an inherent logic that translates well to the beginning, middle and end structure of a film. The most compelling expression of an event may be found before or after the main activity, where one can gain a better understanding of how the relations between people, objects and situations might both challenge and support an idea of community. Daisy-May Hudson made her debut film, *Half Way* (2016), about her family's impending homelessness. The film begins with the happy event of Hudson's graduation from the University of Manchester but this soon comes into contrast with the preparations for her family's eviction from their council-owned home. Apart from heartfelt storytelling, the success of this film resides in the juxtaposition of these two contrasting and critical events.

A publicity poster for Daisy-May Hudson's film, *Half Way*

HALF WAY

A film by Daisy May-Hudson

Official Selection
Homeless Film
Festival
2015

Building scenes and bridges

Narrative does not progress through individual shots alone, but through the ways that these connect together in sequence. Commonly these sequences comprise a number of wide, medium and close shots that work together to describe a process of some sort. The sequences are themselves then brought together as scenes in a film. For example, the content in the narrative arc of an event film is a collection of process sequences punctuated by moments of testimony. Recording in key situations should give you a wide variety of ways to build scenes and to connect them together. Journeys made on foot or by vehicle can provide an informative and exciting way to travel between the scenes in a film and also help to explain significant shifts in time and space. Guided tours are particularly useful when it comes to explaining geography but they can also be used to connect characters to individual processes. If your aim is to explore differences in individual perception, then everyday processes and events can become a tyranny. In this case, an essayistic approach that uses imagination beyond the concrete confines of everydayness might suit your story better.

Character development

Viewers should be encouraged to engage with the protagonists of a film. A connection with the people in your film will help audience members stay connected to your story and provoke them to care about the wider implications of the actions they are witnessing. Viewers come to know protagonists through the ways you reveal personal information about them. A balance between likeability and controversy tends to hold the attention of most audiences, so filmmakers often aim to develop attachment to a character before they start sowing seeds of doubt. Using material created with the triangle of action technique to demonstrate how people physically engage in their activities adds authenticity to a story. By demonstrating how this action affects them emotionally, you add a vital subjective context. This is especially important for principal protagonists that might be required to act as an authority on the subjects you are exploring.

Do not ignore the possibility of including yourself as a character in your film. The most common way to do this is to make your initial intentions explicit at the beginning of the film, followed by an indication of how the fieldwork challenged or supported them. This will add an important reflexive element to your ethnography that can help to bridge any conceptual gap between the audience and the fieldwork participants. If you are struggling to plan a film that involves multiple characters, try to give equal time and effort with each of them (see p. 134). By spending an equal amount of time under similar circumstances, hopefully you will end up with roughly the same amount of footage for each person. This will allow you to cut between characters as your narrative progresses from beginning to end. Unless you are thinking of using only voice-over to express your presence in the film, it is vital that you cover these possibilities with good-quality audio and visual material that includes yourself, recorded while you are still in the field.

Narrative signposting

Viewers need orientation if they are to understand the route that you have taken through your documentary story. Without clues, what may seem like a wonderful and creative journey to you can appear confusing and frustrating to those arriving at your subject for the first time. There are a variety of ways to signpost an edit, some more literal than others. If you have recorded images of road signs, houses or other signifiers of place, then this material will quite literally help you to establish new locations. In a film with an episodic structure, an inter-title card or a line of voice-over can help to explain a relationship or indicate a rupture in the narrative. Try to read the responses of a test audience to understand what type of signs might be necessary. This will also help you see at what point in your narrative audience members lose their way. If you bring in an editor to help, they are unlikely to have been on location with you so they can act as a fresh pair of eyes, eager to establish locations and relationships in a way that attends to the human need for narrative coherence. Without the help of an editor you must attempt to revisit your field site conceptually with renewed excitement and wonder. The aim is to convey a sense of arrival with the potential to excite viewers about the journey ahead and then establish them on the voyage once it begins.

Incorporating spoken words

Fieldworkers encounter words frequently because they are a vital strategy by which humans both reflect on and challenge the order in their world. Words are encountered in filmmaking through formal interviews, as spontaneous moments of

testimony or in recorded conversations (see p. 113). The sounds that protagonists use to express thought and emotion in a film help to define their character, and they happen most often alongside images of synchronous action. Speech offers a way of communicating what remains hidden or invisible. However, if it is used injudiciously it can dominate a film and move it towards the sort of explanation or interpretation that might be better expressed in writing. If we follow the popular maxim of 'show rather than tell', words are considered of secondary importance to the actions that often come before they are spoken. Having said this, voiced narration is remarkably efficient at providing contextualising information and it can also work particularly well as a form of inner dialogue, expressing the unity or disjuncture between perception and expression. Andrew Irving adopts this method in his research into the experiences of people living with HIV/AIDS in New York's Lower East Side. His filmed ethnography, *New York Stories,* aims to research and represent the realms of inner expression that constitute people's lived experiences of urban space but remain beneath the surface of their public activity (Irving 2017).

If you are aiming for continuity in your narrative through a sense of temporality in action, then avoid returning to the same visual interview throughout the story, as this will give the impression that time has not progressed. However, if you remove the visual and aural signifiers that can fix it in time this problem will be mitigated to some degree. With this in mind, wherever possible try to record interview and testimony without background noise, so that if necessary it can be used to signpost a narrative or as a reflexive device. Voice-over narration is also useful when the filmmaker wants to justify their position in the narrative of the film, either as an authority or as an apprentice. This is particularly effective when the presence of the author is made explicit from the beginning of the film and their subjectivity has been developed alongside other protagonists. When filmmaking is used for research some practitioners are tempted to overburden voiced narration with details, or to over-emphasise the academic authority of the fieldworker. Try to avoid this and instead keep voice-over concise, using easy to understand terms that reveal something about the position of the speaker. It is common to see images of a narrator at the beginning of the film, to establish their presence – unless, like Gary Tarn in his film *Black Sun* (2005) you are telling the story of someone whose sight has been taken away and you want the audience to experience a similar limitation in this sense.

It is not usual in filmmaking intended as a means for discovery to begin the editing process with a pre-written narrative voiceover. Scripted dialogue can distract an editor in their search for the performative aspects of recordings that challenge research assumptions and add drama to narrative storytelling. Narration that appears to be voiced from outside moments of actuality is sometimes referred to as 'voice of God' because of its unnatural omnipresence. Using voice-over of this sort can make a film appear dogmatic and render protagonists inept in the face of a greater authority. Additionally, any film that makes excessive use of voice-over runs the risk of developing dependency for this type of spoon-fed information in audience members. Sometimes devices from outside the context of the story are required in retrospect to plug holes in the narrative if appropriate material cannot be found in the original recordings. And in the essay film, narration provides a context in which to imagine new possibilities and other subjectivities.

(*Above*) Rajive McMullen preparing to be interviewed for *The One and the Many*

(*Right*) Improvised lighting on location for *The One and the Many*

Music

Music is the opium of cinema.

Trinh T. Minh-ha
author of **When The Moon Waxes Red** (1991: 59)

Music has the ability to alter our capacity for feeling beyond what is normal, so its use in films aimed at experience-led research is sometimes viewed with scepticism. It is more common for an ethnographic filmmaker to show emotion in their story through carefully recorded facial expressions, reactions and verbalisations, which are considered more authentic and less imposed by the author. Vocal and instrumental music that does not connect strongly with the subject matter of a film can carry us away from the reality we are seeking and lead us into a personalised imaginary scape where intersubjectivity diminishes. Audience members can come to depend on the harmonies as an indicator to how they should feel at any given moment in the narrative and then become dissatisfied if this crutch is removed. However, when the pitfalls of addiction are avoided, music can increase both the ability of a filmmaker to understand their own fieldwork and the creative ways an audience can engage with that work.

If we carefully consider our reasons for adding music then it can be useful at any stage in the development of an ethnographic film project. I asked two musicians, collectively known as the band Walk, to write a soundtrack for *One Long Journey* (2016). Rik Warren and David Schlechtriemen had previously written a song called *Ain't No Shame in Coming Home* that seemed to fit the themes of the film, but the lyrics were confusing for me. Vik's journey encompassed his whole lifetime and this latest dream, to build a boat and sail it home, seemed like a heroic adventure for a man in his seventieth year rather than a shame. Later I discovered how this journey had another more strategic meaning. Vik struggled to unite his need for closeness to family with a desire for personal independence, so he sought a place far away from home to process his thoughts and emotions. The boatyard became somewhere for Vik to fix damaged relationships by focusing on a dilapidated vessel. As filming gave way to editing, the music of *Ain't No Shame* found its way into every part of the narrative, eventually settling at the end. Through this process I began to see more clearly how notions of bravery and shame connect to feelings of loneliness, success or failure. Vik failed in his ambition to reach London by boat but he succeeded in uniting his family, who rallied around him when he returned to the boatyard, and there is no shame in that. Walk wrote many more songs for our film, inspired by the various edits of the material and through their own interactions with Vik. The vocal and instrumental music they made both supported and challenged my understanding of Vik and his grand adventure, and it became part of a dialogue with how I chose to edit the sequences of the film. The soundtrack grew out of the fieldwork and analysis and then back into it again, and for that reason I consider its use a tool for ethnographic discovery.

Try to be subtle with your use of music, so viewers are not overwhelmed by it. Observational filmmakers who hope to preserve a sense of closeness to the subject matter sometimes use sounds that have been recorded on location in a rhythmic way to produce an effective soundtrack. This approach was used to good effect in *Taste of Hope* (2019), where the filmmaker Laura Coppens takes atmospheric sounds from an employee-owned, co-operative tea factory in the south of France struggling to survive in a neoliberal world as the basis for a techno-inspired soundtrack. By connecting actuality to an original music score, the changes in narrative pace and feeling inspired by the music appear entirely contingent on the action. Yasmin Fedda adopted a similar approach in her short film *Breadmakers* (2007). Here the sounds of bread trays being removed from an oven and tins emptied onto cooling racks are sampled to provide music for the title and credit sequences of the film. Consider using single notes, drones or tones to augment your soundtrack, rather than music with its own narrative progression if you sense that this interferes with the actuality. Never return to the same piece of music, unless for comic effect, as this will dispel any sense of progression in your film. Music and illustrative sounds should be placed at an appropriate level in the audio mix, so they do not obscure important moments of action or dialogue.

Aside from the technical issues outlined above and the continuity problems caused by radios mentioned in Section 3, there are other things to consider when using music. The onus is on the filmmaker to determine whether or not permission is required from the rights holder for its use. Some recordings are covered under a 'copyleft' or fair usage policy that is published on the internet but others are subject to more limited terms. In this case permissions can sometimes be secured with an intellectual and property rights clearance document similar to the one in Appendix 2. Clearing rights can be a lengthy and expensive process, so it is a good idea to begin seeking permission early on in the edit, and certainly before you have committed yourself to using the music. If you cannot obtain the necessary permission in writing, then you may not be able to broadcast the work, even to the smallest of audiences. There are different rules for closed screenings, student film festivals, public events and broadcasts. To use pre-recorded music in a film, you usually need permission from the writer, performer and publisher of the work. An internet search followed

Rik Warren (left) and Andy Lawrence (right) during a recording session in Andy's basement for *One Long Journey*

by a few telephone calls will usually get you to a person you can negotiate this with. Lawyers that deal with clearance issues differentiate between music that occurs on location and music that is purposefully applied to a narrative by the author. If you have chosen not to pursue clearance for music and you are questioned by a broadcaster or university administrator – or worse, prosecuted by the owners of the rights to that music – then your only defence might be to argue that the music does not contribute significantly to the appeal of your film. In actual fact, a soundtrack, wherever it comes from, has a very great impact on how audiences receive a film.

Technique and style

Editing is a process that mimics thinking, and styles of cutting a film reflect broader ideologies. An approach that developed in fiction filmmaking in the USA during the first quarter of the last century, typified in the feature film *Birth of a Nation* (1915) by D. W. Griffiths, emphasised continuity in the form of wide shots and long takes. In many ways this was seen to legitimate the actions of pioneers seeking new places to live, regardless of the obstacles that confronted them. Such epic storytelling appealed to documentary filmmakers such as Robert Flaherty, who adopted many of the same techniques to narrate his romanticised portrait of Inuit life. A Soviet Russian style of editing, seen in the work of another feature filmmaker, Sergei Eisenstein, developed around the same time but to different ends. His approach included rapid montage of close-up action as an engine to drive narrative and to express disjuncture – this was adopted later by Vertov as a means to convey documentary ideas. Today, there are many alternative styles for editing a film that have extended from these geographical regions, but it remains true that the selection of images and sounds, speed and style of cutting, and ways of joining, separating and manipulating recorded material all contribute theoretical ideas to the narrative of your film. The primary task for ethnographers is to experiment with techniques to see how they can be combined into a style of editing that is sympathetic to the lifeworlds that we are exploring, rather than those we are already familiar with.

Whatever style of cutting you decide to adopt, it should be consistent throughout the narrative and established early on, so that an audience can learn how to read your film. New styles of editing that appear without motivation from the content can seem like mistakes, and therefore distract viewers from their engagement with the subject matter. Individual techniques that fall within a particular style affect the way that material is perceived and they are useful if you want to signal a shift in gear of narrative pace. It is a useful exercise to look for examples of the techniques outlined below in your favourite films and try to recognise how they are used to influence the storytelling.

The long take

If we think about filmmaking as gathering materials to build a structure, then the idea of recording uninterrupted sequences makes sense. A three-metre-long piece of timber can be sawn into three one-metre lengths, but these cannot so easily be rejoined in a way that retains the strength of the original plank. Similarly, human movements, gestures and interactions are interrelated, so recording these without interruption enables us to examine this relationship and present it to others with structural integrity. As we make editing decisions, the software references original material with a record of our ideas but it does not alter it in any way, so no actual cutting occurs. It is therefore important to record long takes in the field so they can either be used in their entirety or cut down in length. The difficult question that remains is when to cut.

Visual cuts

Multiple cutting points are built into a shot but it is not always obvious which one to choose. Completed actions, looks, gestures and natural wipes – for example, made by passing vehicles – can all help to motivate a cut. If you are editing your own material it is tempting to cut at the last opportunity when often the first is more effective. For example, if the attention of a protagonist alters with a subtle expressive gesture, then this is a cutting point. The turn of their head is another point you could make an edit, and physically walking away is yet another. If you choose the first cutting point your editing will develop a fast pace and remain focused around the action. If, however, you ignore these points, or consciously bypass them, you run the risk of your audience cutting before you do and leaving your film.

Sound cuts

Steven Feld (1994) developed an 'acoustemology' of practical ideas, built around the relationship between sound and sentiment, as an approach to research through listening and hearing. The same ideas can be applied to create atmosphere in the soundtrack of a film and you can also use them to inspire the cutting of visual sequences. An editor who works with sound that is synchronised to pictures can use it to make powerful cutting decisions. Humphrey Jennings made his film poem *Listen to Britain* (1942) at a time when radio was the most common way to share information, and this visual story is driven entirely by mechanical sounds and voices. Moments in the action, on or off camera, that are signified by strong and clear audio can be used as cutting points both in and out of a film sequence. This works well because of the way that human beings perceive sound all around them as a constant stimulus but see through a much narrower frame. A sighted person operates with a bank of sounds that they associate with pictures, regardless of whether or not they see those images. Consequently, a car door slamming, a rumble of thunder, a shout or a siren can all motivate development in a narrative without the need to immediately visualise the source of that sound. You can choose to cut to an associated image quickly or decide to hold out for longer in order to build suspense. Either way, using sound to help your cutting will evoke a more naturalistic feel in your film and also inject dynamism into the edit.

Matching action

To create a believable cinematic juxtaposition between two shots in a continuity scene, we must first consider how we perceive movement in space in our everyday lives. In his theory of relativity, Albert Einstein indicated that any movement in space implies a movement in time, and the video editor must consider this rule of relative indices for each cut they make. Let us take the famous example of the hand-assisted goal by the Argentinian footballer Diego Maradona, which put England out of the World Cup quarter finals in 1986. Imagine this as an edited sequence. The wide shot sees Maradona leaping for the ball, but when we cut to the close angle, the ball is already sailing past the goalkeeper and Maradona's arm is only signalling his joy at scoring the opening goal of the match. This appears natural because the close-up shot 'picked up' the action at a later point in time than where we left the wide shot – missing the vital moment where Maradona's hand makes contact with the ball. If the two shots were cut together without this separation in time, the relativity of time and space would be denied and the scene would 'feel' wrong. The controversy around this goal was heightened by the fact that viewers around the world saw it as a three-dimensional reality rendered in two dimensions. The more significant a cut in space, the greater the amount of time that needs to pass between the close-up and the wide angle shot. The illusion of continuity is developed as the action is progressed to whatever cutting point allows the impression that space has been covered, whereas on the timeline there is not even a 25th of a second between the shots. In practical terms, if you cannot get an edit like this to work then try shortening or lengthening it on both sides of the cut, by varying degrees, until it feels right.

Hard cuts

Strong narrative progression can be achieved by cutting synchronised sound and picture in unison. A hard cut is experienced as honest, where what you see is what you get, without recourse to trickery or refinement. For this reason most documentary filmmakers begin their assembly and rough cutting using hard cuts. It is also much easier to move chunks of synchronised material around the timeline until you discover the best position for them in your narrative. Most hard cuts will eventually be softened using a split method (see below), where sound arrives before the image, to mimic the way that we experience events in real life. However, occasional hard cutting can keep an audience alert or add power and authenticity to a sequence.

Soft cuts

The joins between individual sounds are usually softened with a fade of varying intensity at the point where they merge, mimicking the continuous way that humans hear audio in real-life circumstances. Images, on the other hand, are cut in the blink of an eye and never experienced by human beings as merged, unless something is seriously wrong. You may want to express the passage of time, or some sort of simultaneity as a concept in your film, with a fade, dissolve or wipe between two images. In practice, usually either the material does not suit the transition because it is unstable or continuously moving, or there is a more effective cut you could make that maintains the tension of actuality in your film. For this reason, dissolves are a rarity in ethnographic filmmaking.

Split-cuts and the idea of leading sound

A common method to connect two shots is by separating the sound and image slightly, to create a staggered or 'split edit'. Like most editing techniques, this one draws inspiration from the way humans experience environments with their bodies. We hear a mixture of sounds first and then respond by looking in the perceived direction of a sound that we have isolated in our imagination because it most catches our attention. Only then do we focus on an image that we associate with that experience. Because this is a common way that people act in their sensory environments, it follows that it is the usual style of cutting in a film. Sound leads image in the split edit and it is actually quite rare in cinema to introduce an image before the sound. This technique is also referred to as the 'J' cut because of the shape that the edited sequence creates on a software timeline. A less common variant of the split transition is known the 'L' cut, also because of the shape it makes on the timeline. Here the audio from a preceding scene overlaps the subsequent images. This is useful to express the disappearance of a vehicle or the distance that develops between a protagonist and the scene they are leaving behind.

Continuity and discontinuity

Filmmakers who attempt to understand the logic used by their research participants tend to want to convey this knowledge to an audience preserving some of the naturalism. For this reason, a continuity style of editing, using split-cuts and matching action to replicate the processual nature of complete actions, suits this type of work. Those seeking to express discontinuity in their work may want to disrupt reality, to create space for imaginative theory. Sequencing techniques such as rapid montage, or the parallel cutting of events that occur for a number of protagonists simultaneously, are not naturalistic. They do not evoke a type of perception that is achievable in real life, but they are capable of expressing ideas in your film. When attempting to describe working conditions in a factory, for example, you may need to make more radical jumps between sequences to demonstrate the way that humans manipulate their environments to suit their perceived needs. For multiple sequences to work in parallel, each situation, character and location should be well established, so that the audience recognise when they return to that same situation, and also understand why you have chosen this style of editing. As a foundational rule for editing in parallel, always

ensure that actions are complete before cutting away to another scene and occupy the same amount of narrative time with each location or protagonist.

Overlay

An essay film often requires bringing together eclectic materials into a single narrative idea. To achieve this we can think conceptually about how images and sounds connect through texture, composition, movement and rhythm, as well as notionally. In this instance, you might use spoken words as a platform on which to layer non-synchronous images and other sounds, in order to better express ideas. Considering similarities in movement, colour or composition of images can also offer a new direction to your work, which might have previously escaped the thinking and writing process. Without the guiding light of an inherent narrative, such as a process or journey, it is easy to get lost in the infinite possibilities for arranging a scene that includes overlaid images and voice-over, so screening the work to a test audience can be useful way to trial your ideas.

Tips and tools for editing

- Remember to set a sequence to '**dual-mono**' if you have used two microphones, as most timelines default to stereo.

- Use **keyboard shortcuts** to speed up editing, such as 'J', 'K' and 'L' to play cuts backwards, pause or play forwards.

- Get into the habit of using **control-S** to **save** your work frequently.

- Find the menu-based command to '**duplicate**' your sequence each time you make a significantly different cut, and rename each progression so that you can return to earlier ideas.

- Look for a command that will enable you to **toggle** between the panelled layout of all your software windows and a full-screen viewing window when you want to check the effectiveness and flow of an edit.

- Revert to previously saved **workspaces** if your windows appear out of place, or they become awkward to use.

- Use a **stabiliser** function to reduce unwanted camera shake and improve movements. This is usually found in the effects palette.

- **Slow down** clips with little or no movement to make them longer. This is useful for establishing shots or cutaways if the recording is too brief, or parts of it are unusable.

- Use an '**unsharp mask**' to correct out of focus shots, but be aware of the balance between grain and clarity.

- When adding titles during rough cutting, apply **default transitions** of fifteen frames in length and then adjust these later in the fine cut.

- It is still important to examine **safe margins** for title and action using wire frames, even for screens that claim to scan the whole of an image.

- When applying **effects**, look for simple solutions in the edit but aim to improve your shooting in the long run. Effects work across the complete sound and image of a clip, unless you work with time-consuming key frames, masks and notches.

- Use the **synchronise** tool to match sound that has been recorded on a separate device from the images. This is achieved by comparing the waveform pattern on the high-quality audio recording with the lower quality guide track that has been recorded in sync with the images. This is remarkably accurate but you may still need to make small adjustments to ensure it is frame perfect. It is best to synchronise the quality audio with the image and 'group' these together before you start cutting. You can then delete the low-quality guide track and make detailed edits that might be hard to synchronise later on.

Angélica Ascarza Mendoza and her daughter Maribel Ascarza Mendoza viewing a rough cut of *Entre Memorias* at their home in Ayacucho, Peru

Feedback

*Lead me from illusion to truth and
from darkness lead me to light.*

The Pavamana Mantra
Brihadaranyaka Upanishad

During a recent trip to India, a seeker told me that in order to achieve wisdom I should try to cultivate patience, concentration and sweetness. He continued by saying that I should dispense with faith, hope and glory as they each draw the aspirant into murk and illusion and away from the light of reality. In terms of filmmaking, it seems to be true that the greatest obstacle to transforming one's work into something wonderful is an overarching attachment to the fantasy that the first rough cut will appear to others as it does to us. Faith, hope and glory are employed in equal measure by filmmakers, right up until the moment an audience offers an alternative reading of the work. So to prevent unpleasant surprises, it is useful to learn how to take advice and assess the response of an audience to test screenings.

Receiving editorial advice

When you edit material that you have also recorded, it can be difficult to get a perspective on it that allows you to see its narrative potential. For this reason, any director who is also carrying out the recording and editing relies heavily on guidance from others. Try to avoid telling your editorial adviser all about your film in words before you have shown them a cut. Your story should be understood by the way you have edited the material; if it is not, then you need your adviser to demonstrate how and why this is the case. Editorial advisers can sometimes act more like editors, attempting to reshape your film according to their own ideas. The specific advice they offer is not the only solution and you may find a way that suits your own style better. The important thing is that you recognise the problem. There is no point in arguing with an adviser or attempting to gain their sympathy by listing the reasons why problems exist in your work – this will only push you deeper into the darkness of narrative obscurity. Try to listen patiently and concentrate on how they respond to your work. Feelings cannot be wrong and they are rarely provoked without cause, so it is essential that you respect every reaction and understand how your film has triggered them.

Work-in-progress screenings

Screening work in progress to a critically engaged audience of colleagues, fellow filmmakers or other specialists is another good way to concentrate your mind on potential flaws in the work. A film feels different when it is shown to an audience to how it feels when watched alone. At the Granada Centre for Visual Anthropology we adopt the departmental seminar format, inviting practitioners from various discipline areas to contribute to discussions around a film project as it develops. These sessions have helped PhD students, visiting fellows and staff to complete work that they would otherwise finish in relative solitude. At this stage it is best to court criticism rather than attempt to suppress or control it. Avoid intimidating people who know less about the subject of your film than you, with long preambles before the work

has been screened. As with editorial advice, do not try to gain sympathy from an audience by listing all the reasons why you have not realised your ambitions for the work. Do, however, prepare yourself for a rough ride and allow time to accommodate the extra editing that will be needed after this edifying experience. If viewers tend to agree on a reading of your film and on the order in which the scenes appear, then your film may be near completion – but it is more often the case that disagreement reigns in such screenings. If so, you have probably not succeeded in hooking your audience in the first five minutes, and rather than follow the narrative that you intended they have rearranged the scenes themselves, to make better sense of the story. Do not despair at comments that seem cruel and insensitive; instead, make a note of each individual remark, looking for ideas that will help you to find your way through to the next cut.

It is part of an ethical and shared approach to consult fieldwork collaborators whenever possible, and certainly at some point during the cutting of a film. Commercial documentary makers are unlikely to do this, as most broadcast production contracts forbid it. Thankfully we do not operate under such constraints. Researchers rely on the continuation of fieldwork relationships and a shared approach to making knowledge. It can be difficult and appear contrary to purpose to invite comments from the people who appear in your film, especially if they object to scenes that you like very much, but once you have their support you will feel more confident to push your film gently into controversial areas. Involving your fieldwork participants in the editing may also produce interesting insights into their ideas and expectations for your filmmaking, which in itself may be useful material for your research.

Daniel He at a public screening of *British Born Chinese*

Titles and credits

Words have been used to contextualise film narratives since the advent of cinema. Most films use words in some form or another and they play an important role in translating and crediting information that cannot otherwise be easily expressed through image and sound. Observationalists who use inherent structures such as events, journeys or performances as a way to organise their films tend to shun the use of words, preferring to use recorded sequences of images and sound to guide their audiences. Essay filmmakers and those who work with episodes and diary structures use more titles, inter-titles and name tags to explain the complicated arrangements that can exist in these types of ethnographies.

Title

The name of a film is significant because it points to key issues in the story that can contextualise the author's intentions. A provisional 'working title' is a good starting point, but be prepared to change this as the work develops. Think about how a title serves the main ideas that are being driven throughout your film. Try different titles in place during the rough cutting, so that they become part of the overall narrative arc. Select a font for its readability and consider style and motion effects carefully for how they suit the subject matter. Do not fill the screen with text – this may look good in the small editing window of your computer but it can be overpowering on a cinema screen.

Inter-title

'Inter-titles' are wording that appears between the scenes of a film, to provide information that is absent from the recorded material but vital to the progression of a story. They are favoured by ethnographic filmmakers as a less imposing way to signpost a narrative than voice-over narration. If you choose to use inter-titles then sentences should be presented in easy to understand terms and kept as brief as possible. Avoid placing too much information on one page as this can be hard to comprehend and it is unlikely that an audience will retain more than the first couple of lines. To address the imperative for simplicity, inter-titles are constructed using a simple font in white on a black background and then faded up and down between scenes, or they may adopt a more elaborate font placed over images. Laurent Van Lancker uses both styles of inter-title in his film *Kalès* (2017),

An uncertain future awaits migrant men in a jungle of tents at the French port of Calais. Video still from *Kalès* by Laurent Van Lancker

about the tented 'jungle' near the French town of Calais, where refugees and migrants gathered until it burnt to the ground. Van Lancker opens his collaborative experiment in sensory filmmaking with a quote from Dante's *Inferno*. Each line of text in a white font is revealed individually on a black screen until the message is made clear. The same technique is used towards the end of the film with another quote from the same author, but this time laid over the images. The lines that Van Lancker selects underline the importance of home and security and the tragedy for those who have lost them. There is no voice-over or commentary in the film; instead, viewers are left to find their own way through the shattered existence that the film depicts, but the words offer some guidance in a journey that might otherwise have seemed overwhelming and disorientating.

Subtitle

Documentary filmmaking takes private acts and makes them public, so context matters a great deal. It is important that viewers understand the words spoken by protagonists both in terms of their meaning and their performative qualities. When you add subtitles to a film you are contributing words to an already thick description of sound and images, so they should be integrated with this rather than offer an alternative way of reading the film. For this reason, I avoid the use of text-based grammatical devices in subtitles, such as parentheses, commas, full stops, italics and so on, unless absolutely necessary. A specific problem comes up when adding subtitles in the same language as the film is voiced in: whether to subtitle using a direct presentation of slang or swear words, or clean up the dialogue and translate it to an

official tone. I favour as direct a rendering as possible, one that carries the colourful meaning intended by participants, so long as this is not too obscure to be understood by a general audience. It is necessary to undertake some degree of translation when a dialect is particularly strong or if your work is to be shown to an international audience who simply would not understand the nuances of the original language.

From a technical perspective there are two types of subtitles, those that can be exported as a separate file or those that are 'burnt in' to a media export – the former is the most versatile option. Editing software includes facilities for creating 'closed captions': text that is not permanently burnt into the image but instead offers an option to export a 'sidecar' file called a 'SubRip Title', or SRT for short. Selectable options are exported along with the file, to help with formatting and translation to other languages for online players, DVD authors and third-party users. Look for a current video explainer online that shows you how to create closed captions in your chosen software.

It is possible to spend many days formatting subtitles and then discover that a primary platform you want to export to does not accept that particular format. To avoid this, test your entire workflow in a thirty-second section of your film and then upload that to whatever platform you are using, taking note of whether the results are what you expect.

Other than format, there are a number of issues you need to consider when making subtitles, which I have summarised overleaf:

Font, size and colour (only for burnt in captions, as exported SRT files have third-party defaults applied to them)   The overall style should be sympathetic to the images. A sans serif font, such as Arial in medium bold, is easiest to read. Size will vary according to the resolution that you are working with but the subtitles should always be readable and not dominate the screen. White and yellow are the two most popular colour choices for subtitles because they offer the greatest contrast to the lower-third portion of an image.

Style of subtitling   Keep sentences short and summarise the speech of a protagonist if necessary, but do not overtly change their words or misrepresent what they are saying. It may be necessary to translate vernacular speech using formal vocabulary and it is a decision for each filmmaker whether to include swearing. A maximum of seven words per line and two lines in total is recommended.

Subtitling across cuts   Avoid this as viewers tend to read the subtitle twice when it rests across a cut.

Spacing and position of subtitles   For stylistic reasons and to give the viewer the time the eye needs to recognise a new subtitle, it is best to leave space between titles. Check the position of your subtitles with the wire frame guide that can be activated in your viewer window. All titles should be placed within the inner 'title safe' frame.

Suitability of recorded material for subtitling (consider this in the field before you start recording)   Is there adequate space for a subtitle below the mouth of the person speaking? Is the image too bright or full of contrast for the subtitles to be readable? Does movement within the frame distract from the subtitle? Is the clip of an adequate length to accommodate a subtitle? A minimum of four seconds is recommended.

Credits

No documentary film is a one-person show. The credits at the end of your film acknowledge those who have contributed to the completion of your project and they are evidence of a reflexive and ethical approach that is important in academic work. You might be the producer, director, cameraperson, sound recordist and editor, but to acknowledge yourself in all these roles will appear immodest and make your work look under-supported. It is common therefore to summarise your own roles in the production with 'a film by', so as not to overburden the credits with references to yourself. At the other extreme, thanking everyone in your life will diminish the help that you received from contributors to the film, so be selective and accurate in how you credit people and check thoroughly for spelling mistakes.

Fine cutting

It may be necessary to walk away from an edit for a few days, to regain your perspective and find solutions to lingering problems. This is an opportunity to take a last look through the entire body of your recorded material. You will be surprised what you recognise now that you understand everything so much better. You may discover interesting answers to those problems that you had been wracking your brain about in the edit suite. Once the elements of a story are all finally in place, but before the film is exported, examine each cut closely for minute disruptions in the progression of the narrative and look at how individual shots and sounds match and flow.

Moni Baba communicating with spirits in the
cremation ground at Tarapith

Visual transitions

The precise examination of each edit is much easier if the clips you temporarily placed on tracks above the main action are brought down to 'V1' on a single track (unless you are superimposing images onto one another). This makes it easier to zoom in to the timeline and tweak each edit by rolling back and forth, frame by frame, until a cut is smooth and has the impact you are looking for. It is only by moving beyond the structuring process and concentrating in minute detail that one sees just how much work is necessary at this polishing stage. Final Cut Pro uses an 'intuitive' system for editing, so it is less easy to control the video and audio tracks manually. It is also easier to colour correct when video clips are placed on a single track.

Colour and luma correction

Altering colour casts that have been generated by poor white balancing in mixed lighting conditions and adjusting brightness and contrast in the image both help to unite the visual elements of a film. This is considered a primary stage of colour correction and it is aimed at consistency and re-establishing a natural look for your images. You may decide to go further than this and use a 'look up table' or LUT to enhance the visual appearance of your film. LUTs are sets of data that have been pre-programmed in your editing software that establish colour and luma (brightness) settings to give a specific look to your film, such as sepia for a retro appearance. This secondary level of cinematic colour grading,

which can also be achieved manually, is intended to increase expressive possibilities with the use of technical enhancement rather than emphasise the natural characteristics of your images, so it is not favoured by observational filmmakers. As distinct categories of approach become blurred, so degrees of technical enhancement find their way into ethnographic filmmaking more comfortably at both production and post-production stages. Some software promotes automatic correction but this is inadequate for our purposes. The same principle of manual control we discussed in Section 2 is applied at the editing stage, to ensure artistic control over the work.

Most editing programs include technical **scopes**, which are necessary to accurately assess the impact of colour and brightness changes as they are applied to the images of your film. Technical scopes are important because video screens used for monitoring purposes vary greatly in quality and in the way they represent colour and contrast, so a graphical representation of your images helps you assess their qualities regardless of the vagaries of monitors. Two scopes that are particularly useful are the **Y-Waveform Luma**, to check brightness and contrast, and the **Red, Green and Blue (RGB) colour parade**, to inspect colour balance (see opposite, above). A luma waveform should present a good balance of contrast across the entire broadcastable range of 0–100 on the scale. An RGB parade should include equal amounts of red, green and blue in the highlights, midtones and shadows, with perhaps a small increase in any one of these to represent natural colour casts caused by blue sky, green grass or a red light, for instance. Overall you are aiming for consistency between shots, so you may need to tone up or down an image, even if it looks correct on the scopes, to match it with the images that come before or after it.

There are four basic areas of colour correction that have an impact on the presentational quality of individual images and help you to develop shot-to-shot consistency. These are brightness, contrast, saturation and hue, for which I have provided summary information overleaf. They can be assessed using scopes – try comparing your own images to the luma and colour range shown in the picture to the right. The overall aim is to unify the individual images in a film sequence so they look like integral parts of the same scene, regardless of how, when and where you recorded them.

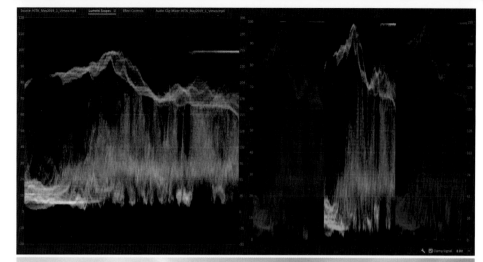

Luma and RGB scopes in the Adobe Premiere Pro interface (top) showing brightness and colour for the image (right) of Martin Ccorahua photographing the cast of his film, *La Maldición Del Inca*

Brightness lifts the gamma regions and overall gain of an image. This can be achieved by increasing exposure at the time of recording, which is why it is sometimes represented as an 'exposure' setting in the editing software. The effects that its adjustment has on an image can be seen in the luma scope.

Contrast ensures a maximum range between light and dark areas of an image. Do not 'crush' the black areas or 'overblow' the whites. Adjusting contrast lifts the exposure and simultaneously lowers darker regions. These can be adjusted independently by selecting either 'exposure', 'midtones' or 'shadows' on the sliders. Contrast is also assessed with the luma scope.

Hue and colour balance can be adjusted to give a more naturalistic look to your images. Altering the hue will help to mitigate distracting colour casts caused by ambient reflections. Adjusting the colour temperature with a slider or wheels will help to rectify problems caused by incorrect white balancing. A slider bar ranges between cool blue tones and warmer reds, and can be adjusted along its scale until the desired look is achieved. Aim for equal amounts of red, green and blue in all areas of the image. Hue and colour balance adjustment can be assessed by using the RGB scope.

Saturation is the amount and intensity of colour in an image. Increasing it will reinvigorate colours that have been washed out because of poor lighting, and lowering it will tone down colours that can become overly rich. Again, aim for consistency. Even if an individual shot looks correct you may need to add saturation or desaturate slightly to match the other shots in a sequence. Saturation can be seen in the RGB scope by the density of the colour in any part of the wave pattern.

Editing and mixing sound

Most audio is edited in sequence along with the pictures at the rough cutting stage but some sounds are added after this to strengthen the soundtrack. This is necessary because of differences in the way that microphones with specific pick-up patterns convert audio into raw data, and the more comprehensive ability of the human ear to separate and position a variety of sounds according to affect. We may also wish to apply creativity in this area to help explain three-dimensional geography within the two dimensions allowed by a cinema screen. Because hearing so often precedes seeing, what happens in a soundscape off-screen can be as important as those sounds we directly associate with the pictures we are seeing. Equally, you may need to eradicate completely, or reduce in their impact, unwanted sounds that have crept in because of poor recording technique, the limits of equipment or environmental factors.

Any sounds that have been added need to be merged into the soundscape of a film – this process is referred to as 'mixing'. A multitude of dials and switches are used for a professional sound mix and it remains an option to send your film in this direction, once you have finished working on it yourself. In this part of the book, however, we will look at how to edit and mix sound using tools found in the same software package that you used for rough cutting your film. There are some basic technical details that need to be covered before we can look in more detail at the actual editing and mixing of sound.

you require two separate tracks to house two independently recorded channels, rather than one stereo track. This setting is adjusted along with the format and timeline settings when you begin a new project. If you neglect to set this correctly then the two mono signals from your separate microphones will be shown as the left and right components of a single stereo pair and appear on one track of your editing timeline. You will still hear the two channels separately through each audio monitor, if you have been consistent when inputting your microphones. If you export the film in mono, these tracks will be summed together and played equally from each speaker. But if you do not export in mono, your audience will hear the same sounds, recorded from different distances with different quality microphones, through each separate speaker, which will create a distorted impression of the

Martin Salmonson mixing sound for *One Long Journey* at Futureworks in Salford

Dual-mono or stereo

The default timeline setting for most editing software is one video track and one audio track, which uses separate left and right channels as a stereo pair. This is because software manufacturers assume you will be recording in stereo. However, when recording a documentary it is also likely that you will have chosen to use two mono microphones instead of a single stereo one (see pp. 46–8). If that is the case, to prepare the tracks for editing, or to mix between mono sources and delete redundant safety or guide tracks, this fact must be established on the editing timeline. For this to happen

A stereo audio track shown next to the same clip with dual mono tracks.

soundscape you are attempting to recreate. It is also much easier to select which sounds you want to keep and which you would like to discard if the two microphones you have used to record your film appear in a consistent way on two separate tracks.

If you have not created a dual-mono timeline then select the problematic audio clip by accessing the 'audio options' and change the timeline setting from stereo to dual-mono. Each mono recording associated with that clip will then appear on its own track. You will need to repeat this process for each clip that has a similar problem. The audio patterns will remain graphically similar because they represent the same audio recording from a slightly different perspective, but as you zoom in closer on the timeline differences in the peaks and troughs of the waveform will become apparent. When combining stereo and mono recordings on a single timeline, with the intention of exporting a stereo mix, use the default timeline setting for stereo and separate each of the dual-mono recordings onto their own stereo tracks. Remember to position these individual sounds by panning them to the left, right or most commonly the centre, of the eventual sound mix.

Track-laying

When rough cutting is complete you will need to 'unlink' the sound from its image in order to weave it together using split-edits for leading or trailing sound, layering and transitions to soften the cutting points. Remember, audio is experienced as continuous, so even if sudden sounds appear in the mix there is always an undercurrent of sustained noise. To prepare for this

it is important to be consistent with your use of tracks for the different types of audio that feature in your project.

A1 - **Mono directional microphone for synchronous sound**
A2 - ditto (to allow for chequerboarding - see below)

A3 - **Radio-controlled microphone for synchronous sound**
A4 - ditto

A5 - **Studio microphone used for voice-over narration**
A6 - ditto

A7 - **Wild track**
A8 - ditto

A9 - **A track that can be used for room tone**
A10 - ditto

A11 - **Music**
A12 - ditto (four tracks are required for stereo sources)

When tracks are laid in this way it is much easier to deal with repetitive problems that require attention across an entire audio track – with audio filters and consistent volume changes, for example. Track-laying enables 'chequerboarding': subsequent sounds from a single source are alternated on two tracks, allowing a more creative sound mix. This process creates a pattern in your audio tracks reminiscent of the board used in a game of chess or chequers. Without chequerboarding it is not possible to alter the length and type of audio transitions that can be used. Final Cut Pro approximates this process automatically, which can be confusing for an experienced editor who is used to manually laying tracks but useful for the novice who is not interested in how to lay foundations for a smooth edit.

Adding sound

You may wish to add other sounds into the mix to compensate for thin or weak recordings. Try to choose these from within the wild-track material that you recorded on location to ensure they are appropriate to your field site. If this is not possible then you can search online for sounds, most of which exist as copyright-free. Some repository websites, especially those dealing with environmental noises and animal or bird sounds, tag the recordings they house to a location map so you can select geographically appropriate sounds for your film. You may also want to record what is referred to as 'Foley' sounds, named after the American sound-effects artist Jack Foley, who pioneered this technique in the 1920s. These are sounds recorded during editing and after the main filming has ended, usually because you forgot to collect them on location or the ones that you possess are not of high enough quality. Common examples are footsteps, creaking doors, bicycle wheels and animal noises, but any subtle sound can get lost in the general hubbub when recording a fast-paced documentary. This added audio helps to reinvigorate a soundtrack and draw the attention of an audience to important details in the film. Some editing software offers a selection of sound effects from within the program and significantly more as third-party plug-ins. Take care to edit this new audio into your mix at the correct level, usually louder for nearer sounds and quieter for those that occur at a distance.

Dealing with unwanted sound

Distracting sounds can be filtered to reduce their impact or cut out entirely. Noise reduction and equalisation filters help to overcome audio problems created by mobile phones, wind, air-conditioning units, boom handling and traffic. These filters are included in the audio effects palette of most editing software. **Low pass filters** mitigate unwanted high frequencies, such as mobile phones, and **high pass filters** bypass annoying low frequencies, such as wind, traffic and handling noise. Notch filters address one specific frequency, which can be useful if there is a continuous unwanted sound in your recording, like an electrical hum at 20 kHz. When a voice seems partially obscured by unwanted noise, you can bring it forward by reducing the frequency presence of the unwanted sound. You may not be able to eliminate the unwanted sound completely, as this would unduly distort the tonal range of the voice; instead, adjust the frequency notch until the voice becomes dominant over the unwanted noise and leave it there. Unwanted sounds that alter in pitch or include more than one tone are harder to deal with as they occur across a broad range of frequencies. For blips, clips and volume peaks in sound, cut out the problematic section and paste in a clean part from a nearby segment of the recording or from the one minute of room tone you have recorded (see p. 104), using a three-frame cross-fade to join these together. If this does not work then reduce the volume by adding four key frames around the problematic sound and dragging down the central section by about 12 dB, or whatever is required. The considerable difficulties experienced when attempting to 'clean up' audio in post-production should encourage you to pay more attention to its importance in the field next time you record sound.

Audio transitions

To avoid audible clipping in and out of a sound, it is common to place fades of varying length at the beginning and end of audio edits, to soften the cut. If the audio tracks are laid correctly, then fades can be applied to clips individually to allow for variation in the way sounds enter and exit the soundtrack. Avoid cross-fading clips in equal parts, which will create a smooth, uninteresting and unrealistic audio mix. Transitions are not only intended to even out unequal sound recordings, but also provide a way to accentuate certain sounds in the ways that they appear in actuality. The length of a cross-fade mimics how that sound triggers our attention in real life, so some are lengthy and others short or exponential. Transitions with constant power retain the signal strength for both clips equally, by locating a midpoint from which to cross-fade from one sound to another. Exponential fades use a curve pattern to alter the speed of arrival or exit of a sound; they are useful for sounds that appear and disappear quickly, like car engines and sirens. Experiment with all the options available to you and aim to create a dynamic sound mix where audio and image both drive narrative progression.

The most common audiovisual edit in a continuity style of editing is the split-cut (see p. 150). This slight separation of sound and image mimics human reaction and interaction, so it helps to create a naturalistic feel in an edited film sequence. Hard cuts, which are something that happens less often in real life, are also used judiciously to alert an audience to a point of interest or signal a shift in narrative gear. Strong foundations in editing are built with simple decisions that make use of both sound and image to motivate cutting. This is one reason that I recommend students begin learning to edit by using only hard cuts to explore the power of synchronised sound and picture in a process sequence (see p. 14). Another reason is that it is a relatively simple approach that offers a way beyond a tyranny of continuity and a route towards creative storytelling. These foundational skills can be assessed in any of the films listed at the back of this handbook to see how the internal rhythms of shots and sounds drive their narratives.

Editing spoken words

People are inclined to repeat themselves and search for coherence in their own words as they speak. It may be best to radically alter the way a statement is voiced if the expression is so unclear that you think an audience might lose the thread of what is being said. It is easier to reorganise a sentence when you are using overlay as a method to mask the cuts, as is the case in many essay-type films. However, it is also possible to truncate and make minor alterations to observational films with the judicious use of cutaways. And if the audio has been recorded without background sound then frames of silence between each word or longer pauses can be exploited to make the incision. If a person speaks rapidly, or rolls their words into one another, use three-frame cross-fades to soften the impact of a word that has been cut in half. If words are unclear then try to cut them out and paste the same word from another part of the dialogue. Use sections of the minute-long recording of room tone on a spare audio track to mask bad cuts and unify sentences that have been reorganised. Room tone can also be used if there is a constant presence of ambient sound in your recording. In this case, paste a segment of the room tone that matches that of your scene underneath the dialogue and then extend this beyond the cut, adding a long fade so the audience are not distracted by the sudden disappearance of the ambient sound. If you are editing words spoken in synchronicity with images, try to cut on gestures and glances or other visual aids that help to motivate the cutting. Perspective is important when mixing sound of any type. For example, as a way into a scene, recordings of voices made at close proximity can be positioned at a lower level beneath an exterior wide establishing image of a house or window, and then increased to their maximum output level as we cut to inside the house where the people are speaking.

Output levels, consistency and range

For theatrical screenings in large cinemas sound is usually amplified and therefore more volatile, so you may be required to lower the output level by 12 dB to ensure the sound does not distort in this setting. If you are intending to share your work on the internet then a theatrical mix will be too quiet, even when the volume is turned to full on domestic equipment, so here peak levels should be exported at -1 dBFS or just below. Do not push the mix to 0 dBFS, as the loudest sounds in your mix will certainly distort. If in doubt an export level of -6 dBFS should be used.

It is important to establish loudness levels at the beginning of an audio mix for each type of sound you are using in your film and then place these on separate tracks (see p. 164). Once track-laying is complete you can mix to one master level on each set of tracks and then increase or decrease the complete sound mix for various outputs as the sounds will remain the same relative to each other. Voices are commonly loudest in an audio mix, with other sounds positioned below them. Raise or lower volume by degrees of 3 dB, otherwise you will not notice the difference. To achieve consistency you must use your ears and a peak level meter. The listening volume of audio monitors should be set at the beginning of a mixing session and then not altered – otherwise the sound of the final mix will be as inconsistent as the choice of listening volume. Level meters are for checking that sounds are within peak limits but they do not indicate how a mix feels, so use your ears for this. It is acceptable to use headphones to roughly edit audio, but it is always best to mix sound using studio monitors with a wide dynamic range, placed according to the mono, stereo or surround requirements of your film. To avoid the gradual creeping up or down of levels during a mixing session, it is a good idea to move randomly across a timeline between sections of the film, especially when you are trying to establish consistency in loudness.

As with images, variety develops interest, so wherever possible establish a good range between loud and quiet sounds in your film. Silence is never absolute – there is always some noise present, however subtle. Using moments of quietness that are punctuated by noise is far better than a general level of unfocused sound. Sound that has been well recorded appears on a graphic timeline in the shape of the Swiss Alps: sharp peaks and deep valleys with discernible space between. The audio you export along with the final cut of your film should also have this appearance.

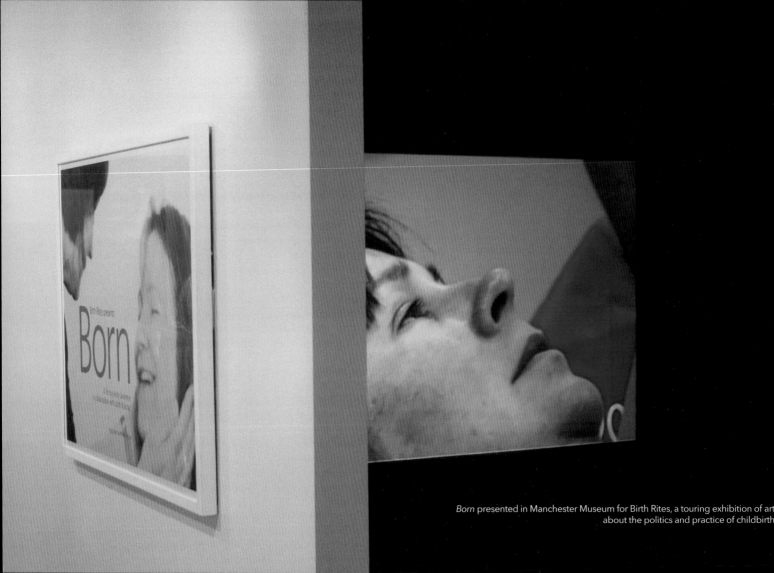

Born presented in Manchester Museum for Birth Rites, a touring exhibition of art about the politics and practice of childbirth

Mastering

Once the picture is locked, colour corrected, audio mixed and titles and credits are firmly in place then it is necessary to watch the completed film through twice without pausing, to check that everything is as it should be. Place at least three seconds of black video at the beginning and check that both audio and image fade up and then fade to silent blackness at the end of the film. Ensure that all active tracks are selected. You are now ready to make a final export of the film at its highest quality, along with any other compressed versions that may be necessary.

Export and delivery

To retain the highest quality, export your film using the exact same image and audio settings as the original recordings. This setting is often referred to as 'same as source'. Check that the frame rate and aspect ratio are consistent with the originals and the data rate is high enough for a master copy – 50 Mbps or higher is currently recommended but this rises each year that technology improves. Check that the audio is set correctly to stereo or mono, depending on how you have mixed the sound. If you are unsure about this, centre all the tracks by selecting a mono output. Make sure the export audio peak level is high enough to be heard on domestic computer equipment but that it will not distort: -6 dBFS is a good standard. Also ensure that the audio is of a high enough quality – at least 16 bit, 48 kHz. Once the export is complete, store this file as an 'edited master' in at least two separate places along with the other deliverables, such as synopses and iconic images. The editing software can then be used to compress the film using a portable codec with a lower data rate for sharing online, such as the popular QuickTime H-264, which produces an Mpeg-4 file. For films intended for cinema release select Digital Cinema Print (DCP). This will create a very high-quality set of files stored in a folder that is only accessible with cinema equipment.

If you are producing a film for video on demand (VOD), broadcast or festival screening you may wish to include an industry standard starting time-code, followed by colour bars and audio mix-level tone. This will enable a broadcaster to set their equipment in line with how you have graded the colour in your film and at an audio level appropriate to the output levels of the sound mix. Most broadcasters and some festivals have clear guidelines about export levels and delivery format, so check these first.

Artwork

As the editing nears completion there are usually a few images that seem to express the content of the film particularly well and tend to linger in the imagination. These can be exported from a timeline as still frames, for use in online galleries, websites, banners, thumbnail images for online video players, posters, postcards and book illustrations. Look for images that convey their content powerfully and simply, such as those shown overleaf. If you want to add text to an image then select a frame with less detail that can be darkened, defocused or tonally muted, so that the writing is readable. Export each still frame at its highest quality. This is usually defined by the way an image has been recorded but it can be slightly improved by exporting at a higher resolution or by using a different codec. The popular JPEG format is acceptable for screen-based applications, but because it compromises quality in favour of portability it is not suitable for print purposes. The resolution of print items should be increased to 300 dpi or above using software such as Adobe Photoshop and then exported using a high-quality lossless codec such as PNG or TIFF. Images can be enhanced for these purposes by adding contrast using the same software. *Born* was recorded in standard definition using the DV25 codec at a screen resolution of 72 dpi, often in very low light. The image that I used for the A1 poster of this film, was extracted from the edited film sequence using Avid Media Composer and then saved as a TIFF. This was imported into Adobe Illustrator by the designer, who increased the resolution to 600 dpi and then altered the contrast, brightness and framing to make it more suitable for the postcard, poster and gallery materials. The artwork for *One Long Journey*, also pictured here, was generated in a similar way but here the designer turned the photograph into a line drawing.

This page (*top to bottom*) The image used by Ross Phillips to develop publicity material for *One Long Journey* | Ross also created materials for *One Long Journey* that helped with crowdfunding | A video grab from *Born* used as a basis for poster art | The artwork for *Born* was adapted to fit across doors that led into a cinema space | Cath Webb's exhibition poster for *Born*

Facing page (*clockwise from top*) A production still of Dan He and Kevin But taken during filming for *British Born Chinese* | The screening poster required a large amount of information | DVD cover artwork for *The One and the Many*, using still images from the film | DVD cover artwork for *The Lover and the Beloved*, also using still images from the film

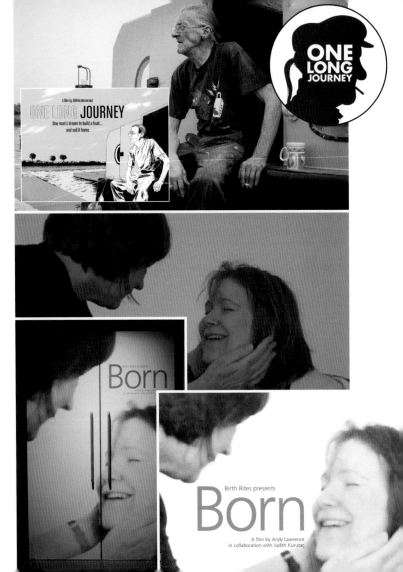

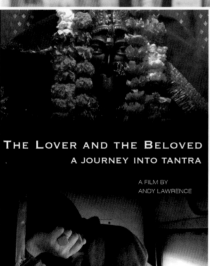

THE LOVER AND THE BELOVED

A JOURNEY INTO TANTRA

A FILM BY
ANDY LAWRENCE

Documentary Educational Resources   www.der.org 617-926-0491

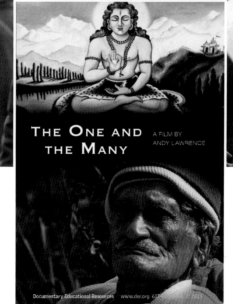

THE ONE AND
THE MANY

A FILM BY
ANDY LAWRENCE

Documentary Educational Resources   www.der.org 617

BRITISH INTER-UNIVERSITY CHINA CENTRE PRESENTS
A PUBLIC LAUNCH SCREENING AND DISCUSSION

BRITISH BORN CHINESE

A Documentary film exploring the experience of two boys growing up in Manchester a generation after their parents first came to the UK

5:00pm - 7:00pm
30th April 2015

Manchester Central Library
St Peters Square
Manchester
M2 5PD

Free entrance by reservation on Eventbrite:
**www.britishbornchinese.
eventbrite.co.uk**

For more details see
www.allritesreversed.co.uk/britishbornchinese

There will be a discussion following the film with the first published British Born Chinese writer, PP Wong, Senior Lecturer in International Relations, Dr. Véronique Pin-Fat and the director of the film, Andy Lawrence.

PP Wong is the first British born Chinese novelist to secure a publishing deal in the UK. Her novel The Life of a Banana covers the topic of racial bullying in London. It has been longlisted for the Bailey's Women's Prize for Fiction. She was born in Paddington, London and she spent her childhood moving between London and Singapore. She is a freelance writer and also the Editor-in-Chief of www.bananawriters.com The website is a voice for East Asian and South East Asian writers.

Dr. Véronique Pin-Fat is Senior Lecturer in International Politics at the University of Manchester and is the Director of Undergraduate Studies for the School of Social Sciences.

Andy Lawrence is a filmmaker in residence and lecturer in visual anthropology at the Granada Centre for Visual Anthropology, University of Manchester.

SECTION 5
Distribution

I've a feeling we're not in Kansas anymore.
*Dorothy from **The Wizard of Oz** (1939)*

Images and sounds that have been created in the field take on new meanings when they are presented in a viewing room or cinema. Ethnographic stories are edited for a public audience but they often rely on experiences that have been recorded in private. To some degree, a film is constructed by an author's imagination of the audience it is intended for and this is then adapted by viewers themselves, who contribute to the recreation of meaning through their own immersion in the film's content. The relationships that audience members develop with the protagonists of a film become something new, a cinematic experience entwined in the public act of viewing, which is quite different to the private experience of fieldwork. Previous sections have attempted to show how cinematic tools and techniques are used to relate the unfolding of experience to its narration through affect and the senses. Now that construction work for the film has ended, you may want to think carefully about how filmmaking negotiates this shift from personal experience to publicly accessible commodity, and what this process contributes to knowledge and understanding.

A film should not need extra information to make it an edifying experience, but that does not mean writing cannot be practised alongside filmmaking. A film expresses theoretical considerations in the way it is recorded and edited but you may want to publish more substantial written work that reflects on the methods you

(*Left*) An audience of research participants at the premiere screening of *Entre Memorias* in Lima, Peru

(*Facing left*) A flyer for the screening
(*Facing right*) Filmmaker Martha-Cecilia Dietrich speaking to her collaborators and other audience members at the screening

Charla y Proyección de

Entre Memorias

Un documental sobre memorias
diversas en Perú Posconflicto

Realizado por Martha-Cecilia Dietrich
Reino Unido/Perú 2015

5. de Marzo 17.00–18.30

Lugar de la Memoria, la Tolerancia
y la Inclusión Social LUM
Bajada San Martín 151, Miraflores
Tel. 7192065

www.lum.cultura.pe

have used, or elaborates on aspects of ethnography, or introduces new ideas associated with your fieldwork. The theoretical scope of a film is limited to some degree by the concrete nature of the contexts in which it is made. Concentrating on the ethnographic present can inhibit an imagination of the future because of the weight of evidence that gathers around the way things are in the moment they were recorded. Both writing and filmmaking make use of montage to disrupt this order as well as to present continuity. An ethnographer must strike a balance between using moments of recorded actuality to test existing ideas and referencing the same moments to inspire new ideas. Within a broad research project we can use the praxis of filmmaking to write more engagingly about the possibilities that lie beyond the narratives of our films.

The main story of this handbook resides in the processes of making images, sound and stories. That is not to say that sharing the final cut of a film, writing or taking account of audience opinion are less important, but rather that they lie at a slight tangent to the practical activities involved in the empirical art of filmmaking for fieldwork. The last section of this book is therefore shorter than the others. In it, I offer summary advice about how to attract a wider audience to your filmmaking. If you are an aspiring documentarist, you may want to showcase your work at film festivals, as this can help you secure a distribution deal for your current project and receive your next commission. If you are working in a research environment, film festivals also provide a forum to get your work published. Most university research evaluation frameworks accept media other than writing on equal terms, but to contribute to your research output, it must receive recognition from a festival jury or reviewer, have a cinema or TV release, or be or published by a recognised distributor.

Sharing your work

It is not usual to feel wholly positive about a film immediately after completing it. I find that six months usually passes before I can watch work that I have directed without being critical of its failings. However, once you overcome this doubt it can be a pleasant experience to share something that you have taken care to produce, especially with fieldwork participants who have contributed so much towards its making. This section is dedicated to a variety of ways that can extend the reach of your work.

Returning work to fieldwork participants

Whatever degree of authority you assert over the direction of a project, it can never imply total authorship. Responsibility for the impact of a film project, whether positive or negative, lies with the director because they have intervened to make personal experiences accessible to a wider public. The consequences of that intervention may, however, be felt more acutely by the research participants. Perhaps you anticipated this in your research preparation but much has changed since then. In a code of ethics that honours our commitments to research partners, it is important to return work in its completed form to research partners before it is distributed widely. If you have screened a rough cut to protagonists or sought their advice throughout the cutting then you should also to let them know when you have arrived at the final cut. It is legitimate for a filmmaker not to want to change anything at this late stage, so you may need to negotiate some aspects of your film. Try to be open to the points raised by others and gentle as you press your case. After a short amount of time has elapsed, or perhaps with a second viewing of the work, most protagonists can be won over if there is a problem. But if the problem is significant, it is easier for you to adjust a film at this stage, rather than later when more opinions have settled on it.

Online video platforms

Once a deal has been struck with research participants and you have secured the necessary rights to music, archive or any other third-party materials, you can begin looking for tools that will help you share your work in a public arena. Some websites offer video streaming services free of charge, or for a small additional payment they include more advanced distribution and sales features. This is a good option if you are beginning your career and want to establish a portfolio of work. Currently, YouTube and Vimeo command the airwaves but other services are available. Vimeo On Demand offers an associated self-distribution service that allows you to set a monetary fee for the rent and download of work. Additional materials, similar to those previously found as extras on a DVD, such as artwork, alternative cuts and filmmaker commentaries, can also be included in the package. These platforms offer digital download of your film for distribution purposes at no extra cost, which can be useful for the submission of festival screeners and other complimentary copies. To operate a site such as this, beyond paying an initial fee you are also required to upload artwork, log line, synopses and an appropriately sized export file of your finished film using specified codecs.

Sarai Ramirez-Payá (left) reviewing material with a participant in her research project

Websites and social media

Template-based website services offer a cheap and easy way to summarise your filmmaking activities and create an online portal for your films. Applications for this purpose are included free of charge with a cloud subscription to some post-production software, or as an add-on to a host subscription for your domain name. If you are lucky you can buy an internet domain with your own name, or the name of your research or documentary filmmaking project; if not, then think of a suitable title for your filmmaking activities. My personal name is quite common, so I chose 'filmmakingforfieldwork.co.uk' for the way that it related to the type of work I was interested in. Videos for streaming that you have uploaded to platforms such as Vimeo and YouTube can also be embedded into your website, along with a gallery of production stills, log lines and synopses, production credits, festival appearances and links to social media. Additionally, it is useful to have some background information about yourself – sometimes referred to as a 'filmmaker biog' – and a link to written publications that connect with your filmmaking. Keep a back-up of all the elements of your website and look for easy-to-use software that can be replaced if the service is withdrawn or goes out of fashion. A website is a good place to cultivate your presence as a filmmaker and it won't be long before you have an impressive catalogue of work to display.

Social media is a useful though capricious means to inform people about the progression of your film project, and a way to alert them to festival and other screenings. You can add a graphic link on most website templates that will connect users to associated social media sites. There are also websites intended specifically for the purposes of film festival submission, such as the popular FilmFreeway. This site acts as an intermediary, channelling submissions to festivals that have accepted their services. They come and go with relative rapidity, so look for whatever is current when it is time to submit your film to festivals. A key feature of submission sites is the way they help you to organise your material to suit festival criteria. As well as log lines and synopses, you will have to add five or six production stills, the technological specifications of your film and state whether the film is your debut in directing documentaries.

Participants of the F4F™ Summer School provided an iconic image for our website that illustrated what Filmmaking for Fieldwork as an organisation aims to deliver

Writing about your work

Elaborating academic ideas beyond the narrative of a film is one reason to write about your work but there are other reasons. Longer written statements that outline the dramatic potential and key areas of specialist interest in your film will assist reviewers in their assessment of your work and help festival organisers consider your film for screening. Short pithy statements help publicise a film on websites or in newspaper articles and entertainment listings. Or you may be completing a doctoral thesis or research project, where the main output is written and therefore you are required to contextualise the filmmaking component in a substantial piece of ethnographic writing.

Log line and synopses

The 10-word log line used to summarise your research idea at the planning stage has helped maintain direction in the work throughout the filmmaking, even if it has changed considerably. This will prove its worth again now as you attempt to distribute the finished film. The log line, in whatever form it has ended up, is a good way to catch passing attention from website traffic, but these ten words also provide a basis from which to expand a synopsis. I have seen log lines with as few as three words. Synopses summarise the narrative arc of your film, as well as eliciting main characters and ideas in as few words as possible. Commonly 50- to 250-word versions are required for festival submission and to explain your film on video on demand (VOD) sites or DVD covers. Longer versions are useful if you work in a research environment where you have to submit your work

for evaluation. Here the emphasis is on the originality of your approach and a clear indication of the study areas you are contributing to.

10-word
One man's dream to build a boat and sail home.

50-word
Following his seventieth birthday, Vik Pengilly-Johnson decides to leave the south of England for one last adventure. He exchanges the confines of his lonely flat for a self-built boat and when this vessel encounters troubled waters, Vik is drawn ever closer to the home that he thought he had left behind.

100-word
One Long Journey follows Vik Pengilly-Johnson as he attempts to fulfil a lifelong dream. Vik exchanges his lonely flat in the south of England for the broken shell of a river cruiser that he found in a northern boatyard. To the dismay of his family, Vik announces at his seventieth birthday that despite having no money he will rebuild the boat and sail it home. Unable to let his father go alone, Vik's eldest son accompanies him and when their little vessel encounters troubled waters, they are drawn ever closer to the home Vik thought he had left behind.

250-word
One Long Journey follows Vik Pengilly-Johnson as he attempts to fulfil a lifelong dream. What ensues is a drama of impossible

loves set on English waterways where a home is lost and found. Vik was born in the north of England and after a spell in the army he moved south to work in a safari park where he found love and made a family. Years later, Vik became separated from this family and loneliness grew within the solitary confines of his small flat. Yet a strong bond of love persisted, bringing the Johnsons together in times of difficulty.

To the dismay of his family, Vik announces on his seventieth birthday that he is leaving home. Despite having no money, he tells them of his intention to rebuild the broken shell of a river cruiser that he found in a northern boatyard and sail it home. Unable to let his father go alone, Vik's eldest son travels with him and together they renovate the dilapidated boat. Cracks soon emerge in this uneasy relationship when the task takes on new dimensions as Vik's dreams become real and the little boat enters troubled waters.

The filmmakers use observational cinema methods and an original music score by electro-blues duo Walk as ethnographic tools to explore the nature of dreams and familial love. The film is an attempt to involve viewers in this arduous but ultimately rewarding journey.

… and so on

(*Clockwise from top left*) Vik during one of many attempts to make the windows on his boat secure | Vik's son, Kelly Johnson | Kelly and Vik attempting to resolve a disagreement about work procedures | Vik looking ahead to the Journey

The accompanying statement

The type of writing included in an extended statement is different from the synopsis because it does more than summarise the overall narrative arc of a film and key academic ideas. Video journals that are aimed at extending the use of filmmaking for research purposes expect you to position your work in discussions about the development of methods and also to be explicit about the unique contribution you are making to knowledge. Whether you are completing a doctoral thesis, writing an essay or aiming to publish, it is useful to begin by reflecting on your approach and to test these ideas thoroughly in writing. Here is what the publishers of the audiovisual research journal *Sightlines* concluded in their second volume:

> *The peer review process raised the contentious issue of the extent to which one can identify and evaluate research by watching the finished film. It is clear that in many cases the reviewers felt that a supporting statement of some form was necessary. In our guidelines to the filmmakers, we left it open to them to decide on the nature of the supporting material provided. The responses varied from an audiovisual essay, to a short research statement and the equivalent of a full journal article. However, it is clear that, in most cases, the way that this supporting material is written or presented has a significant bearing on how a peer reviewer can evaluate a film as research.*
> (***Sightlines: Filmmaking in the Academy***, *vol. 2, 2017*)

Theoretical ideas are applied to a film at each stage in its production, with the intention that they melt into the ethnographic landscape of the finished work. For this reason you may want to make explicit how you have arrived at the final version of your story. At this point it can be useful to dig out your research proposal and use this as a basis to elaborate such a thesis (see pp. 34–6). Begin structuring your essay under the same headings that you used earlier to describe your methods and the ideas that informed them. Then use these to preface analytic explanations and the conclusions you arrived at by undertaking the fieldwork and editing. This will help a reader to understand your research journey and evaluate the discoveries you have made along the way. In a wider ethnography it is useful to explain your reasons for excluding some of the recorded material from the film, for example because of length constraints or ethical reasons. Elaborating on your ethical approach and how this worked in practice helps other filmmakers to focus on similar issues in their own work, like where to place a camera and microphones.

Do not be afraid to write about your failures. The problem with many academic essays, especially those that concern the writer's own filmmaking, is that they try to underline the indisputable success of the work, whereas it is through moments of confoundment that we most often learn to reconsider ways of thinking and acting. I discovered this myself when reflecting on the making of *One Long Journey*. The initial aim of this project was to document Vik's triumphant river journey from Manchester to London in a self-built boat. We had in mind that this would culminate in his arrival on the River Thames in London, with our musical band playing on the deck of the little boat as it passed beneath Tower Bridge. Here we imagined the closing scenes being filmed by a large number of our crowdfunding backers, who would cheer Vik along the last leg of his glorious journey. But when our principal protagonist decided to abandon his trip soon after setting off, a depression set in amongst the filmmakers. It seemed that the hopes they carried for our collective endeavours had all been in vain. In fact, reality was

asserting its right to demonstrate a deeper truth to us, and in times like these, documentary filmmakers just have to continue filming patiently until a new destiny reveals itself. Despite our despondency, the final scenes of *One Long Journey* became some of the strongest in the film. It was necessary for us to innovate alternative endings, both physical and metaphorical, in order to save the film of Vik's adventure. What we discovered lay in a look of resignation on Kelly's face as he returned to meet his father, in Vik's resilience in the face of his apparent disaster as he dragged his little boat home and the shots of an empty canal, open skies and boatyard gates shutting. We gathered as much material as possible while the story challenged our assumptions and presented new possibilities, and then we moved on to the edit.

Documentary filmmaking is a creative pursuit that follows our ideas to the extent that actuality can support them. The process works well when our imagination helps us to design artistic interventions that contribute towards narrative expression, but less well if we ignore how these can become disconnected from the real lives we are exploring. When I came to write about *One Long Journey* I realised how the adventure and bravery that I perceived initially in Vik's endeavour had diverted my attention from his more humble attempts to deal with common fears. In unpacking this ethnographic dilemma, I also began to think more deeply about the practical research ideas that I have detailed in this handbook.

Vik redirecting his journey back to the boatyard

Film festivals and screening events

It is rare that a research film that discovers its own dimensions through its making finds a mainstream broadcast slot, as these tend to be established before the work is commissioned. Film festivals and public screenings remain the best way to draw attention to your work. It is here that a film is showcased alongside other exemplar work, chosen by a panel of fellow filmmakers to enter a competition for prizes in a variety of categories. This may sound trivial for work that is guided by a search for knowledge and understanding, but in fact it is a rigorous process where strong work can find its way to a wide audience. Film festival selection is considered similar to peer review in writing – but the 'best of the fest' for one person is the worst for another, so do not read too much into a failure to be accepted. A filmmaker who selects the pursuit of knowledge as their goal, rather than the satisfaction of an audience, must accept moments of rejection. Whatever the outcome, this stage in filmmaking has a special part to play in the research process. Dialogues that you create with reviewers, festival selection committees and audiences all help you to understand a subject better, so in this sense you have achieved your goal regardless of whether your work is accepted or rejected at a festival.

From a purely pragmatic perspective, it is desirable to win awards for your filmmaking. Accolades do not fundamentally change the work but they do help to build confidence. There is a time during most projects when one becomes convinced that the film will sweep the table of awards, and equally there are moments when we feel certain that the work is doomed to failure. A more balanced indication of whether a film can reach its objectives is achieved through feedback screenings (see p. 154). Use this information to address a specific tier of film festival that is appropriate to the standard of your work, otherwise you can waste a lot of time, money and optimism. There is a range of mainstream documentary film festivals – the associated kudos is determined by the renown of the festival and the size of the prizes it offers, which also determines the financial cost for submission. Film festivals raise a significant amount of their revenue from inappropriate submissions, most of which are dismissed after the first five minutes of viewing, or earlier if the film does not match the submission criteria. Top tier festivals such as Sundance, Sheffield Independent Documentary Festival and the Independent Documentary Festival in Amsterdam like to be considered first, so the general rule is that you submit to these as a priority and then work your way down to smaller film festivals in your local neighbourhood. Most academic-related films that unpack detailed ideas around a specific subject will not be considered for mainstream festivals but they are valued at smaller events that focus on the subject area of your research. Most discipline areas have related film festivals, and there is usually a niche within these for even the most esoteric subjects. Do not underestimate these festivals; they are often free to enter and organisers occasionally provide accommodation and travel expenses so that you can attend the screening. Here you enjoy a friendly, conference-like atmosphere, surrounded by people who are knowledgeable about your subject and interested in your film. Keep a record of each screening, as this will be an important resource when you assess the impact of the work.

José Carlos Agüero chairing a discussion with Martha-Cecilia Dietrich about her PhD research and film collaboration in Lima, Peru

Fieldwork participants might express an interest in accompanying you to festival screenings, or you may want them to be there to help deal with questions, or simply because you like them. This is generally a good idea. If fieldwork is shared and we consult on editing then why not also make screenings inclusive? Problems can occur if the response of an audience is not anticipated, or if fieldwork participants have not been prepared for how the content of a film can feel different in a public space. If you have been working intimately in the field then it can be a significant shock when a public audience treats your film like an object for analysis and criticism – even more so if they do not like your protagonists for some reason. A work-in-progress screening of your film in public, during the editing, can help test the water but it cannot cover all eventualities. This means it is a good idea to brief participants before festival or other public screenings, especially when a critical academic audience may be looking to trip you up. It is also a good plan to listen to your own briefing. A film is a personal statement and some viewers may not be sensitive to that. If the audience react badly to the content, or they perceive an oversight on your part, they may want to punish you for it. Try not to react to this. Their response is a gift that you choose whether or not to accept. Reactions say a lot about the person acting; they cannot be wrong, but equally they do not express the problem from all perspectives. When a filmmaker remains open to comments, the research process continues each time the film is screened.

Film festivals are an excellent context in which to gain an introduction to the ideas discussed in this book. If you have not yet started making your own films, then consider attending one or two events and engage with some of the critical debates with filmmakers present.

Publication

Filmmakers working in a university context are required to publish their work in a way that is searchable and available to other researchers. If you have not yet managed to secure a mainstream distributor then you may want to consider first publishing your film as a journal 'article'. For the purposes of university research evaluation, I would argue that a film can be considered alongside a book publication if it extends from a significant body of research. Value is added to this submission if the film is selected for a film festival, receives an award, is taken by a distributor and given international release and subsequently reviewed favourably, or cited by peers. Films submitted to video journals can be considered equivalent to written articles if they are accompanied by a statement and published peer reviews.

Peer review and journals

A very intense and gripping film, 'Born' is marked by an immediacy and purity of instance. The images in this film are hard to confront yet the film leaves us quiet and composed for it subtly gestures towards man's ultimate insignificance before nature.
Aparna Sharma,
Review of Born for **The Women's Feature Service** (2009)

Finding other people to write about your film will help new audiences engage with your work and raise your profile as a filmmaker. This in turn will help you to fund and distribute future film projects. If your film does well at festivals, reviewers will seize on this success and write about your film without being prompted to do so. But in most instances it is necessary to contact potential reviewers yourself or submit your film to a peer-reviewed journal. A review by a newspaper columnist who is not a specialist on the subject matter can provide an accurate reflection of how the film communicates your ideas to a wider audience. Distributors of films submit work for peer review on your behalf and they use extracts from the writing of responders as a way to promote your film on websites, postcard flyers and in catalogues. You can request that the entire review is shared with you in a Cloud document so that it adds to the general compendium of your film journey.

Peer-reviewed journals that deal specifically with research-based filmmaking tend to publish film or artworks alongside a written statement by the filmmaker, similar to that discussed earlier. If the peer reviewer agrees then their response is published alongside your own written statement, with or without their name attached to it, depending on their preference. Journals usually set out a number of criteria for peer reviewers to consider in their assessment of the contribution your work makes to an area of academic research. It is useful to bear these in mind when writing a statement.

> - Is there evidence of a particular question, issue or problem that is explored?
> - Is there evidence of innovation (in form or content for example)?
> - Is the work contextualised within specific social/artistic theoretical fields?
> - Is there evidence of new knowledge, interpretation, insights or experiences?
> *(Sightlines: Filmmaking in the Academy, vol. 2, 2017)*

At the time of writing this handbook, video journals (see Appendix 4 for examples) are still in the process of establishing academic standards for reviewing ethnographic films. Unlike written articles, where an author may be requested by reviewers of the work to revise and resubmit, a film is usually accepted or rejected according to how it is presented at first viewing. This may change as more practitioners submit their work to journals and moderators are forced to be more selective. I suggest that a basic set of criteria is established for selection, relating to running time, the technical quality of image, sound and editing and overall narrative coherence, a system that can also be applied to the evaluation and marking of student films. In this way the subjective aspects of evaluation can be separated from the more widely understandable assessment criteria.

Distributors and video on demand

Not so long ago, individual copies of films were sold on analogue tape, digital video disk (DVD) or Blu-ray. Publishers acted as intermediaries, selling your wares across networks that only they could access. Today, most commercial distributors concentrate solely on video on demand (VOD), which is something that you can operate yourself, using networks of social media to promote easily accessible and relatively cheap online sales platforms. Book publishers have also changed the way they incorporate films. As recently as 2011, the anthropologist and Africa specialist Richard Werbner published his film *Holy Hustlers* on DVD, along with a full-length ethnographic monograph (Werbner 2011). Today a VOD copy of the film would most likely be linked to the publication via an online website.

Tools for self-publishing are available online and much of what you need will come packaged with your editing software. So it may seem like a pointless exercise to involve a third party who will inevitably reduce your profit share to well below 50 per cent. Do bear in mind, however, that a small percentage of something is worth more than 100 per cent of nothing. By securing the backing of a publisher you can devolve areas of expertise into specialist hands that will extend the reach and increase the profile of your work, probably resulting in more sales. Work that is globally distributed by a respected company is considered equal to a book publication in terms of research output, regardless of reviews. Many distributors do not accept unsolicited submissions and they prefer to collect films at festivals, once they have already been through a sifting process. You can alert distributors to your work by email, but be strategic about when and how you do this – for example, after it has been accepted by one or two festivals, or received a favourable review, would be a good time. Most academic discipline areas are connected to companies that specialise in work associated with their arena, so search for these instead of attempting to attract publishers at random. Look at the existing film catalogues held by a distributor and think carefully about how your own work can fit in to these.

Floating filmmakers on Dal Lake in Srinagar, India

AFTERWORD

The journey continues

Every sensation shares the same characteristic: it arises and passes away, arises and passes away. It is this arising and passing that we have to experience through practice.

S. N. Goenka
teacher of **Vipassana meditation**

The craft of filmmaking extends infinitely in all directions. It is as varied as the subjects we choose to film and limitless as the human imagination. We are on the cusp of interesting changes in the ways that documentary is being made. I hope this handbook will be useful for people who choose new formats as well as those who opt for established ones. It is important to consider what techniques and approaches can be carried forward and what methods need to be developed to serve new ideas and technologies. Students require practical solutions to the problems they encounter with 'i-docs' (Aston et al. 2017) – a term used to collectively describe 360-degree video, VR, desktop documentary, interactive gaming and augmented reality. Many of these problems will be the same as those discussed in this book, such as where to place the camera and microphones, how to read a fieldwork situation or relationship and when to take risks. Some issues will be different, such as how the involvement of the filmmaker can be limited in order to create more scope for an individualised and interactive experience within a flexible narrative.

Most ethnographic documentary encourages the *maker* to engage critically and reflexively with the production of knowledge in the field. Recording a two-dimensional film is a way of acting in the world, as an extension of seeing and hearing, and editing can be considered akin to reflective thinking and telling stories. Technology that seeks to extend this experience into three dimensions, where 'viewers' are encouraged to move physically within a space, does offer something new and immersive for the audience of our work. Here discussions extend to a polyphony rather than the triangular relationship that we are used to negotiating between audience, subject and filmmaker. Gaming can be used as an ethnographic resource to introduce students to the lifeworlds of others, helping them to understand how it feels to be part of that world.

The empirical techniques that I have outlined in this handbook are fundamentally altered when they are applied to these emergent forms. VR, for example, has a deliberately limited narrative that allows those who experience it to make certain choices, also limited in scope. Selecting shot size, moving with the camera, as well as detailed analysis and juxtaposition in the edit suite, are for the most part left to those who consume the VR experience, rather than being directed by those who are making it. Looking closely with a camera and microphones through a triangle of action in key situations such as processes, testimonies and events, or gathering a variety of shots and sounds that can be used to think through the puzzle of a narrative edit, are limited in VR to an expression as close to an 'actual' experience as possible. This reduces the scope for an author to use more imaginative modes of documentary storytelling that rely on allusion and metaphor. It is not necessarily the experience of others but our own that is brought to the fore in VR, which can reduce alterity and objectify the other as something 'to be experienced'.

Each new project we begin requires us to think again about why we want to make a documentary *film*. Filmmaking says different things from writing, and from i-docs, because it is a different type of epistemological practice. Filmmaking for fieldwork has value because an ethnographer tries to understand the world from as many perspectives as possible. You may want to inspire a new way of writing or thinking, and there are texts that examine how an audiovisual approach to writing ethnography can unlock new avenues for research (Cox et al. 2016; Rose 2016; Pink et al. 2016; Pink 2013; Grasseni 2009). Fewer texts have detailed the practical stages that lead to an overtly artistic expression of academic work.

The empirical art of filmmaking for fieldwork involves cinematic tools and techniques that serve a research agenda. It applies description, in image and sound, to analysis and expression through ethnographic storytelling. This work is collaborative because the people we call research participants inform our methods and guide our actions with a camera and microphones, as well as influencing the style of editing we choose. I have tried to show how knowledge about making films can help a researcher to think not only about the being of a subject but also its becoming. And I hope that I have demonstrated how ethnography can extend to a wider audience through the way that cinematic problems are unpacked in the field and resolved through narrative editing.

Selecting equipment that suits a subject is of far greater importance than chasing the latest tools available in an ever-changing marketplace. Cinematic skills improve with practice along with our ability to understand the subjective realities that guide us in our work and our awareness of what affects and orientates the lifeworlds of others. When we arrive in the field, we search for fresh answers to the documentary imperative under new circumstances, repeating each stage described in this handbook. Theory is applied to begin with, but very soon one is presented with pragmatic issues, such as where to place the camera and microphones and how to get close to the people we are working with in key situations. Understanding how our own gestures, movements and interactions are embedded in recordings unlocks a dramatic way for us to carry a sense of this enactment into the film. Learning how to access and deal with archival material will open up a vital resource, especially when key situations are not available for the story we are attempting to recount.

Ultimately fieldwork experience must be distilled into a single sensory expression built through careful study and playful editing. Rough cutting constitutes the bulk of this work and it also represents the role of analysis in academic research, where theory-making is explored and expressed through the styles of cutting that we choose. Even colour correction, sound mixing, titles and mastering contribute to description and analysis and they are vital to the overall ethnographic qualities of a film. These are technical aspects of the documentary task that can obliterate the whole process if they are not well executed.

As the filmmaking process is made public, fieldwork relationships diminish in intensity but they grow in importance as the film affects its audience. The processual nature of cinematic praxis helps a researcher to look closely into those personal narratives and then relate them widely. The empirical nature of this art inspires reflexivity, where the creativity of a filmmaker is woven inseparably with that of research participants. All parties, including the audience, are subject to change inspired by this documentary cycle. Freelance and broadcast documentary makers often run more than one project simultaneously, moving quickly from one subject to another, but research filmmakers tend to develop a continuity in their work that reveals itself gradually and retrospectively over many years. It is therefore necessary to allow space to reflect on your completed work, and use the words of your reviewers and the responses of your audience to help decipher the way forward.

This book holds cinema craft as its principal interest: more specifically how the process of making a two-dimensional film about human actuality shapes our understanding of the world around us. I have discussed how the dual processes of describing and analysing are linked to recording and editing a film. Photography did not replace painting. Cinema did not replace photography. Rather, many of the skills developed in fine art came to inform the empirical art of documentary filmmaking. I close this book with an eye to the future, and as certain as I can be that everything will change, so too I am quite sure that much of it will appear to remain the same.

The author and his daughter in virtual reality

ACKNOWLEDGEMENTS

I wish to thank my colleagues at the Granada Centre for Visual Anthropology, in particular Paul Henley for his support and guidance during the years we spent teaching together and Rachel Fox for inspiring me to think differently about my teaching. Anna Grimshaw, for developing my interest in cinema and research when I was first a student at the GCVA in the mid-1990s. Birth Rites Collection, Freie Universität Berlin, Universität Bern, and The Futureworks School of Media in Manchester have all offered me contexts to develop the pedagogical ideas in this book and I am grateful to Helen Knowles, Steffen Köhn, Michaela Schäuble and Paul White for this. I am indebted to my fellow teachers at the F4F™ Summer School, in particular Kieran Hanson and Jón Bjarki Magnússon, who helped me with the technical sections on camera systems. Elena Barabantseva, William Callahan, Roger Canals, Lee Gallagher, Erica Lawrence, Max Pendleton and Richard Werbner all read draft versions, adding precision and clarity to the text. I dedicate this book to my children, Olaf, Leo and Alma, who provided a continual source of inspiration through their own engagements with media and filmmaking. A very special thanks is reserved for my wife and partner, Martha-Cecilia Dietrich, who offered detailed suggestions and support at every stage in the development of the manuscript.

Additional to my own images, I would like to acknowledge the use of photographs taken during our Summer Schools and thank the participants who agreed to their inclusion in this book. Here I must also thank: Jonathan Purcell who acted as stills photographer for my films *The Message*, *Born* and *One Long Journey*; Peter Ran during the production of *British Born Chinese*; Jon Tipler for the photos he took whilst recording sound for *The Lover and the Beloved* and *The One and the Many*; Rohan Jackson, for his friendship and photos during years spent living aboard narrowboats on English canals and travelling in India; and José Luis Fajardo for his pictures from the screening sessions of Martha-Cecilia Dietrich's film, *Entre Memorias* and while we were on location in Peru for *Horror in the Andes*. My students who have subsequently produced films using the methods described in this book have kindly allowed me to use images from their work. Particular thanks here goes to Elena Barabantseva, Lloyd Belcher, Kate Blackmore, Ben Cheetham, Kieran Hanson, Emma Harris, Daisy-May Hudson, Stephen Linstead, Jón Bjarki Magnússon, Sarai Ramírez-Payá, Peter Ran, Lea Vinter Sonne, Tom Turner and Rachel Webster. The gratitude I feel towards the people who welcomed me into their lives with my camera should also be acknowledged in this book, as it is their images and stories that contribute the most compelling elements to it. Here I wish to thank Mark Gwynne-Jones, Judith Kurutaç, Rajive McMullen, Kevin But, Daniel He, Vik Pengilly-Johnson, Kelly Johnson, Martin Ccorahua and the National Union of Mineworkers in Barnsley. It was my great pleasure to work with Abbey Akanbi remotely during the COVID-19 lockdown, creating illustrations and a cover for the book and Dave Rodgers of Double Dagger on the design and layout.

Lastly, I thank my students for giving me the reason to write this handbook and Tom Dark, David Appleyard and the team at Manchester University Press for their hard work, encouragement and support in completing it.

PICTURE CREDITS

Jón Bjarki Magnússon setting up a landscape shot near the Sauðanes Lighthouse on the northern coast of Iceland for *Half Elf*. Photo by Magnús H. Traustason. **p. iv**

Rachel Webster recording the geography of a Bakarwal valley in Jammu, northern India, for her PhD research. Photo by Andy Lawrence. **p. vi**

Kevin But. Photo by Ben Cheetham courtesy of AllRitesReversed. **p. x**

Mira. A photomontage installed as open-air cinema in the gardens of Jodrell Bank Observatory, UK, for the Radio Halo (2000) exhibition of site-specific art curated by Helen Knowles. Photo and artwork by Andy Lawrence courtesy of AllRitesReversed. **p. xii**

Andy Lawrence (right) consulting research participants about the framing of his film, *The Lover and the Beloved: A Journey into Tantra*. Photo by Jon Tipler courtesy of AllRitesReversed. **p. 3**

Daniel He, appearing in the first public screening of Elena Barabantseva's film collaboration, *British Born Chinese*. Photo by Kieran Hanson. **p. 6**

Kevin But (left) and Daniel He (right) filming in Manchester for *British Born Chinese*. Photo by Ben Cheetham **p. 9**

Jón Bjarki Magnússon filming his grandmother, using a Blackmagic Pocket Cinema Camera rig with Zoom H4N and Sennheiser MKE600 during filming for *Half Elf*. Jón graduated with

his film and accompanying thesis from the Masters in Visual Anthropology programme in Berlin. Photo by Trausti Breiðfjörð Magnússon. **p. 11**

Rajive McMullen's bookcase, on location for *The One and the Many*. Photo by Andy Lawrence. **p. 13**

Andy Lawrence (far left) and Rajive McMullen (centre left) filming with Ma Durga Nath (centre right) and Shobha Nath (far right) at their house in Haridwar. Photo by Jon Tipler courtesy of AllRitesReversed. **p. 16**

Moni Baba in the cremation grounds at Tarapith in north-eastern India, from *The Lover and the Beloved*. Photo by Andy Lawrence courtesy of AllRitesReversed. **p. 18**

Elena Barabantseva consulting Kevin But. Photo by Kieran Hanson. **p. 20**

Martha-Cecilia Dietrich filming with Ayacuchean women in Peru for her PhD research and film *Entre Memorias*. Photo by Andy Lawrence. **p. 21**

Jon Tipler casting his shadow for *The Lover and the Beloved*. Photo by Jon Tipler courtesy of AllRitesReversed. **p. 23**

Remnants gathering in the Manchester Ship Canal. Photo by Andy Lawrence. **p. 25**

Kiera photographed by her father moments after she was delivered by caesarean section at Royal Blackburn Hospital, from *Born*. Video still by Andy Lawrence courtesy of Birth Rites Collection. **p. 30**

Lloyd Belcher recording street scenes in Hong Kong for his PhD research with his mirrorless

camera mounted on a gimbal. Photo by Gabriella Belcher. **p. 33**

Martin Ccorahua directing his film, *The Curse of The Inca*, on location in Ayacucho, Peru. The making of this film was the subject of Martha-Cecilia Dietrich's research film, *Horror in the Andes*. Photo by Andy Lawrence courtesy of AllRitesReversed. **p. 36**

Anja Vogel using a Sony NX7 camcorder for an F4F™ workshop at the University of Bern. Photo by Andy Lawrence. **p. 38**

Andy Lawrence operating a Canon 5D on location for *British Born Chinese*. Photo by Peter Ran courtesy of F4F. **p. 39**

Eleanor Featherby using her phone to make a film about the Cross Bones graveyard at London Bridge during an F4F™ workshop about smartphone filmmaking for Birth Rites Collection. Photo by Rebecca Lennon courtesy of Birth Rites Collection. **p. 42**

Michaela Schäuble immersed in a virtual reality experience. Photo by Martha-Cecilia Dietrich. **p. 43**

Peter Ndagi filming an event as a participant of the F4F™ Summer School in Manchester. Photo by Kieran Hanson courtesy of F4F. **p. 44**

Jon Tipler recording atmospheric sound with his microphone for *One Long Journey*. Photo by Kieran Hanson courtesy of AllRitesReversed. **p. 45**

Hlín Olafsdóttir operating a boom microphone with Zoom recorder attached during filming for *Half Elf*. Photo by Jón Bjarki Magnússon. **p. 49**

Jon Tipler listening to the sound of a rusty sign with his microphone fully protected from the wind. Photo by Kieran Hanson courtesy of AllRitesReversed. **p. 50**

Lana Askari recording the sound of an event as a participant of the F4F™ Summer School. Photo by Kieran Hanson courtesy of F4F. **p. 51**

Emma Harris demonstrating how to organise cables around her Canon C100 camera while filming in Tamil Nadu. Photo by Sarai Ramírez-Payá. **p. 52**

Zoom H4N recorder attached to a Blackmagic Pocket Cinema Camera rig. Photo by Trausti Breiðfjörð Magnússon. **p. 53**

Jón Bjarki Magnússon setting up a tripod for a landscape shot in Iceland. Photo by Magnús H. Traustason. **p. 56**

Jón Bjarki Magnússon battling an Icelandic storm with his monopod. Photo by Hlín Olafsdóttir. **p. 57**

Jón Bjarki Magnússon operating his Blackmagic Pocket Cinema Camera rig. Photo by Trausti Breiðfjörð Magnússon. **p. 57**

Kevin But, Daniel He and their Tai Chi teacher as seen through the Kinotehnik viewfinder loupe of a Canon 5D DSLR camera. Photo by Peter Ran courtesy of F4F. **p. 58**

Participants of the F4F™ Summer School scrutinising a Premiere Pro timeline. Photo by Kieran Hanson courtesy of F4F. **p. 60**

Participants of the F4F™ Summer School using luma scopes to assess brightness and contrast in their images. Photo by Olaf Lawrence courtesy of F4F. **p. 63**

Mari Korpela (camera) and Devrim Aslan (sound) working in unison to record a

Manchester market for the F4F™ Summer School. Photo by Kieran Hanson courtesy of F4F. **p. 73**

Audio selection switches on a panasonic GH sound interface (top) and channel inputs on a Canon camcorder. Photo by Andy Lawrence. **p. 75**

Kelly Johnson (left) and Vik Pengilly-Johnson (right) working late into the evening on *Rif Raft*. Photo by Jonathan Purcell courtesy of AllRitesReversed. **p. 78**

Fading light on set for *The Curse of the Inca* during filming for Martha-Cecilia Dietrich's film, *Horror in The Andes*. Photo by Andy Lawrence courtesy of AllRitesReversed. **p. 80**

The three-point lighting set-up used for filming *Black Snow*. Photo by Andy Lawrence. **p. 83**

Rajive McMullen during his journey into Tantra. Artwork by Andy Lawrence from a photo by Jon Tipler courtesy of AllRitesReversed. **p. 84**

Andy Lawrence (centre) preparing to film with Hari Nath Pagal (left) en route to Kamakhya Devi in Assam. Photo by Jon Tipler courtesy of AllRitesReversed. **p. 87**

Tom Turner (left) and Vik Pengilly-Johnson experiencing a difficult moment on location for *One Long Journey*. Photo by Ben Cheetham courtesy of AllRitesReversed. **p. 89**

Judith Kurutaç (left) and Helen Pusey (right). Artwork by Cath Webb from a video still by Andy Lawrence, courtesy of Birth Rites Collection. **p. 91**

Martha-Cecilia Dietrich using an L-arm bracket to steady her handheld camera. Photo by Andy Lawrence. **p. 93**

Tom Turner (left) and Ben Cheetham locking-off a tripod shot on the front of Vik's boat for *One Long Journey*. Photo by Jonathan Purcell courtesy of AllRitesReversed. **p. 95**

The image created by Ben's camera. Video still by Andy Lawrence courtesy of AllRitesReversed. **p. 95**

Andy Lawrence using a plastic dolly discovered on set to create moving shots of a commemorative statue during filming for *Black Snow*. Photo by Stephen Linstead. **p. 96**

Vik Pengilly-Johnson demonstrating the rule of thirds in photographic composition whilst filling a water container. Photo by Jonathan Purcell courtesy of AllRitesReversed. **p. 97**

Matthew Jones, the Assistant Principal of William Hulme Grammar in Manchester, helped us to negotiate ethical issues while filming Daniel He at school for *British Born Chinese*. Photo by Ben Cheetham courtesy of F4F. **p. 97**

Shooting through an object can add interest to the framing and context to the main subject. Photo by Jonathan Purcell courtesy of AllRitesReversed. **p. 98**

Sarai Ramírez-Payá (right) explaining to her research participants how to place a microphone. Photo by Emma Harris. **p. 102**

Jon Tipler with a four-track Edirol recorder on his Sound Devices field mixer, used to record stereo and surround sound for *The Lover and The Beloved*. Photo by Andy Lawrence courtesy of AllRitesReversed. **p. 110**

Martha-Cecilia Dietrich using basic equipment to help research participants understand the techniques that she used to record her film *Entre Memorias*. Photo by Andy Lawrence. **p. 111**

Kieran Hanson (recording sound) and Andy Lawrence (camera) with Dr Elena Barabantseva (centre) as she interviews Daniel He (far left) and Kevin But for her research film *British Born Chinese*. Photo by Peter Ran courtesy of F4F. **p. 115**

The image of Dan and Kevin that developed from this scene. Video still by Andy Lawrence. **p. 115**

Rodney Kelly and his family watching a rough cut of Kate Blackmore's *Objects of Resistance*. Kate graduated with her film and accompanying thesis from the Masters in Visual Anthropology programme in Berlin. Photo by Kate Blackmore. **p. 117**

Andy Lawrence using an ARRI magic arm to position a Canon 5D with a 50 mm lens to record close-up shots of Kevin riding his bike. (It may be safer to use an action camera for this purpose but in this instance the shots were relatively controlled.) Photo by Kieran Hanson. **p. 118**

Lloyd Belcher using a gimbal to facilitate smooth walking shots of himself as the principal narrator of his PhD film, *Nepalese Drug Users in Hong Kong*. Photo by Gabriella Belcher. **p. 120**

Jón Bjarki Magnússon filming his grandfather eating lunch. Photo by Trausti Breiðfjörð Magnússon. **p. 121**

Two 800 W halogen lights used to record images from the National Union of

Mineworkers archive in Barnsley, for *Black Snow*. Photo by Andy Lawrence. **p. 123**

A gift from the Miners Federation of Great Britain to Mr Benjamin Pickard MP of Barnsley, for his 'persistent labours' on behalf of mine workers during the 'Great Lock-Out' of 1893. Photo by Andy Lawrence courtesy of the National Union of Mineworkers. **p. 124**

Rajive McMullen visiting a tantric yogi in the Assamese Jungle during filming for *The Lover and the Beloved*. Video still by Andy Lawrence courtesy of AllRitesReversed. **p. 127**

Georgina Howard using her phone to explore the library at Guy's Hospital in London during an F4F™ workshop about smartphone filmmaking for Birth Rites Collection. Photo by Rebecca Lennon courtesy of Birth Rites Collection. **p. 131**

Vik Pengilly-Johnson at his workbench. Photo by Jonathan Purcell courtesy of AllRitesReversed. **p. 132**

A publicity poster for *One Long Journey*. Artwork by Ross Phillips from a photo by Jonathan Purcell courtesy of AllRitesReversed. **p. 133**

A close-up of Vik at work. Photo by Jonathan Purcell courtesy of AllRitesReversed. **p. 138**

A publicity poster for *Half Way*. Courtesy of Daisy-May Hudson. **p. 142**

Rajive McMullen preparing to be interviewed for *The One and the Many*. Photo by Andy Lawrence. **p. 145**

Improvised lighting using tinfoil and a bent coat hanger to shield and direct 100 watt tungsten light bulbs. (Always check that

you are not overloading the circuit even if it is protected by a breaker, and that the cable you are using to connect lights is rated for the correct amps.) Photo by Andy Lawrence. **p. 145**

Rik Warren (left) and Andy Lawrence (right) during a recording session for *One Long Journey* in Manchester. Photo by Kieran Hanson courtesy of AllRitesReversed. **p. 147**

Martina Krajňáková and Elisabeth Ogle enjoying editing during the F4F Summer School. Photo by Kieran Hanson courtesy of F4F. **p. 148**

Angélica Ascarza Mendoza and her daughter Maribel Ascarza Mendoza viewing a rough cut of *Entre Memorias* at their home in Ayacucho. Photo by Martha-Cecilia Dietrich. **p. 153**

Daniel He, appearing at a public screening of *British Born Chinese*. Photo by Kieran Hanson. **p. 155**

An uncertain future awaits migrant men who find temporary refuge in a jungle of tents at the French port of Calais. Video still from *Kalès* by Laurent Van Lancker courtesy of Polymorfilms. **p. 156**

Moni Baba communicating with spirits in the cremation ground at Tarapith. Photo by Andy Lawrence. **p. 159**

Luma and RGB scopes in the Adobe Premiere Pro interface. Screengrab by Andy Lawrence. **p. 161**

Martin Ccorahua photographing the cast of his film, *La Maldición Del Inca,* on location in Ayacucho, Peru. Video still from *Horror in the*

Andes by Martha Cecilia Dietrich courtesy of AllRitesReversed. **p. 161**

Martin Salmonson mixing the sound for *One Long Journey* at The Futureworks Studio in Salford. Photo by Andy Lawrence. **p. 163**

A stereo audio track shown next to the same image with dual-mono tracks. Screen grab from Adobe Premiere Pro. **p. 163**

Born as it was presented in Manchester Museum for the Birth Rites (2009) touring exhibition of art curated by Helen Knowles, about the politics and practice of childbirth. Photo by Jonathan Purcell courtesy of Birth Rites Collection. **p. 168**

The image used by Ross Phillips as a basis to develop the *One Long Journey* publicity poster. Photo by Jonathan Purcell courtesy of AllRitesReversed. **p. 170**

Ross Phillips created online publicity materials for *One Long Journey* that helped with crowdfunding. Artwork by Ross Phillips courtesy of AllRitesReversed. **p. 170**

A frame grab from *Born*, used to develop the artwork for the film. Video still by Andy Lawrence courtesy of Birth Rites Collection. **p. 170**

The exhibition poster for *Born*. Artwork by Cath Webb from a photo by Andy Lawrence courtesy of Birth Rites Collection. **p. 170**

The artwork for *Born* was adapted to fit across the doors that led into a cinema space at The Glasgow Science Museum. Artwork by Cath Webb courtesy of Birth Rites Collection. **p. 170**

A production still of Dan He and Kevin But taken during filming for *British Born Chinese*,

used as the basis for a publicity poster. Photo by Ben Cheetham. **p. 171**

A screening poster for *British Born Chinese*. Courtesy of Elena Barabantseva. **p. 171**

DVD cover artwork for the DER release of *The One and the Many*, using still images from the film. Artwork by Frank Aveni from video stills by Andy Lawrence courtesy of DER. **p. 171**

DVD cover artwork for the Documentary Educational Resources (DER) release of *The Lover and the Beloved*, using still images from the film. Artwork by Frank Aveni from video stills by Andy Lawrence courtesy of DER. **p. 171**

An audience of research participants at the premiere screening of *Entre Memorias,* at the Lugar de la Memoria (LUM) in Lima, Peru. Photo by José Luis Fajardo. **p. 172**

A flyer for the screening of *Entre Memorias* at the LUM. Artwork by Lisa Ifsits from a photo by Martha-Cecila Dietrich. **p. 173**

Martha-Cecilia Dietrich speaking at the premiere screening of her collaborative film, *Entre Memorias*. Photo by José Luis Fajardo. **p. 173**

Sarai Ramírez-Payá (left) reviewing material that she recorded with a participant in her research project. Photo by Emma Harris. **p. 175**

Anne Toftelund Jensen (right), Mathilde Maitrot (centre) and Ran Muratsu (left) enjoying the camera at the F4F™ Summer School. Photo by Lea Vinter Sonne courtesy of F4F. **p. 176**

Vik Pengilly-Johnson during one of his many attempts to secure the windows of his boat,

Rif Raft. Photo by Jonathan Purcell courtesy of AllRitesReversed. **p. 178**

Vik looking ahead to his journey. Photo by Jonathan Purcell courtesy of AllRitesReversed. **p. 178**

Vik's son, Kelly Johnson. Photo by Jonathan Purcell courtesy of AllRitesReversed. **p. 179**

Kelly and Vik attempting to resolve a disagreement about work procedures. Photo by Jonathan Purcell courtesy of AllRitesReversed. **p. 179**

Vik redirecting his journey back to the boatyard. Photo by Jonathan Purcell courtesy of AllRitesReversed. **p. 181**

José Carlos Agüero chairing a discussion with Martha-Cecilia Dietrich at the LUM to answer questions about her PhD research and film collaboration. Photo by José Luis Fajardo. **p. 182**

Floating filmmakers on Dal Lake in Srinagar, India. Photo by Andy Lawrence **p. 186**

Andy Lawrence and Alma Dietrich-Lawrence trying out immersive documentary. Photo by Martha-Cecilia Dietrich. **p. 190**

LIST OF FIGURES

APPENDICES

1 Kit list

Filmmaking equipment is in a state of perpetual innovation, so the internet is the best place to check for the latest solutions. Below is a list of generic items that comprise a comprehensive DSLR or mirrorless kit. You can use this as a summary checklist alongside the information in Section 2, to make sure you have considered all the tools you might need for a filmmaking for fieldwork project. The lens sizes given here are appropriate for a full-frame 35 mm sensor, so you will need to adjust these if you are using any other size of sensor. Ethnographic filmmakers operating on a limited budget often choose a camcorder with an integrated lens and XLR audio interface, although you may also want to use an audio mixer if you are planning to work with a sound recordist.

A basic shooting kit comprises:

  Camera body
  Zoom lens: 28–105 mm or whatever came with your camera
  Battery
  Data card
  Headphones
  Microphone: directional type

But you may also want to consider the following items:

Kit bag with rain cover
Large enough to carry all of your equipment easily, including a laptop and backup drive(s), but small enough to travel as hand luggage on a plane. Use a rain cover to make your kit less conspicuous and harder to access when travelling.

Spare batteries or battery grip
Make sure you have enough of these if you are working where there is no power supply and using low-capacity DSLR and mirrorless batteries.

Lenses
50 mm f1.7 or equivalent prime lens – a good lightweight, bright, versatile and usually cheap lens.
35 mm prime or pancake lens if you are operating alone and need to get close.

Filters
NDx4 (6-stop option), if operating in bright conditions.
UV or skylight, to protect the lens.
Note: buy these to suit your largest lens and then purchase step-up rings for smaller lenses. Sometimes sold as a kit with ND filters.

Viewfinder loupe
For clearer, daylight viewing of LCD screen.

Monitor
Camera-mountable 5" type. For controlled shoots where precision and image control is vital. These work well with a camera rig.

Tripod
The sturdier the better, but balance this against ease of use and portability.

Monopod
If you are working in cramped conditions.

Gorillapod
Useful for attaching lights or when you have limited space. Will not support a camcorder or heavy DSLR camera.

Spare data cards
Many small-capacity cards that each store an hour of footage is an alternative to fewer high-capacity cards.

Hard drive(s)
For backing up your material in the field. Solid state drives are best.

Laptop computer
Any lightweight laptop that can transfer data fast. If you do not need to edit in the field you can look for cheaper options.

Audio mixing device
A high-quality option when you are working with a dedicated sound recordist or if you are strong enough to operate with it attached to the base of a camera.

Pre-amplified sound interface
A lightweight and budget option if you are working alone. Some DSLR and mirrorless cameras have their own dedicated models but any powered interface that accepts at least two XLR inputs and allows you manual control will suffice (four XLR if you are using an ambiasonic system).

External recorder
This is useful when you also want to record sound without images. Look for a device that can be inputted to a camera and mounted alongside it when working solo.

Quality microphone
Mono directional or MS stereo or multifunctional ambiasonic. Consider whether it is best to use a powered or unpowered microphone.

Videomic
Ideal when you are operating alone or require 'zoom' features. These come in a variety of options but the lowest quality is best avoided.

Wireless microphone
Useful if you are working alone or with a recordist, especially on an observational-type shoot. Do not use this instead of your principal microphone.

Closed-back audio monitors
Look for headphones that block out extraneous sounds and have a flat response for accurate and detailed field recordings.

Wind cage
The only way to deal with strong wind. A full wind cage is expensive and bulky but a scaled down 'Super-Shield' is a good compromise.

Softie and pistol grip

If wind is not excessive then this lighter and cheaper alternative to a cage will be enough to both support and protect your microphone from interference.

Boom pole

A 2 m extension is adequate for most documentary purposes and it will be easier to use and lighter to carry than a longer pole. Look for a four- or five-stage extension.

Shock mount

A suspension mount is necessary if you are attaching the microphone directly to the camera.

Audio cables

3 m XLR boom cable male-female (M-F).
3–5 m mixer loom (L and R XLRs and tape return) if working with a soundperson or separate cables.
2 x 45 cm XLR M-F cables for working solo.

Audio bag

Consider using a separate bag if you are carrying a lot of audio equipment.

LED video light

Many lights accept Sony NP-F batteries but some are rechargeable via USB. Consider whether you will attach these to your camera or a stand. A head torch seems like a good idea but in practice it does not offer much help.

Three-point lighting kit

Three lights, stands, power and filters. It is rare to carry one of these into the field but some projects require more sophisticated lighting. LED, halogen or tungsten options are available at a range of prices.

Reflector

The type with silver on one side and white on the other are a good option for reflecting light into dark spaces when no power is available. These require human operation to work well as reflectors but they can also be useful to record objects on a white background.

Lighting and grip case

If you are carrying a lot of lighting equipment.

Rechargeable AA batteries

For microphones, lights, mixers and recorders.

Solar power charging

When there is no access to mains or auxiliary supply.

Camera rig

When you are able to carry bulky kit and do not need to operate discreetly.

L-arm flash bracket

When you need cheap lightweight kit that you can operate discreetly.

Gimbal

When you require ultra-smooth tracking and walking shots.

Lens cloth
Always keep one in your camera bag.

White card
It is worth carrying a small, rigid, non-reflective white card in a side pocket of your camera bag, specifically to establish colour balance.

Cable ties
Plastic or velcro types have multiple uses.

Tools
Small screwdrivers, a sharp penknife and tiny pliers are always useful. Carry whatever tools are specific to your camera and a hex key to tighten your tripod when it works loose. A soldering iron is also useful for fixing cables.

Camera tape
Specialist cloth tape that does not leave a sticky residue.

Gaffer tape
Useful when you need to secure cables for health and safety reasons, fix your tent, rucksack or waterproof coat and make covers for your equipment.

Water or dust cover for your camera
These can be awkward to use and expensive if you are buying manufacturer recommended products. A plastic carrier bag usually does an adequate job if the correct holes have been cut into it and reinforced with gaffer tape.

Compass
Useful for planning establishing shots or finding your way home from a misty mountain.

Camera manual
In case you encounter a fault or forget how to select a function.

Participant information and personal release forms
Store these in a waterproof wallet and photograph all completed forms as a backup.

Stills camera
A good-quality photographic camera capable of recording at least 300 dpi is useful to produce production stills for written articles and publicity purposes.

Notepad and pen
For those times when your smartphone runs out of power.

Insurance
In case you lose it all …

2 Forms

1 Personal release forms are signed by each principal contributor to a film – anyone whose contribution would mean the project could not be completed if it could not be used. These forms are not a strict legal requirement in the UK, where one is at liberty to film in a public space, but they do help collaborators understand the implications of the filming encounter to a limited extent and imply the right for you to use the recorded material.

2 Location release forms are signed by those with authority over properties or sites where you are filming. These forms are intended to mitigate against prosecution for trespassing or vandalism and to establish an appropriate separation of responsibilities between you as the filmmaker and the landowner.

3 You will need a form covering intellectual property rights if you intend to use music or any other audio or visual archive, created by anyone other than yourself, in your eventual film.

4 To fulfil the terms of ethical clearance required by most university and other research institutions, it is necessary to gain informed consent from research partners who play a significant role in your fieldwork, or anyone you anticipate may be affected by the outcomes of your work. Forms for this purpose are an extension of the personal release form and they come in two parts:

Part one is a participant information sheet detailing the discussion topics that must be covered to give those you are working with as full an understanding as possible of the implications of your project.

Part two is an informed consent form, which is signed by both the researcher and fieldwork participants as an agreement that part one of this process has been completed satisfactorily. Informed consent aims to safeguard the wellbeing of your co-fieldworkers, whereas personal and location release forms secure the legality of your production.

There is more information on production release forms in Ascher and Pincus (2013: 739–47). For a detailed discussion about 'evidence, ethics and politics in documentary' see Bill Nichols (2016), *Speaking Truths with Film*. For the particularities of research-based filmmaking and ethical clearance I recommend the relevant chapters in Marcus Banks and David Zeitlyn (2015), *Visual Methods in Social Research*. And for a discussion of how an ethical approach informed the research method of an F4F™ project, see the article 'Encountering vulnerabilities through "filmmaking for fieldwork"' (Barabantseva and Lawrence 2015).

The following sample forms are intended as templates only. They should be adapted to your own purposes including up-to-date and geographically relevant information that suits your project. These forms can be downloaded for use in your own project from www.manchesterhive.com/filmmaking-resources.

Personal release form

Name _____

Project _____

To whom it may concern.

I agree to the recording and/or broadcasting of the contribution and/or interview given by me to you, and hereby give all consents necessary for the reproduction, exhibition, transmission, broadcast and exploitation thereof in perpetuity throughout the universe by all means and media (whether now known or hereafter invented) without liability or acknowledgement to me, and without inspection or approval.

You shall be entitled to cut and edit the above-named contribution as you deem fit and you shall not be obliged to include all or any part of the same in any programme.

All opinions expressed by me in this film project are mine and made of my own free will. All activities carried out by me in this film project were undertaken of my own free will.

Yours faithfully,

Name _____

Signature _____ Date _____

Address _____

I am a parent (or guardian) of the minor who has signed this release and consent form and I hereby agree that I and the said minor will be bound by all the provisions contained herein.

Name _____

Signature _____ Date _____

Location release form

Date _____

Name _____

Project _____

This is to confirm the arrangements made between those named above ('we' or 'us') and you whereby you have kindly agreed to make available to us the premises ('Premises') at _____

For for the purposes of filming exterior/interior scenes in connection with the film project named above ('the Film'), under the following terms and conditions

The Premises will be made available to us on _____

We shall have the right to exploit the material filmed at the Premises in any medium, whether now known or hereafter devised, without any restrictions whatsoever.

You confirm that you are fully entitled to grant us the right to film at the Premises and that no further consents are necessary.

You confirm that we will own the entire copyright and all other rights in the films, photographs and recordings made at the location.

We shall have no obligation to use the material that we film at the Premises in the Film.

We shall ensure that the Premises are left in good order after use. You agree we can make changes and alterations to the Premises provided that we return the Premises to the condition we found them in, and we agree that we shall be responsible for any loss or damage directly arising from our use of the Premises.

We would be grateful if you would confirm your acceptance of these terms by signing and returning the enclosed copy of this letter.

Yours faithfully,

_____

Master synchronisation licence agreement

'[Title of film]'

The following terms have been agreed between [licensing company name and address]

('the Licensor') and [name and address of production company]

('the Licensee') with respect to the Master(s) (as defined in clause 1 below) to be included on the soundtrack of the feature film which the Licensee intends, but does not undertake, to produce, provisionally entitled [title of film]'

('the Film' – which expression shall include excerpts and extracts from the Film as well as the Film itself):

1. **The Master:** [name of track and performer/writer] ('the Master(s)'). The Licensor hereby confirms that it owns and is entitled to grant to the Licensee the rights referred to in clause 3 below throughout the world.

2. **Usage:** up to [length of music required] seconds of the Master(s) to be included on the soundtrack of the Film.

3. **Rights granted by the Licensor to the Licensee:**

(a) The non-exclusive right to include the Master(s) on the soundtrack of the Film and to exploit the Film worldwide in perpetuity in any and all media now known or hereafter invented, including without limitation by means of all kinds of theatrical, non-theatrical, videogram (including without limitation by means of digital versatile disc and video on demand) exploitation and also by means of all kinds of free, basic, pay, satellite, cable and all and any other forms of television exhibition and by means of public exhibition in commercial, non-commercial and educational institutions.

(b) The non-exclusive right to include the Master(s) both in and out of context on all trailers, advertisements and other advertising and promotional materials created in connection with the production and exploitation of the Film.

4. **Term:** in perpetuity.

5. **Licence fee:** [agreed amount in words and £000 figures]

payable on signature of this agreement and it is agreed that no further payments shall be made to the Licensor by the Licensee in respect of the licence of the Master hereunder.

6. **Session musicians:** the Licensor confirms that there are no session player fees to pay with regard to the original recording of the track and that the musicians were paid a one-off fee at the time of the recording.

7. **Credit:** the Licensor shall receive a credit on the Film in the form:

[Name of track]

_____

[Written by]

_____

[Performed by]

_____

[Courtesy of]

8. **Assignment:** the Licensee shall be entitled to assign this agreement to third parties *provided that* the Licensee shall remain liable to the Licensor for its payment obligations hereunder.

9. **Termination:** the Licensor shall not have the right to injunct or in any way restrain the exhibition, promotion or exploitation of the Film or any of the allied and ancillary rights connected therewith for any cause whatsoever. Any claim by the Licensor in respect of the Master(s) shall be limited to a claim for damages.

10. **Governing law:** this agreement shall be governed by English law and the parties hereto hereby submit to the non-exclusive jurisdiction of the English courts.

Please confirm your acceptance of the above terms by signing both this agreement and the enclosed copy in the space indicated. Please then return one fully signed original to us, whereupon a binding agreement shall exist between us.

For and on behalf of   For and on behalf of

[Production company]   [Licensing company]

Participant information sheet

Informed consent Part one

[Your university/faculty/school/department]

[Note: this is a sample sheet and can be adapted according to the nature of the research project (e.g. whether it is an undergraduate, taught postgraduate or postgraduate research project)]

Suggested headings:

- What is the title of the research?
- Who will conduct the research?
- What is the aim of the research?
- Why have I been chosen?
- What would I be asked to do if I took part?
- What happens to the data collected?
- How is confidentiality maintained?
- What if I do not want to take part or I change my mind?

- Will I be paid for taking part in the research?
- How long will the research last?
- Where will the research be conducted?
- Will the outcomes of the research be published?
- What benefit might this research be to me or other subjects of the research?
- Contact for further information
- What if something goes wrong?

Name of participant giving consent

Date   Signature

Name of person taking consent

Date   Signature

Informed consent

Informed consent Part two

[Your university/faculty/school/department]

[Insert title of dissertation/project/research]

If you are happy to participate please read and sign this consent form:

I confirm that I have read the attached information sheet on the above project. I have had the opportunity to consider the information and ask questions, and these have been answered satisfactorily.

I understand that my participation in the study is voluntary and that I am free to withdraw at any time without giving a reason and without detriment to any treatment/service.

I understand that the interviews will be audio/video-recorded.

I agree to the use of quotations that are anonymous/attributed to me (delete as appropriate).

I agree to take part in the above project.

Date   Signature

3 Recommended viewing
(including films cited in this handbook)

Below is a list of documentary films that offer some historical background to the ideas described in this handbook and underline the potential for filmmaking as epistemic practice. I have included student work made with no budget alongside films produced with considerable financial backing. I have not included a summary of the films as they are all searchable online.

Nanook of the North – Robert Flaherty (1922)
Drifters – John Grierson (1929)
Man with a Movie Camera – Dziga Vertov (1929)
Rain – Joris Ivens (1929)
Land without Bread (Las Hurdes: Tierra San Pan) – Luis Bunuel (1933)
Song of Ceylon – Basil Wright (1934)
Listen to Britain – Humphrey Jennings (1942)
Meshes of the Afternoon – Maya Deren (1943)
Trance and Dance in Bali – Margaret Mead and Gregory Bateson (1952)
Night and Fog (Nuit et Broulliard) – Alain Resnais (1955)
I, a Black (Moi, Un Noir) – Jean Rouch (1958)
Chronicle of a Summer (Chronique d'un Eté) – Jean Rouch and Edgar Morin (1961)
A Joking Relationship – John Marshall (1962)
The 7-Up Series – Michael Apted (1964–present)

Bob Dylan: Don't Look Back – D. A. Pennebaker (1967)
Titicut Follies – Frederick Wiseman (1967)
Jaguar – Jean Rouch (1968)
To Live with Herds – David MacDougall (1972)
Grey Gardens – Albert and David Maysles (1976)
News from Home – Chantal Akerman (1977)
Reassemblage – Trinh T. Minh-ha (1982)
Celso and Cora: A Manila Story – Gary Kildea (1983)
Shoah – Claude Lanzmann (1985)
Forest of Bliss – Robert Gardner (1986)
Sherman's March – Ross McElwee (1986)
Handsworth Songs – John Akomfrah (1987)
The Thin Blue Line – Errol Morris (1988)
Surname Viet, Given Name Nam – Trinh T. Minh-ha (1989)
The Leader, His Driver and the Driver's Wife – Nick Broomfield (1991)
Blue – Derek Jarman (1992)
The Belovs – Victor Kossakovsky (1993)
The Boatman – Gianfranco Rosi (1993)
Memories and Dreams – Melissa Llewelyn-Davies (1993)
Metal and Melancholy – Heddy Honigmann (1993)
Time of the Barmen (Tempus de baristas) – David MacDougall (1993)
Gallivant – Andrew Kötting (1996)
The Gleaners and I – Agnès Varda (2000)
Bombay Beach – Alma Har'el (2001)
Duka's Dilemma – Jean Lydall and Kaira Strecker (2001)
To Be and to Have (Etre et Avoir) – Nicholas Philibert (2002)

Aileen: Life and Death of a Serial Killer – Nick Broomfield and Joan Churchill (2003)
Tarnation – Jonathan Caouette (2003)
Black Sun – Gary Tarn (2005)
Grizzly Man – Werner Herzog (2005)
Sisters in Law – Kim Longinotto (2005)
Breadmakers – Yasmin Fedda (2007)
Transfiction – Johannes Sjøberg (2007)
Born – Andy Lawrence (2008)
Sweetgrass – Ilisa Barbash and Lucien Castaing-Taylor (2009)
Guilty Pleasures – Julie Moggan (2010)
Manenberg – Christian Vium and Karen Valtorp (2010)
Nostalgia for the Light – Patricio Guzmán (2010)
Pink Saris – Kim Loginotto (2010)
Holy Hustlers – Richard Werbner (2011)
The Lover and the Beloved – Andy Lawrence (2011)
Shooting Freetown – Kieran Hanson (2011)
The Act of Killing – Joshua Oppenheimer (2012)
Leviathan – Lucien Castaing-Taylor and Véréna Paravel (2012)
The One and the Many – Andy Lawrence (2012)
Stories We Tell – Sarah Polley (2012)
Two Years at Sea – Ben Rivers (2012)
Descending with Angels – Christian Suhr (2013)
Manakamana – Stephanie Spray and Pacho Velez (2013)
The Look of Silence – Joshua Oppenheimer (2014)
Between Memories (Entre Memorias) – Martha-Cecilia Dietrich (2015)
British Born Chinese – Elena Barabantseva and Andy Lawrence (2015)

Clouds over Sidra – Gabo Arora and Chris Milk (2015)

Griot – Daniel Lema (2015)

Intimate Distance – Steffen Köhn (2015)

The Man who Loved Books – Roger Canals (2015)

Cameraperson – Kirsten Johnson (2016)

Half Way – Daisy-May Hudson (2016)

Notes on Blindness – Peter Middleton and James Spinney (2016)

One Long Journey – Andy Lawrence (2016)

Black Snow – Stephen Linstead (2017)

Calais (Kalès) – Laurent Van Lancker (2017)

Nepalese Drug Users in Hong Kong – Lloyd Belcher (2017)

Objects of Resistance – Kate Blackmore (2017)

This is my Face – Angélica Cabezas Pino (2017)

Untitled – Michael Glawogger and Monika Willi (2017)

Knots and Holes: An Essay Film on the Life of Nets – Mattijs van de Port (2018)

Red Earth White Snow – Christine Moderbacher (2018)

Theatre of War – Lola Arias (2018)

For Sama – Waad Al-Kateab and Edward Watts (2019)

Great Walls – William Callahan (2019)

Horror in the Andes – Martha-Cecilia Dietrich (2019)

Taste of Hope – Laura Coppens (2019)

Half Elf – Jón Bjarki Magnússon (2020)

Some works are available in the *Ethnographic Video Online Series* and other collections at Alexander Street Press.

4 Further reading
(including texts cited in this handbook)

Books and articles:

Alter, Nora M. (2018) *The Essay Film After Fact and Fiction*. New York: Columbia University Press.

Arendt, Hannah (1994) 'Understanding and politics (the difficulties of understanding)' in J. Kohn (ed.) *Essays in Understanding 1930-1954*. New York: Harcourt, Brace and Company, pp. 203-327.

Ascher, Steven and Edward Pincus (2013) *The Filmmaker's Handbook: A Comprehensive Guide for the Digital Age*. London: Penguin Books. A useful definitive reference guide to the technical problems of filmmaking.

Aston, Judith, Sandra Gaudenzi and Mandy Rose (eds) (2017) *i-docs: The Evolving Practices of Interactive Documentary*. New York: Wallflower/ Columbia University Press.

Balson, Erika and Hila Peleg (eds) (2016) *Documentary across Disciplines*. Cambridge, MA and London: MIT Press.

Banks, Marcus and David Zeitlyn (2015) *Visual Methods in Social Research* (2nd edition). London: Sage.

Barabantseva, Elena and Andy Lawrence (2015) 'Encountering vulnerabilities through "filmmaking for fieldwork"'. *Millennium: Journal of International Studies* 43(3), pp. 911-30.

Barbash, Ilisa and Lucien Taylor (1997) *Cross-Cultural Filmmaking*. Berkeley, LA and London: University of California Press.

Battaglia, Giulia (2014) 'Crafting "participatory" and "collaborative" film projects in India'. *Anthrovision* 2.2 http://journals.openedition.org/anthrovision/1416.

Batty, Craig and Susan Kerrigan (eds) (2018) *Screen Production Research: Creative Practice as a Mode of Enquiry*. Cham, Switzerland: Palgrave Macmillan.

Benjamin, Walter (1999) 'The task of the translator' in *Illuminations: Walter Benjamin*. Edited and with an introduction by Hannah Arendt. Translated by Harry Zorn. London: Pimlico, pp. 70-82.

Berger, John (1977) *Ways of Seeing*. London: British Broadcasting Corporation and Penguin Books.

Callahan, William A. (2020) *Sensible Politics: Visualizing International Relations*. New York: Oxford University Press.

Callahan, William A. (2015) 'The visual turn in IR: documentary filmmaking as a critical method'. *Millennium: Journal of International Studies* 43(3), pp. 891-910.

Chen, Nancy N. and Trinh T. Minh-ha (1994) 'Speaking nearby' in Lucien Taylor (ed.) *Visualizing Theory: Selected Essays From V.A.R. 1990-1994*. Oxford and New York: Routledge, pp. 433-51.

Cox, Rupert (2017) 'Sound, anthropology of' in Hillary Callan (ed.) *The International Encyclopedia of Anthropology*. New York: Wiley Blackwell.

Cox, Rupert, Andrew Irving and Christopher Wright (eds) (2016) *Beyond Text? Critical Practices and Sensory Anthropology*. Manchester: Manchester University Press.

Crawford, Peter and David Turton (eds) (1992) *Film as Ethnography*. Manchester and New York: Manchester University Press.

Deleuze, Gilles (2006) *The Fold: Leibniz and the Baroque*. London: Continuum.

Favero, Paolo S.H. (2018) *The Present Image: Visible Stories in a Digital Habitat*. Cham, Switzerland: Palgrave Macmillan.

Feld, Steven (1994) 'From schizophonia to schismogenesis: on the discourses and commodification practices of "World Music" and "World Beat"' in S. Feld and C. Keil (eds) *Music Grooves*. Chicago: University of Chicago Press, pp. 257–89.

Gardner, Robert and Akos Ostör (2001) *Making Forest of Bliss: Intention, Circumstance and Chance in Nonfiction film: A Conversation between Robert Gardner and Akos Ostör*. Cambridge, MA: Harvard Film Archive and Harvard University Press.

Grasseni, Christina (ed.) (2009) *Skilled Visions: Between Apprenticeship and Standards*. New York and Oxford: Berghahn Books.

Grimshaw, Anna (2001) *The Ethnographer's Eye: Ways of Seeing in Anthropology*. Cambridge: Cambridge University Press.

Grimshaw, Anna and Amanda Ravetz (2009) *Observational Cinema: Anthropology, Film, and the Exploration of Social Life*. Bloomington, IN: Indiana University Press.

Heider, Karl G. (1990) *Ethnographic Film*. Austin: University of Texas Press.

Henley, Paul (2020) *Beyond Observation: A History of Authorship in Ethnographic Film*. Manchester: Manchester University Press.

Henley, Paul (2009) *The Adventure of the Real: Jean Rouch and the Craft of Ethnographic Cinema*. Chicago: University of Chicago Press.

Henley, Paul (2006) 'Narratives: the guilty secret of ethnographic documentary?' in Metje Postma and Peter Ian Crawford (eds) *Reflecting Visual Ethnography: Using the Camera in Anthropological Research*. Hoejbjerg and Leiden: Intervention Press and CNWS Publications, pp. 376–401.

Henley, Paul (2004) 'Putting film to work: observational cinema as practical ethnography' in Sarah Pink, Laszlo Kurti and Ana Isabel Afonso (eds) *Working Images: Methods and Media in Ethnographic Research*. London: Routledge, pp. 109–30.

Irving, Andrew (2017) 'New York stories: narrating the neighbourhood'. *Ethnos: Journal of Anthropology* 82(3), pp. 437–57.

Jackson, Michael (2013) *Lifeworlds: Essays in Existential Anthropology*. Chicago and London: University of Chicago Press.

Jackson, Michael (2002) *The Politics of Storytelling: Violence, Transgression and Intersubjectivity*. Copenhagen: Museum Tusculanum Press.

Köhn, Steffen (2020) 'Desktop documentary: screens as film locations' in Phillip Vannini (ed.) *The Routledge International Handbook of Ethnographic Film and Video*. Abingdon and New York: Routledge.

Linstead, Stephen A. (2018) 'Feeling the reel of the real: framing the play of critically affective organizational research between art and the everyday'. *Organization Studies* 39(2–3), pp. 319–44.

Loizos, Peter (1993) *Innovation in Ethnographic Film: From Innocence to Self-Consciousness, 1955–1985*. Manchester and New York: Manchester University Press.

Lunch, Chris and Nick Lunch (2006) 'Insights into participatory video: A guide for the field'. InsightShare. Available for free download from https://insightshare.org.

MacDonald, Kevin and Mark Cousins (1998) *Imagining Reality: The Faber Book of Documentary*. London: Faber and Faber.

MacDougall, David (2006) *The Corporeal Image: Film, Ethnography, and the Senses*. Princeton and Oxford: Princeton University Press.

MacDougall, David (1998) *Transcultural Cinema*. Edited with an introduction by Lucien Taylor. Princeton and Oxford: Princeton University Press.

MacDougall, David (1994) 'Whose story is it?' in Lucien Taylor (ed.) *Visualizing Theory: Selected Essays From V.A.R. 1990–1994*. Oxford and New York: Routledge, pp. 27–36.

Małinowski, Bronisław [1922] (2014) *Argonauts of the Western Pacific: An Account of Native Enterprise and Adventure in the Archipelagoes of Melanesian New Guinea*. London and New York: Routledge.

Marks, Laura (2000) *The Skin of the Film: Intercultural Cinema, Embodiment, and the*

Senses. Durham, NC and London: Duke University Press.

Minh-ha, Trinh T. (1991) *When The Moon Waxes Red: Representation, Gender, and Cultural Politics*. New York: Routledge.

Murch, Walter (2001) *In the Blink of an Eye: A Perspective on Film Editing* (2nd edition). Los Angeles: Silman-James Press.

Nichols, Bill (2017) *Introduction to Documentary* (3rd edition). Bloomington: Indiana University Press.

Nichols, Bill (2016) *Speaking Truths with Film: Evidence, Ethics, Politics in Documentary*. Berkeley: University of California Press.

Pink, Sarah (2013) *Doing Visual Ethnography* (3rd edition). London: Sage.

Pink, Sarah, Heather Horst, John Postill, Larissa Hjorth, Tania Lewis and Jo Tacchi (2016) *Digital Ethnography: Principles and Practice*. London: Sage.

Rose, Gillian (2016) *Visual Methodologies: An Introduction to Researching with Visual Materials* (4th edition). London: Sage.

Rouch, Jean [1974] (2003) 'The camera and man' in *Ciné Ethnography*. Edited and translated by Steven Feld. Minneapolis and London: University of Minnesota Press.

Sharma, Aparna (2018) 'Practices of making as forms of knowledge: Creative practice research as a mode of documentary making in northeast India' in Craig Batty and Susan Kerrigan (eds) *Screen Production Research: Creative Practice As a Mode of Enquiry*. Cham, Switzerland: Palgrave Macmillan. pp. 161-76

Sjöberg, Johannes (2008) 'Ethnofiction: drama as a creative research practice in ethnographic film'. *Journal of Media Practice* 9(3) pp. 229-42

Sobchack, Vivian (1992) *The Address of the Eye: A Phenomenology of the Film Experience*. Princeton and Oxford: Princeton University Press.

Suhr, Christian and Rane Willerslev (eds) (2013) *Transcultural Montage*. New York and Oxford: Berghahn Books.

Tarkovsky, Andrey (1998) *Sculpting in Time: Reflections on the Cinema*. Translated from the Russian by Kitty Hunter-Blair. Austin: University of Texas Press.

Ten Brink, Joram and Joshua Oppenheimer (eds) (2012) *Killer Images: Documentary Film, Memory and the Performance of Violence*. London and New York: Wallflower Press.

Vaughan, Dai (1999) 'The aesthetics of ambiguity' in *For Documentary: Twelve Essays*. Berkeley, LA and London: University of California Press, pp. 54-83.

Walderman, Diane and Janet Walker (eds) (1999) *Feminism and Documentary*. Minneapolis and London: University of Minnesota Press.

Werbner, Richard (2011) *Holy Hustlers, Schism, and Prophecy: Apostolic Reformation in Botswana* (DVD included). Berkeley, LA and London: University of California Press.

Zemp, Hugo (1988) 'Filming Music and Looking at Music Films'. *Ethnomusicology* 32(3) pp. 393-427

Journals concerning film as research practice:

Anthrovision from VANEASA
Publishes articles including audiovisual material and promotes innovative ways of writing in an academic framework.

Journal of Anthropological Films
Curated by the Nordic Anthropological Film Association (**NAFA**), this journal offers a selection of ethnographic documentaries available for viewing and peer review.

Sensate
A peer-reviewed, open-access, media-based journal for the creation, presentation and critique of innovative projects in the arts, humanities and sciences, based at Harvard University.

Sightlines Journal and Conference
Primarily an audiovisual publication designed to showcase films made in a research context in the higher education sector. The filmmakers are usually academic staff or doctoral students, often but not always based in the screen production discipline.

Visual Ethnography
Frequently has articles on audiovisual research methodology. Older editions are open access.

INDEX